DILEMMAS OF
DOMINATION

DILEMMAS OF
DOMINATION

THE UNMAKING OF THE AMERICAN EMPIRE

Walden Bello

Metropolitan Books
Henry Holt and Company
New York

Metropolitan Books
Henry Holt and Company, LLC
Publishers since 1866
115 West 18th Street
New York, New York 10011

Metropolitan Books™ is a registered
trademark of Henry Holt and Company, LLC.

Library of Congress Cataloging-in-Publication Data
Bello, Walden F.
    Dilemmas of domination : the unmaking of the American empire / Walden
Bello.—1st ed.
        p.   cm.
    Includes bibliographical references and index.
    ISBN 13: 978-0-8050-7402-4
    ISBN 10: 0-8050-7402-3
    1. United States—Foreign economic relations.   2. United States—Foreign
relations—2001–   3. United States—Military policy.   4. Globalization.
I. Title.
HF1455.B377 2004
337.73—dc22   2004056106

First Edition 2005

Designed by Betty Lew

Printed in the United States of America

10   9   8   7   6   5   4   3   2   1

To

秀美

CONTENTS

DILEMMAS OF DOMINATION

INTRODUCTION

A Southern Perspective on the
Crisis of the Empire

On November 2, 2004, the most significant electoral contest in the world took place in the United States. Yet only 115 million people participated in an exercise that the British Broadcasting Corporation described as "a truly global election," the results of which would drastically affect the future of the vast majority of the world's people. To be exact, the choice of only slightly over 59 million people mattered in a decision of global consequence. Hundreds of millions outside the borders of the United States were rooting for the Democratic candidate, John Kerry, mainly because he was not George W. Bush, and they stood by helplessly as the latter won a second term owing to the support of people who saw the rest of the globe as a threat to their privileged status.

A not dissimilar situation existed over 2,000 years ago, when the fate of several million people who inhabited the area bounded by Spain in the West and Syria in the East, Gaul in the North, and Africa in the South was decided in factional struggles among a handful of citizens in the city of Rome. Like this earlier people, today's global population is hostage to the dynamics of political competition and political succession in an imperial republic.

This book is, first of all, written from the point of view of an observer from the global South, on the imperial periphery, where Washington's far-flung legions are stationed to maintain global order. Only recently have Americans begun to think of their country as an empire. But for those of us subjected to repeated imperial interventions—incursions designed to uphold the interests of a distant power—empire is an everyday reality.

Why is this experience important? Because it profoundly affects the perspective that we bring to events. This notion became quite clear to me in the aftermath of September 11, 2001. At that time, the French newspaper *Le Monde* editorialized: "We are all Americans now." It was speaking for the French, for Europeans maybe, but certainly not for somebody like me. My reaction to September 11 was expressed in an article I wrote a few days after the horrific event:

> The assault on the World Trade Center was unpardonable, but it is important not to lose perspective, especially a historical one. . . . The scale and consequences of the September 11 attack are massive indeed, but this is not the worst act of mass terrorism in U.S. history, as some U.S. media are wont to claim. The over 3000 lives lost are irreplaceable, but one must not forget that the atomic raids on Hiroshima and Nagasaki killed 210,000 people, most of them civilians, most perishing instantaneously. One may object that you can't compare the September 11 attack to the nuclear bombings since, after all, Hiroshima and Nagasaki were targets in a war. But why not, since the purpose of the nuclear bombings was not mainly to destroy military or infrastructure targets, but to terrorize and destroy the civilian population?

In contrast to the European reaction, I pointed out, the response to the September 11 event in the South was muted. A survey would probably reveal that

> while many people in the Third World are appalled by the hijackers' methods, they are not unsympathetic to their political objectives. As one Chinese-Filipino entrepreneur said, "It's horrible, but on the other hand, the U.S. had it coming." If this reaction is common among middle class people, it would not be surprising if such ambivalence towards terrorism is widespread among the 80 per cent of the world's population marginalized by current global political and economic arrangements.

The underlying motivation behind September 11, I suggested, was a sense of injustice and outrage. These two emotions were directed at the twin pillars of U.S. policy in the Middle East: first, the needs of the peoples of that region are subordinate to America's strategic and economic interest in Middle Eastern oil; second, the United States must provide unstinting support for Israel. Unless the United States abandoned these policies and addressed the roots of terrorism in injustice and inequality, I argued, "there will always be thousands of recruits for acts of terrorism."[1]

At the time, these comments outraged many readers, a number of whom branded me as an apologist for terrorism. I suspect that the article would still strike a raw nerve among some readers in the North today.

What is more, my fundamental analytical approach has provoked heated disagreement. I take the view that the moment of greatest triumph for an individual, an institution, or a system may also exhibit its vulnerabilities. The shadow of defeat accompanies every victory. Winning the battle may accompany defeat in the larger war, as was the case with the United States Pyrrhic victory during the Tet Offensive in Vietnam.

A few days after George W. Bush landed on the deck of the USS *Abraham Lincoln* to declare American victory in Iraq on May 1, 2003, I wrote: "This point may sound surreal after the massive firepower we witnessed . . . [but] there is good reason to think that [the United States] is overextended. In fact, the main strategic result of the occupation of Iraq is to worsen this condition of overextension. Washington's goal is to achieve overwhelming military dominance over any rival or coalition of rivals. This quest for even greater global dominance, however, inevitably generates opposition, and it is in this resistance that we see the roots of overextension."[2]

If my analysis of September 11 aroused anger, the commentary on May 1 evoked ridicule from some readers, who saw it as the ultimate in wishful thinking. "Which planet are you on?" was not an uncommon reaction, even among some fierce critics of the United States. Today that counterintuitive view does not seem so strange after all.

CRISES OF GLOBAL CAPITALISM

This book, which is about the crisis of the American empire, is focused on the interrelated dilemmas of imperial economics and imperial politics. Actually, three crises threaten to convulse the empire: a crisis of overproduction, a crisis of overextension, and a crisis of legitimacy.

Crisis of Overproduction

The economic core of the empire is an expansive capitalist mode of production, one that is based on the extraction of profit from the accumulation and investment of capital. Today global capitalism is distinguished by the hegemony of the U.S. economy, both as a market for goods and as a destination for capital. Roaming the world, U.S. transnational corporations function as agents for capital accumulation and production. Their drive for profit makes capitalism both relentlessly expansive and prone to contradiction or to crises. One crisis is rooted in the contradiction between the increased consumption of natural resources and the production of waste and finite ecological space. A second stems from the more intense conflict between the minority in command of productive and financial assets and a majority with little control over these. Related to this is a third crisis, on which we shall focus our discussion: the widening gap between the growing productive potential of the system and the capacity of consumers to purchase its output. This gap has increased in recent years because of the radical free-market policies pushed by the global elite, which have depressed the incomes of working people in both the North and the South while concentrating wealth in the hands of a small minority. Termed variously as overproduction, overcapacity, or overaccumulation, this dynamic has resulted in declining growth rates in the center economies and disappearing profits in the industrial sector. It has also resulted in global financial speculation becoming the central source of profit and capital accumulation.

Crisis of Overextension

The development of capitalism and of markets has accompanied the development of states, or "systems of domination," to use the felicitous phrase of the sociologist Max Weber. Although states have promoted the expansion of capital both at home and abroad, governments recognize the need for restraint to ensure social stability or to protect and promote the competitive ability of capitalist elites. States are not simply at the beck and call of the economic elites as cruder versions of Marxism would have it. Governments function with relative autonomy vis-à-vis the system of production, partly because of their conflicting roles in providing order, supporting capital accumulation, and maintaining social stability. Moreover, nation-states must coexist with their global counterparts. In an international system marked by anarchy, states are driven to maintain or extend their strategic reach.

The wealthy nations tend to develop a grand strategy, or a fundamental approach toward the world—a conflict-ridden process fueled by competition among elites. Contending elites mobilize mass constituencies to provide them with a decisive edge in imposing their policies. The struggle during the Cold War between the strategies of "containment" and "rollback"—between those who sought to prevent the Soviet Union from expanding beyond its post–World War II borders and those who yearned to reverse, or roll back, Soviet conquests in Eastern Europe and elsewhere—is an example of competitive dynamics.

In addition, the drive to extend the state's strategic reach may run up against, and even outstrip, the resources available for achieving its ambitions. Such an eventuality is the source of the second crisis of the U.S.-dominated global system: overextension or overstretch. In pursuit of undisputed military supremacy wedded to unlimited economic and political goals, the Bush administration courted trouble even before the invasions of Afghanistan and Iraq. But by making Afghanistan and Iraq exemplary wars—demonstrations of American invincibility—it ended up exposing the limits of its military strength. It thereby provided an unintended lesson to U.S. foes in the global South: one can fight the U.S. military to a stalemate—and in guerrilla warfare, a stalemate is a triumph for the guerrillas.

Crisis of Legitimacy

The third major crisis is one of legitimacy. Ideologies are central to creating and maintaining not only the economic but the social conditions for capital accumulation, both domestically and abroad. Ideologies legitimate the system.

In the legitimation process, the subordinate classes (the citizens of a superpower, for instance) assent to the control of the dominant elites. Legitimacy, rather than force or coercion, is the linchpin of social order. In Western capitalist societies, the enhancement of individual freedom and economic mobility through the operation of the market and democratic representation serves as the ideological cornerstone of legitimacy. More-over, the creation of legitimacy is not just a cognitive process, one that is achieved through an inculcation of values and ideas. It is actively engaged in by members of the subordinate classes themselves—for example, when they participate in elections.

At the international level, similarly, domination cannot simply take the form of coercion. The creation of international or multilateral institutions that seemingly promote universal interests is essential. The development of the Bretton Woods institutions—the World Bank and the International Monetary Fund—was a response to this imperative. A more recent exam-ple is the establishment of the World Trade Organization. Multilateralism involves yielding at least some control and behaving as primus inter pares, first among equals, an actor on whom the rules are also binding. When it encounters opposition, however, the dominant power in a multilateral sys-tem will almost always be tempted to achieve its objectives through unilat-eral means. It is this tension that accounts for the oscillation between multilateral initiatives and unilateral measures in the development of U.S. foreign policy.

Today a crisis of legitimacy pervades the multilateral system and the neoliberal ideology that underpins it. Instead of promoting prosperity, as the major postwar financial institutions promised, corporate-driven glob-alization has proven destabilizing. It has increased poverty and widened inequalities both within and between nations. In pursuit of its narrow interests, the Bush administration has exacerbated this crisis by strong-arming the World Bank, the IMF, and the WTO, instead of taking the longer but more legitimate route of forging consensus. Consequently, international economic institutions have seen their credibility erode, espe-cially in the South.

Alongside the crisis of legitimacy of the multilateral system is the crisis of legitimacy of democracy. Born out of an anticolonial struggle, the United States has found traditional mechanisms of colonial rule problem-atical. To maintain the reality of empire while concealing it, America has resorted to forging dependent political structures posing as carriers of democracy. Dependent democracies, however, have often failed to take root. In many cases, Washington has had to rely on authoritarian regimes to serve its strategic and economic interests, dealing a severe blow to impe-rial legitimacy. The newest attempts to revive the democratic rationale for empire have also failed, because the U.S. government has used the formal mechanisms of civil society to impose harsh programs of economic adjustment on Third World societies. Moreover, U.S. democracy has itself entered a crisis of legitimacy. Transparent corporate domination of the political system, as well as widespread restrictions on the civil liberties of citizens, has diminished the attractiveness of U.S.-style democracy as a model for people in the global South.

CENTRAL CONFLICTS

When these three fundamental crises of empire intersect in volatile and unexpected ways, as they are likely to do, the system's inherent instability and propensity for crisis and unraveling becomes evident.

For nearly fifty years after the Second World War, the conflict between the central capitalist nations, led by the United States, and the so-called Socialist bloc, led by the Soviet Union, represented the dominant global cleavage. Since the collapse of the Soviet bloc in the late 1980s, other tensions have come to the fore.

First, there is the rivalry among the major players. The leading capitalist societies have experienced both interdependence and competition. Interdependence prevailed during the early postwar decades, as the United States supported and derived benefits from the reconstruction of the war-ravaged economies of Europe and Japan. Since the 1970s, however, competition has trumped cooperation. The central economies seek to achieve recovery and growth at the expense of the others. With the formation of the European Union, the competition reached a new level. Political differences on such issues as relations with the South, approaches to environmental problems, and the role of multilateral institutions exacerbate the economic rivalries.

Second, there is the continuing conflict of capital and labor in the North. In the United States, the tensions between the classes have always been marked by racial, gender, and ethnic discrimination and, recently, by increasing antagonisms over social values and other cultural issues. Some commentators prefer to talk of a "cultural civil war" rather than class conflict. Nonetheless, the capital-labor struggle continues in the United States. The power of labor has significantly eroded, and corporations and

Republican administrations have colluded in rolling back the trade union movement. Whether a confrontation looms remains to be seen.

Third, there is the conflict between the major economies of the North and the developing countries of the South, where most of the world's marginalized people, some three billion, are located. More and more, this complex struggle defines the age we live in.

The resistance by northern elites to the demands, by newly independent countries, for political equality and economic redistribution has aggravated this conflict. At the same time, the industrialized world seeks to speed up the integration of the South into the global economy in order to offset the stagnation overtaking the northern economies.

In the first postwar decades, the struggles by the South against domination often took the form of wars for national liberation. While they sometimes deployed the language and ideology of Marxism-Leninism, these enterprises, as in China and Vietnam, had as a fundamental objective the achievement of political independence and economic modernization. There also were non–Marxist-Leninist versions of this goal, as in Nasser's Egypt, Sukarno's Indonesia, Mexico under the Institutional Revolutionary Party (PRI), and the military dictatorships in Brazil and South Korea.

While they were on different sides of the Cold War divide, these left-wing and right-wing governments pursued programs marked by domestic protectionism, government direction of the industrialization process, efforts to cartelize the production of oil and other raw materials, strong regulation of foreign investment, and capital controls. Momentarily, in the 1970s, left-wing and right-wing elites—in Mexico, Cuba, Indonesia, Brazil, Iraq—united under the ideology of the New International Economic Order, which proposed a substantial redistribution of wealth and power from the North to the South. For many of the developing nations, a model of sorts was provided by the Organization of Petroleum Exporting Countries, which brought together regimes as varied as Mu'ammar Gadhafi's Libya, the Saudi monarchy, center-right democratic Venezuela, and Saddam Hussein's Iraq in an ambitious effort to dictate the price of oil and accumulate financial resources.

Ronald Reagan's election in 1980 marked a turning point in the North's drive to roll back the South. His victory was initially seen as a triumph for a new foreign policy elite dedicated to militant confrontation with the Soviet Union and Communism. That it certainly was: the Reagan administration moved quickly to upgrade its strategic arsenal to gain first-strike capacity while seeking to develop a shield against incoming ballistic missiles, the so-called Strategic Defense Initiative. But the actual wars of the Reagan administration—the invasion of Grenada, the intervention in Lebanon, the long effort to bring down the Sandinistas in Nicaragua— were fought against Third World insurgencies, in a continuation of the pattern of U.S. interventions in the Philippines, Korea, Guatemala, Vietnam, and Chile.

Reagan did chart new territory, however, launching comprehensive economic counterinsurgency campaigns to undermine those state-assisted capitalist regimes that had served as the base for such challenges as the New International Economic Order. The right-wing foreign policy circles of the Reagan regime wanted to transform these nations into free-market economies. Trade wars were waged to open up more advanced economies of the South, like Taiwan and South Korea, which were making the transition from developing to developed country. Most decisive, though, were the structural adjustment programs, inaugurated by the IMF, that promoted trade liberalization, deregulation, and privatization. They served as the principal mechanism for disciplining the economic aspirations of the South.

Succeeding American administrations continued the strategy of rollback and resubordination of the South. Under Bill Clinton, structural adjustment was repackaged as globalization. Washington, in collaboration with the IMF and the WTO, speeded up the elimination of barriers to investment and the lowering of tariffs. The more rapid integration of the South into the global economy, also designed to widen the arena for exploitation by transnational capital, was, in turn, critical for northern economies trying to escape the dilemma of their own stagnation.

Thus the intersection of the crises of the imperial system—overproduction, overextension, and illegitimacy—has intensified those traditional cleavages that have long marked the empire. Especially critical today is the North-South conflict, in which the chief battlefields are Iraq and the World Trade Organization. Although the United States remains the world's prime power, its global system of domination is under severe assault and may be in the process of unraveling.

PLAN OF THE BOOK

We begin by examining the grand strategies formulated by U.S. adminis-trations over the last half century. Chapters 1 and 2 focus on the way George W. Bush's open-ended drive for military superiority has provoked a crisis of overextension that leaves the credibility of U.S. military might severely compromised.

Doubts about American military invincibility are compounded by a creeping anxiety about the country's economic prowess. Chapter 3 analyzes the crisis of overproduction and overcapacity underlying the stagnation that has overtaken most of the central capitalist economies. The chapter shows how speculative finance has replaced industrial and manufacturing activity as the prime source of profitability, how China is contributing to the crisis of global overproduction, and how the recent recessions and ane-mic, jobless growth in the United States suggest that the global economy is at the tail end of the long, fifty-year wave of capitalist expansion and decline.

One symptom of that underlying economic pathology is the overbearing position of finance capital. Chapter 4 reveals the way financial speculation increasingly drives global economic activity. The mobility of capital, facili-tated by the elimination of capital and foreign exchange controls, has been extremely destabilizing for developing countries. They have watched them-selves become the darlings of speculative investors at one moment and pariahs the next. With the liberation of finance, economic crises have become more and more frequent and serious, and most of them have occurred in the South.

Upheaval, both political and economic, south of the border preoccupies the imperial center. Chapter 5 discusses the various mechanisms deployed for the containment of the South over the last four decades. It focuses on the roles of the IMF, the World Bank, and the WTO. The dynamics of eco-nomic rollback and resubordination of the South are examined in detail. The chapter zeroes in on the disruptive consequences of structural adjust-ment programs and free-trade policies.

Over the past decade or so, the domineering behavior of northern gov-ernments and financial institutions has undermined their legitimacy in the South. Chapter 6 explores the reaction of the North to this crisis of legitimacy. Multilateral institutions have engaged in lukewarm, incoherent reform efforts, not all of which have enjoyed universal support among northern elites; for instance, Washington scuttled an attempt by the IMF to set up a global bankruptcy mechanism (akin to Chapter 11 in U.S. commercial law) that developing countries might use temporarily to shelter themselves from their creditors. Not surprisingly, reform has foundered, accelerating the crisis of institutional credibility that the reform efforts were supposed to address in the first place.

The unilateralism of the Bush administration has exacerbated relations with the global South. Chapter 7 describes the economic program of the Bush regime. It argues that, under Bush, the U.S. approach to free trade, relations with its allies, and its dealings with the South are subordinated to strategic considerations. Never before has the White House so brazenly advanced double standards, as it arrogantly demands protectionist measures for the United States and free markets and free trade for the rest of the world.

In the end, what people believe to be true will determine the imperial future. Chapter 8 describes the empire's profound ideological dilemma. Who believes any longer in the American promise of democracy—either abroad or at home—a promise that has accompanied the drive for economic expansion and strategic extension? The loss of legitimacy has many sources. Most significant were the subversion of fledgling democracies in the South in the 1980s and 1990s by draconian financial regimes imposed by the North, and the hijacking of the democratic process in the United States by the increasingly heavy-handed influence of corporate lobbyists over the electoral and legislative processes. Yet another factor has been the erosion of individual freedoms by nonconstitutional measures justified in the name of fighting terrorism.

In the conclusion, I explore how the crisis of empire may in fact translate into an opportunity for liberating change not only for marginalized nations but for the people of the United States as well.

CHAPTER 1

The Road to Baghdad

It is not simply that current international law and the institutions it has created cannot assure international security, it is that they are a positive barrier to such security because they hamstring the one state with the power and willingness to intervene on behalf of world order.

George W. Bush takes the doctrine of "democratic engagement" of the first Bush administration, and that of "democratic enlargement" of the Clinton administration, one step further. It might be called "democratic transformation." Or it might be called "liberal imperialism." What is wrong with this noble idea?

PHILIP BOBBIT, *THE SHIELD OF ACHILLES*

There may be good and sufficient reasons to abide by the provisions of a treaty, and in most cases one would expect to do so because of the mutuality of benefits that treaties provide, but not because the U.S. is "legally" obligated to do so.

JOHN BOLTON, U.S. UNDERSECRETARY OF STATE

The behavior of the U.S. government in the international arena reflects, of course, the needs of American capitalism. But the underpinnings of American foreign policy are considerably more complex than this statement suggests.

In dealing with other nations, the United States is also impelled by its drive to extend its strategic reach, to project its power. Which global stances it develops depends on many factors, including the nature and intentions of the country's rivals and the character of domestic politics. Moreover, its offensive and defensive policies are affected by the tension between strategic goals and the resources available for achieving them. The projection of power, in short, is always dogged by the specter of overextension.

This chapter and the next one explore the origins and dynamics of the strategy that evolved after George W. Bush's inauguration, on January 20, 2001, and that led to the quagmire in Iraq. Earlier administrations struggled to resolve the same tension between imperial ambition and imperial means. That's where our search to make sense of the present dilemma must begin.

UNILATERALISM VERSUS MULTILATERALISM— A USEFUL DISTINCTION?

When contrasting the foreign policy of the administration of the younger Bush with that of previous regimes, analysts tend to label the Bush II presidency "unilateralist" and its predecessors "multilateralist." For instance, liberal writers Ivo Daalder and James Lindsay claim that Bush has launched a "revolution" in foreign policy:

> In less than three years in office, he has discarded or redefined many of the key principles governing how America engages the world. He has relied on the unilateral exercise of American power rather than on international law and institutions to get his way. He has championed a proactive doctrine of preemption and abandoned the tested strategies of deterrence and containment. He has preferred regime change to direct negotiations with countries and leaders that he loathes. And he has promoted forceful interdiction and missile defenses to counter weapons proliferation, all the while downplaying support for nonproliferation treaties and regimes.[1]

Liberal analysts do not deny that previous administrations tried to achieve hegemonic ends but assert that they did so in collaboration with other powers and in a way that promoted global stability. To quote G. John Ikenberry:

> The United States could exercise its power and achieve its national interests, but it did so in a way that helped deepen the fabric of international community. American power did not destabilize the world order; it helped create it. The development of rule-based agreements and political-security partnerships was good for both the United States and for much of the world. By the end of the 1990's, the result was an international political order of unprecedented size and success: a global coalition of democratic states tied together through markets, institutions, and security partnerships.[2]

Comparisons of this sort between Bush and his predecessors have three shortcomings as historical analysis: they downplay the role of unilateralism in the unfolding of U.S. foreign policy in the post–World War II period; they exaggerate the break between Bush and his predecessors, although there are significant differences; and they fail to acknowledge that many of Bush's initiatives found precedents in the actions of earlier presidents, including Bill Clinton.

While multilateralism was prominent in the rhetoric of both Republicans and Democrats in the Cold War period, the practice of multilateralism to achieve U.S. objectives was, in reality, limited. In the construction of the anti-Soviet free world, the United States had only a few partners— mainly Britain, and, to a much lesser extent, France, Germany, and Japan. The commitment to act through the United Nations was always selective— that is, only when the world body could be relied on to serve U.S. security objectives, as in the UN-sanctioned police action in Korea in 1950.

Although multilateralism was more than a fig leaf in Europe, where NATO did in fact serve as a formal decision-making structure for security issues, it was nonexistent in Asia, where the United States refused to be constrained by multilateral treaties and organizations set up to achieve collective security.

In East Asia, the United States has assured maximum liberty of movement for its troops by forestalling the creation of a multilateral organization and by establishing a network of bilateral treaties with weaker countries. Freedom of action and unilateralist decision making were legacies of victory in the Second World War; they were maintained by a trans-Pacific garrison state that spanned seven client governments and allies and island colonies grabbed from Japan. Unilateral action, which reached its apogee with U.S. intervention in Vietnam from 1954 to 1975, has continued to be the main avenue of response in the area. Those who speak of multilateralism point to the United States–Japan partnership, but it is really a dependent relationship built on the occupation and then domination of a defeated enemy.

The fact of the matter is that in Asia, the United States did not need multilateral alliances to exercise its power, while in Europe it did. As Ikenberry himself acknowledges, "In Europe, the United States had an elaborate agenda for uniting the European states, creating an institutional bulwark against communism, and supporting centrist democratic regimes," while in Asia, "unchallenged hegemonic power meant that the United States had fewer incentives . . . to secure its dominant position through international institutions that would have circumscribed its independent decisionmaking."[3]

Nor was multilateralism ever a reality in Latin America. There, direct U.S. action was preferred to collective diplomacy to resolve problems, whether in staging the Bay of Pigs invasion in 1961, in removing a populist government in Brazil in 1964, or in supporting a coup against the socialist president Salvador Allende in Chile in 1973 on the grounds that, as Henry Kissinger put it, "I don't see why we should let a country go Marxist because its people are irresponsible."[4]

It is difficult, therefore, to characterize U.S. policy, even before the 1990s, in terms of a black-and-white distinction between multilateralism and unilateralism; unilateralism has always been a central—if not *the* central—feature of U.S. policy. When we consider the 1990s, the multilateralist-unilateralist distinction becomes even more difficult to maintain. A common view is that the instincts of the Clinton administration were multilateralist but that the White House was hamstrung because the Republican-controlled Senate was simply waiting to pounce on its initiatives. A number of analysts have pointed out that Clinton, in his last days in office, did sign the Rome Statute of the International Criminal Court, defying the U.S. military and the Republican senators who intended to veto it. "Assertive multilateralism," an observer has argued, was the preferred strategy of the administration when it took power in 1993, but "faced with congressional and public misgivings, Clinton retreated to a pragmatic internationalism, encapsulated in the mantra of 'multilateral when we can, unilateral when we must.'"[5]

There is reason, however, to doubt the accuracy of this portrait. For, in many areas, the Clinton administration was as unilateralist as any of the preceding administrations. This was certainly the case in East Asia. Here the United States, under Clinton, actively opposed moves to multilateralize the existing security system dominated by Washington. The White House, for instance, systematically subverted the ASEAN (Association of Southeast Asian Nations) Regional Forum (ARF), which, for all its flaws, was a step in the right direction. When the forum was founded in Bangkok in July 1994, Secretary of State Warren Christopher was one of the few foreign ministers of participating governments absent from the meeting—no doubt a calculated move on the part of the United States to underline the lowly status it accorded the organization. Clinton himself denigrated the ARF and other multilateral security initiatives, saying they "are a way to supplement our alliances and forward military presence, not supplant them."[6]

Why was an administration that was so multilateralist in rhetoric so determined to kill an embryonic multilateral system of collective security in the region? The reason was cogently summed up in a report of the Congressional Research Service:

> [A] problem would arise if East Asian governments used the ASEAN Regional Forum and other future regional security consultative organizations in attempts to restrain the United States from acting on certain security issues. The impasse between the United States and the NATO and CSCE countries over policy toward Bosnia-Herzegovina points up the potential for disagreements as Cold War–based mutual security interests decline. Four areas of U.S. security policy in East Asia would appear to be subject to potential differences between the United States and some East Asian governments: U.S. attempts to restrain Chinese missile and arms sales; U.S. policy towards Taiwan, especially if

Taiwan-China relations should worsen; U.S. efforts to prevent North Korea from developing nuclear weapons; and U.S. policy towards Japan's future regional and international military roles. The U.S. Government and friendly East Asian governments might agree on some basic objectives on these issues, but they may disagree on the strategies and tactics to employ. Regional security consultative organizations could be focal points for the airing of such differences.[7]

But fear of future disagreement was not the only reason. Even more central was the fact that, as the conservative analyst Robert Tucker put it, "In Asia much more than in Europe we have clients rather than allies."[8]

When it came to dealing with nonallies, unilateralist saber rattling was sometimes the first rather than the last resort. As the simmering Taiwan-China crisis sharpened in response to Chinese military exercises in the Taiwan Straits in March 1996, the Clinton administration's reaction was classically unilateralist: sending two aircraft carrier battle groups to the area to warn China. Similarly, when it had difficulty getting the United Nations to impose sanctions on Korea over the latter's nuclear reprocessing plant at Yongbyon, the then secretary of defense, William Perry, sent word out that "North Korea's nuclear facilities might be bombed" if a negotiated closing of the facilities could not be achieved.[9]

Targeted bombing, not of North Korea, but of the Sudan and Afghanistan in an effort to kill Osama bin Laden and other Al Qaeda leaders, after the bombings of the U.S. embassies in Nairobi, Kenya, Dar es Salaam, Tanzania, in August 1998, was a unilateralist act through and through, legitimized by a specious appeal to Article 51 of the United Nations Charter, which justifies actions taken in self-defense. The bombing was a serious affront to many members of the international community to whom "the primary responsibility for controlling the actions of a resident [bin Laden] belongs to the local state, precluding direct foreign action even in self-defense until all other steps are exhausted."[10]

But perhaps the most memorable case of unilateralism was the high-altitude bombing conducted against the former Yugoslavia in the spring of 1998, designed to get Serbian police and military forces out of Kosovo, where the population of Albanians was under threat of ethnic cleansing. While the Clinton administration sold the NATO air campaign as necessary to avert genocide, the White House "seemed to disregard the primacy of the Security Council in authorizing the use of force outside of self defense."[11]

It is certainly true that, in the Yugoslavia air strikes as well as the intervention in Haiti early in 1994, Washington cited humanitarianism as a rationale for violating the principles of national sovereignty and collective security. It is also true that, unlike the Bush II administration, the Clinton White House did not undertake military action simply as a cover or an instrument for pursuing strategic interests but appealed to the missionary self-image of American liberalism. Nevertheless, they were unilateralist attacks, and in much of its behavior the Clinton administration sought, when it could, to avoid the constraints of multilateralism.

The multilateral/unilateral distinction, then, provides little help in understanding the uniqueness of the foreign policy of George W. Bush. In this regard, Robert Tucker accurately captures the centrality of unilateralism in foreign policy from Truman to Bush II:

> The multilateralism of the Cold War years was more nearly a qualified unilateralism. The point has often been made that the American diplomatic experience has differed from the experience of other states in that the nation has never had to entertain genuinely cooperative action with other nations. In moving from a relative isolation to global engagement, we did not go from unilateralism to multilateralism but from the unilateralism of a position of isolation to the unilateralism of a position of undisputed leadership over a global alliance. This is not to say that the more recent unilateralism was without any of the constraints real multilateralism must imply, only that the constraints imposed by our allies still left us with a very considerable freedom of action.[12]

GRAND STRATEGIES IN U.S. FOREIGN POLICY

Rather than employing the not very useful distinction between unilateralist and multilateralist administrations, we might better analyze the continuities and discontinuities in the foreign policies of different administrations by enlisting the concept of grand strategy. A grand strategy is the fundamental strategic approach of a national elite toward the rest of the world. It emerges from a dynamic process that involves, among other things,

- specifying the national interests of the society in the global arena;
- identifying the country's enemies and allies from the perspective of these interests; and
- elaborating a strategy to neutralize enemies and harness allies to achieve the national interests.

The formulation of a grand strategy in the United States is greatly influenced by the interplay between the economic and political drives of an advanced capitalist society and the conflict among classes and interest groups.

The United States has a dynamic, expansive capitalist mode of production. Policy making does not originate in the imperatives of economic expansion alone, however. The strategic imperative—the drive of the U.S. state to extend its reach—is also vital. In some areas and some periods, the strategic imperative can be overriding, as was certainly the case with the U.S. expansion into Asia. From the very beginning of the country's drive across the Pacific in the late nineteenth century, commercial opportunities served as ill-disguised rationales to justify acquisition of bases and to project the military and strategic reach of the United States.[13]

Then there is the ideological imperative. The United States is not a nineteenth-century power operating solely on the basis of great-power realpolitik but a modern imperial democracy. In democracies, ideology is a vital element in winning legitimacy for imperial expansion both from the American people as well as from subject populations. Legitimacy is central to the U.S. imperial project.

The imperial enterprise is inherently fluid, unstable, and volatile. The drives for capitalist expansion, strategic dominance, and ideological enclosure operate with relative autonomy, sometimes in complementary fashion, sometimes in conflict with one another. Thus the imperial undertaking is a negotiated and conflict-ridden process in which various factions of the ruling elite, agencies of the bureaucracy, and contending intellectual forces develop competing strategies to achieve what they all claim to be in the national interest. Yet the conflicts are not simply struggles among different elements of the ruling class. The competing elites mobilize popular coalitions to help impose a grand strategy.

Containment as Grand Strategy

During the post–World War II period, the dominant grand strategy was containment. Competing with it and supplanting it, toward the end of the Cold War, was the strategy of rollback.

Containment was essentially a political-military strategy; its central tenet was best expressed by the man universally regarded as its creator, George Kennan: "[T]he main element of any United States policy toward the Soviet Union must be that of a long-term, patient but firm and vigilant containment of Russian expansive tendencies."[14]

In Europe, where containment rested on alliances, especially NATO, national elites enjoyed some decision-making power, although it was seldom exercised against the United States. In Asia, however, containment was deployed unilaterally.

Worried about the gap between goals and resources, containment strategists promoted a carefully calibrated approach that confronted Soviet power at selected global points considered to be of vital interest to the United States.

Liberal containment was the strategy of the so-called Eastern Establishment, which was grounded in old wealth as well as in big finance and corporate capital. This approach found support in the relatively affluent middle and working classes, created by the New Deal–inspired Keynesian reforms in the first postwar decades. Indeed, Big Labor became part of the coalition and was given a key role in promoting anti-Communist unionism throughout the free world.

Rollback: Containment's Rival

Rollback, a grand strategy as old as containment, found expression in National Security Council Memorandum 68, which proposed an open-ended commitment to resist what it saw as Soviet aggression. Whereas containment identified as the enemy a Russian nationalism that respected counterforce, NSC 68 saw the foe as Communism bent on global domination.

Containment defined victory as the prevention of the territorial expansion of Russia and its allied states. To adherents of rollback, victory was the liberation of the "captive nations" that had fallen to Communism via the "projection into the Soviet world" of the "moral and material strength of the free world."[15] Advocates of rollback never forgave Franklin Delano Roosevelt for recognizing Eastern Europe as Stalin's sphere of influence.

Vietnam and the Search for a New Grand Strategy

When liberal containment unraveled after the U.S. defeat in Vietnam, two other grand strategies competed to fill the void: Henry Kissinger's strategic diplomacy and Jimmy Carter's trilateralism. Both Kissinger and Carter based their approaches on one key post-Vietnam premise: that the United States had experienced a relative decline in its power. Carter's portrayal of the "malaise" hounding the nation is well known, yet Kissinger was similarly explicit about dwindling U.S. influence.[16]

Kissinger's solution was to reaffirm the objective of containing the Soviet Union but to use strategic diplomacy as a substitute for force—specifically, to exploit the differences between China and the Soviet Union to isolate the latter, while cultivating traditional alliances with Western Europe and Japan.

Carter worked with a model articulated by the Trilateral Commission, a forum of public figures and leading business executives from the Western industrial countries and Japan. Responding to the crisis of containment triggered by Vietnam and put off by what many members of the commission saw as Kissinger's amoral balance of power politics, they sought a new mechanism of world order, called the "management of interdependence." According to Jerry Sanders, it sought to shift the "emphasis to the economic pillar of containment but without disavowing the military pillar."[17] U.S. leadership would rest on a reinvigorated system of world trade and refurbished economic institutions to replace the defunct international financial order that had been one of the casualties of Vietnam. For selected Third World countries, the trilateralists "envisioned a role . . . in a rationalized world economy that offered them greater promise of economic gain through interdependence than by striking out on an independent course."[18]

Both Kissinger's strategic diplomacy and Carter's trilateralism were vulnerable to the right-wing backlash that gathered momentum in the late

1970s. Republican pundits made fun of the "Carter doctrine," which warned the Soviets against intervention in the Persian Gulf. As for Kissinger, the bulk of his own party disowned him.[19]

Reagan and the Triumph of Rollback

In 1981, rollback as a grand strategy came to power with the Reagan administration. No longer was the aim simply the containment of the Soviet Union. As Richard Pipes, a member of Reagan's National Security Council, put it: "Rather than seek to modify Soviet behavior, the West should assist those forces within the Communist bloc, which are working for a change of the *system*."[20] The Reaganite agenda included abandoning détente, sabotaging nuclear arms limitations agreements like Salt II, and pushing for decisive nuclear superiority over the Soviet Union.

Led by a prominent member of the staff of Secretary of Defense Caspar Weinberger, Richard Perle—the same Richard Perle who enjoyed significant influence in the Bush II administration—a network of anti-SALT advocates campaigned for withdrawal from arms control agreements with the Soviet Union.[21] As one major consequence, the Sixth Single Integrated Operation Plan (SIOP 6) raised the number of potential targets from 25,000 (already far above the number of warheads necessary for assured destruction of the Soviet Union) to "a staggering 50,000 potential targets."[22] But perhaps most ambitious was Reagan's Strategic Defense Initiative, popularly known as Star Wars, aimed at creating a shield against oncoming ballistic missiles. If put into effect, the SDI would have scuttled the Anti-Ballistic Missile Treaty between the United States and the Soviet Union.

The rejection of détente and the pursuit of nuclear superiority over what Reagan called the "evil empire" had a global impact in the early 1980s, similar to that of the Bush doctrine of preemptive warfare, promulgated in 2002. The two programs were key elements of an approach that also included

- preparing the U.S. armed forces to fight a "limited" nuclear war with the Soviet Union.
- upgrading U.S. military capability not just to fight a Europe-focused "one-and-a half-war" (one major war in Europe and a half war elsewhere) but to wage war on several fronts at once.

As Defense Secretary Weinberger put it: "Our long-term goal is to be able to meet the demands of a worldwide war, including the concurrent reinforcement of Europe, deployment to Southeast Asia and the Pacific and to support other areas."[23]

- establishing "maritime supremacy," or the achievement of "outright maritime superiority over any power or powers which might attempt to prevent our use of the seas and the maintenance of our vital interests worldwide" and the transformation of the Navy's posture from sealane defense to one that was "visibly offensive in orientation, [with] offensive power . . . widely distributed throughout the fleet."[24]

Early on, the Reagan administration took advantage of a conflict within the left-leaning government in tiny Grenada to unilaterally invade and institute regime change in that country—armed with a " 'signed, formal request' that it received from the little-known Organization of Eastern Caribbean States (OECS) 'asking for U.S. assistance in assuring their collective security and in restoring democracy to Grenada.' "[25] Also brazen in its unilateralist thrust was the American mining of Nicaragua's harbors and its financing and training of mercenaries—the contras—to bring down the Sandinista government in Nicaragua. And, of course, there was the 1986 bombing of Tripoli and Benghazi in Libya by U.S. warplanes in an effort to kill Mu'ammar Gadhafi.

Change in the Soviet Union was, of course, the centerpiece of the rollback strategy. Its advocates believed that their offensive nuclear and conventional posture, backed up by virtually unrestricted defense spending that made massive government deficits a fact of life in the United States, led to the emergence of the reformist regime of Mikhail Gorbachev and the eventual collapse of the Soviet Union, in 1991. As the Project for a New American Century, whose key figures were central players under Reagan, put it, the "essential elements of the Reagan administration's success [were] a military that is strong and ready to meet both present and future challenges; a foreign policy that boldly and purposefully promotes American principles abroad; and national leadership that accepts the United States' global responsibilities."[26]

Reagan's triumph marked the capture of the Republican Party by the hard right. The Reagan ascendancy entailed the displacement of the patrician Eastern wing that had led the party through much of the early Cold War era. The party's new center of gravity was in the South, the Southwest, and, to some extent, the West. Other vital sources of support included the Christian Right and an increasing number of Jewish voters worried about the firmness of the Democratic Party when it came to the defense of Israel.[27] The business community, of course, was cheered by the antilabor, deregulatory, and anti-corporate-tax proposals of the government. Indeed, Reagan appealed widely to members of the middle class, many of whom saw themselves as victimized by the emergence of the global South in the 1970s—mainly through the soaring oil prices that resulted from the greater bargaining power of the Organization of Petroleum Exporting Countries (OPEC).

The Specter of Overextension in the Grand Strategy

Yet even within the armed forces, showered as they were with the latest in weaponry, there was apprehension about the unlimited scope of military engagement that the Reagan administration seemed to be proposing. The concerns about overextension that had prompted George Kennan to suggest limiting American military and political commitment to selected areas of the globe resurfaced. To many in the military and civilian leadership, Vietnam was a debacle because it had unfolded in an area of little strategic importance. Admiral James Watkins, then chief of naval operations, admitted that because of resource constraints, the rollback strategy would be less ambitious than originally planned: "All tasks cannot be accomplished simultaneously without considerable risk. Thus, our current maritime strategy emphasizes maximum use of the other services and our allies in coalition warfare. . . . We know that any major war conflict will involve our allies."[28]

Indeed, a 1984 exercise, "Pressure Point," run by the Joint Chiefs of Staff, showed that in a conventional war on the Korean peninsula, the United States would run out of ammunition within a month. Moreover, should a crisis in Korea break out simultaneously with one in Central America, troops could not be sustained elsewhere. These findings confirmed the results of a major congressional study that concluded that "United States forces in Korea will have to sink or swim on their own." As a well-known strategic analyst put it, "America's unlimited global military objectives [under Reagan] render almost any conceivable US military means inadequate."[29]

When 241 marines were blown up by a suicide bomber in Lebanon in late 1983, the result was a rapid retreat from a commitment that threatened to become open-ended. What many in the administration saw as a clear case of overextension led the defense secretary to formulate the Weinberger doctrine. It proposed six criteria for involvement in a military conflict: vital U.S. interests were at stake; there was a clear intention to achieve military victory; the political and military objectives of the intervention were precisely defined; there was assurance of significant support from Congress and the American people; there was continual reassessment of the relationship between objectives and the size, composition, and disposition of forces; and force was used only as a last resort.[30]

To many military analysts who took to heart Weinberger's points, the lesson of the Gulf War led by President George H. W. Bush, was not so much the supremacy of the U.S. military but the fact that it took so much to achieve a victory over a fourth-rate army. In Andrew Bacevich's words, "As a feat of arms, the American-led victory in Desert Storm just might qualify as the most overblown achievement since the U.S. Navy, nearly a century before, handily dispatched a rickety Spanish fleet in Manila Bay."[31] Yet at the same time, U.S. resources were so badly strained that had another conflict broken out, things could have gone badly for Washington. To defeat Saddam Hussein, the United States sent 8 out of 18 Army divisions, 6 out of 9 Marine brigades, 6 out of 15 aircraft carrier battle groups, and 10 out of 22 Air Force tactical fighter wings.[32] The Gulf War was a worrisome case of overstretch, especially to subdue a weak military power.

One influential figure conscious of the downside of the conflict—one whose voice was drowned out in the ticker tape parades celebrating the winning of the war—was General Colin Powell, the armed forces chief of staff. He had opposed the launching of the war in the first place, although he had, paradoxically, emerged as one of its main heroes.

Clinton: Globalization and the Uses of Force

Worries about overextension, however, faded away in the early 1990s, with the expulsion of Saddam Hussein's army from Kuwait and, even more important, the sudden collapse of the Soviet Union. The transformation of the global equation posed two alternatives. The first option, represented by the Project for a New American Century and proposed by the Reaganite elements in the Bush I administration, was that of permanent military supremacy. The second, developed by the Clinton Democrats, was the deployment of American power in the service of globalization.

In the early 1990s, the Democrats had not yet resolved the intraparty bloodletting induced by the Vietnam War. The party's liberal containment wing fell apart, while a faction imbued with the antiwar sentiment of the party's 1972 presidential candidate, George McGovern, gained in influence. The Carter administration had tried to forge a centrist position, but it unraveled when the combination of the Iran hostage crisis and the Soviet invasion of Afghanistan forced a retreat to a hard-line containment policy soon dubbed the Carter doctrine. In hopes of retaking the White House, Clinton and other moderates in the party set up the Democratic Leadership Council. Despite their efforts to distance themselves from Carter, Clinton's "New Democrats" were also in search of a centrist position.

Economic Expansion as a Priority. Like Carter's initial efforts, the Clinton people focused on strengthening the economic aspects of global hegemony. For Clinton, the phenomenon of globalization, or accelerated integration of the world's economies, provided a convenient starting point for a distinctive foreign policy. In the view of theorists such as Kenichi Ohmae, a borderless world was in the making, marked by the ascendancy of transnational corporations and the decline of the state. For the Clintonites, foreign policy was to be the handmaiden of globalization, promoting the market forces that were driving it while channeling them in benign directions. Yet the focus on the economic and the promotion of globalization had strategic implications, and Clinton's people were well aware of the link. As the director of intelligence of the National Security Council put it:

> The United States can benefit immensely from this shift because we are well placed to thrive in a globalized political economy. Indeed, a globalized society of market-states plays into and enhances American strengths to such a degree that it worries some states that the United States will become so dominant that no other state will be able to catch up to it.[33]

A month after he took office, Clinton laid out the new strategic direction. With the acceleration of global capital and trade flows, it was "time for us to make trade a priority element of American security." Clinton promised a comprehensive trade strategy that would "open other nations' markets" and "establish clear and enforceable rules on which to expand trade."[34] Clinton and his team, Andrew Bacevich writes, had found the "Big Idea" that would supersede containment; it was the strategy of "Openness": "the removal of barriers to the movement of goods, capital, people, and ideas, thereby fostering an integrated international order conducive to American interests, governed by American norms, regulated by American power, and, above all, satisfying the expectations of the American people for ever-greater abundance."[35]

Bacevich notes that there was really nothing new about the strategy of openness, however, since expansion of markets had been the underlying dynamic of U.S. history. Containment during the Cold War presupposed that "the essential aim of liberal internationalism was to open the world to American enterprise."[36] Yet the centrality of opening markets as an *overt priority* of foreign policy was new. The main global initiatives during Clinton's first term were the creation of the North American Free Trade Area (NAFTA) in 1993 and support for the establishment of the World Trade Organization in 1995. The two institutions served as powerful mechanisms that swept away regional and global barriers to U.S. goods and investments over the next few years.

The commitment to economic expansion as a foreign policy objective was also reflected in the emphasis on opening up East Asia to U.S. capital. Trade liberalization had been a critical concern since the Reagan period, but under Clinton, promoting the flow of investment to East Asia became a priority as well. Not surprisingly, the key international crises of the Clinton administration were economic—the Mexican collapse and bailout in 1994, the Asian financial upheaval in 1997, and the fiasco at the WTO ministerial meeting in Seattle in 1999. Nor was it surprising, given the centrality of economic initiatives in the Clinton White House, that the Treasury Department and the United States Trade Representative (USTR) emerged as the chief foreign policy arms of the administration, overshadowing the Department of State. As one observer noted, the State Department

> has lost ground on what has become a major element of foreign policy, trade negotiations. The USTR has not only filled this role, but has emerged as a major player in foreign policy. Whether in fashioning the lodestone of our relationship with China, the

future of the international trading system in the WTO, or, increasingly, the relationship with emerging third-world economies, the USTR is perhaps one of the most powerful foreign policy agencies in this age of globalization. Yet it is not part of the traditional foreign policy structure, nor does it feel bound by the latter.[37]

Under Mickey Kantor and his successor, Charlene Barshefsky, the U.S. trade representative's office alternated between threatening allies with unilaterally imposing trade sanctions under the so-called Super 301 provision of the U.S. Trade Act and cajoling them to accept Washington's preferred versions of NAFTA and the WTO.

The Treasury Department gained even more influence than the USTR, especially during the Asian financial crisis. As Princeton Lyman has noted: "International financial stability was at stake, but so too was the political stability of important countries like Indonesia and South Korea. The US Treasury nevertheless took the lead in fashioning the US response, while the State Department struggled for weeks to have a seat at the table in order to inject its concerns."[38]

Robert Rubin, Clinton's second Treasury secretary, and Lawrence Summers, Rubin's successor, enjoyed enormous influence over foreign policy. Formerly a senior partner at the Wall Street investment bank Goldman Sachs, Rubin represented, in Washington's pyramid of power, what had become the most dynamic sector of business—finance capital. Summers, former chief economist of the World Bank, had become the prime ideologue of free-market capitalism. They emerged as symbols of what Jagdish Bhagwati, the Columbia University free-trade economist, dubbed the "Wall Street–Treasury Complex." During the most serious foreign policy dilemma of the Clinton administration, the Asian financial crisis, the fate of the global economy and global order was, for all practical purposes, in their hands—a fact underlined by *Time* magazine, when it called them, along with Federal Reserve chair Alan Greenspan, the "Committee to Save the World."[39] Promoting the interests of U.S. banks, investment houses, and bondholders became Washington's overriding consideration during the crisis—marginalizing traditional political and defense concerns—as it dealt with Korea, Russia, Thailand, Indonesia, and Malaysia.

Missionary Democracy. The economic priorities of the Clinton agenda

did not, however, have the effect of sidelining political and military strategies for long. Globalization itself, particularly through structural adjustment programs designed to liberalize, deregulate, and privatize developing
economies, was creating more losers than winners, especially in Latin
America and Africa. The artificial system of nation-states into which the
colonial powers had partitioned postcolonial Africa was breaking down.
And with the end of the Cold War, the discipline of the Communist-
capitalist rivalry, which had kept Eastern Europe together for fifty years,
gave way to those nationalist and ethnic forces that had been simmering
below the surface for generations.

The Clinton team was more sensitive than the first Bush administration
to the ideological dimensions of foreign policy. George H. W. Bush, like
Kissinger, was instinctively a conservative. His foreign policy relied on
realpolitik to maintain global order in the post-Communist world. In
Bush's view, U.S. interests were primary, and he was averse to promoting
democratic reform among authoritarian allies that had supported the
United States in the struggle against the Soviet Union. Thus, as vice president under Reagan, Bush had toasted Philippine strongman Ferdinand
Marcos during a visit to Manila on the occasion of Marcos's victory in the
rigged elections in June 1981: "We love you, sir . . . we love your adherence
to democratic rights and democratic processes."

Strobe Talbott, who served as Clinton's deputy secretary of state,
claimed that the post–Cold War environment demanded more than
realpolitik to keep the nation engaged in the world: "The American people
want their country's foreign policy rooted in idealpolitik as well as
realpolitik."[40] Thus, in the words of Anthony Lake, the national security
adviser, "enlargement of the community of free nations" had to be a central foreign policy goal.[41]

This mixture of liberal messianism and ethnocentrism conveniently for-
got, of course, that the move toward democratization in the 1980s in Latin
America, Africa, and Asia had taken place not because of but in spite of the
United States. Moreover, while Clinton's democratic evangelism was
robust when it came to enemies like Iran and Iraq, the administration
remained virtually silent about those authoritarian regimes, such as
Indonesia and Saudi Arabia, that protected U.S. strategic interests. There
was much greater continuity of policy from Reagan and Bush and on
through the Clinton years than immediately met the eye.

Flexible Force versus the Powell Doctrine. Clinton's key foreign policy staff—Madeleine Albright, for example—felt that the issue of the deployment of U.S. power could not be avoided in the post–Cold War era. The question was under which circumstances to use the nation's military might. Where strategic interests were clearly involved, as in the case of access to Middle East oil, there was not much of a problem. Nor was controversy aroused when Saddam Hussein was pounded from the air to enforce what Washington viewed as the peace terms of the Gulf War. In June 1993, in response to an alleged Iraqi plot to kill former President Bush; in September 1996, when Saddam's troops invaded the Kurdish sanctuary in northern Iraq; and again in late 1998, when Saddam expelled UN weapons inspectors; Washington launched massive air attacks on Iraqi targets.

Moreover, the United States did not hesitate to show the flag in areas it considered its traditional stomping grounds. They included the South China Sea, where, disregarding China's protests, Washington sent two aircraft carrier battle groups in March 1996 in response to China's military exercises during the presidential campaign and elections in Taiwan. The largest armada assembled since the end of the Vietnam War, the deployment was conducted despite a consensus among defense analysts that China had no intention of invading Taiwan.

When the direct interests of the United States did not clearly warrant an intervention, however, things became fuzzy. Here a potential problem surfaced, thanks to the increased pressure for U.S. participation in UN peacekeeping efforts, demand for which surged during the late 1980s and 1990s. The Somalia deployment undertaken by outgoing President Bush in December 1992 and affirmed by the incoming Clinton administration was one in which U.S. vital interests were unclear. When U.S. Special Forces ran into an ambush staged by the warlord General Aideed on October 3, 1993, suffering eighteen dead and scores wounded, domestic criticism rained down on Clinton, making the participation of ground troops in UN operations in which they could suffer casualties something to be shunned at all costs. The consequence was what the diplomat Richard Holbrooke called the "Vietmalia" syndrome.[42]

Avoidance of ground operations did not, however, stop Clinton aides from promoting intervention they felt would enhance U.S. interests and prestige or could be justified on humanitarian grounds. Stung by criticism of its inaction during the genocide in Rwanda in 1994, the Clinton administration took to using ground troop proxies in both Bosnia in 1995 and East Timor in 1999. In East Timor, the Australian-led International Force for East Timor (INTERFRET) moved in to restore order after a campaign of terror waged by Indonesian troops and Indonesian-allied Timorese militias in response to the overwhelming vote for independence by the Timorese people. Behind the scenes, some five thousand U.S. support troops provided communications, intelligence, transportation, and logistics.[43]

In Bosnia, airpower combined with reliance on Washington's proxies on the ground to create a military victory that defeated the Bosnian Serbs and led to the Dayton Peace Accords at the end of 1997. Washington's "Gurkhas," as Bacevich called them after the famous Nepalese mercenaries of the British Army, were the soldiers of the Croat Army. They were trained by the Pentagon-linked private firm Military Professional Resources Inc., which hired former U.S. military officers to carry out a variety of functions, including training proxy troops. As one analyst noted, MPRI had "effectively acted as a mechanism of U.S. policy in the Balkans at less cost and lower political risk than that incurred if the U.S. military were directly involved."[44]

What constituted the vital interests of the United States became murkier as Clinton administration strategists tried harder to define it. Did they lie in isolating nondemocratic regimes? In asserting leadership during humanitarian catastrophes? In containing a long-term strategic threat, as China appeared to be to some in the Pentagon's military and civilian leadership? In creating the political conditions for former Socialist countries to join the market economy? In preventing the diffusion of weapons of mass destruction? In waging a war against the threat of global terrorism? In opposing efforts to weaken the U.S. presence in Europe? In enlarging NATO? In acting as an international gendarme to prevent local conflicts around the world from igniting regional or global conflagrations?

As U.S. interests proliferated, along with conflicts in the post–Cold War world, the Clintonites increasingly valued the country's daunting military power. Yet concerns about overextension resurfaced in influential quarters, especially in the person of Colin Powell. What came to be known as the Powell doctrine was actually an updated version of the Weinberger doctrine.

The Gulf War was thought to fit the Weinberger criteria to a *t,* but even this war, as noted earlier, was initially opposed by Powell, although he contributed mightily to its victory. Nevertheless, Powell endorsed the Weinberger doctrine. He gave it an "Army spin" by "emphasizing that the clear intention of winning should include the use of overwhelming force and that Weinberger's precisely defined political and military objectives should be clearly linked."[45] According to some interpreters of his doctrine, Powell also demanded "a clearly defined exit strategy."[46]

Powell's cautious approach to the use of military power is said to have stemmed from the Army's experience in Vietnam, where the military was nearly shattered by vague war aims issued by a confused civilian leadership.[47] In any event, the Powell approach helped stymie the tendency of the Clintonites to make military commitments wherever they felt the strategic interests of the United States were involved. Les Aspin, Clinton's first secretary of defense, complained that the Weinberger and Powell doctrines "left the president with only two options: force or nothing," and he "argued that a more flexible doctrine, with more options, was required."[48] Madeleine Albright was equally frustrated by the leash that the Powell doctrine seemed to put on the initiatives of the Clinton administration. In her autobiography she recounts Powell's answer to the question of what it would take to intervene in Bosnia, where Bosnian Serbs were engaged in murdering, massacring, and deporting Muslims:

> [H]e replied consistent with his commitment to the doctrine of overwhelming force, saying it would take tens of thousands of troops, cost billions of dollars, probably result in numerous casualties, and require a long and open-ended commitment of U.S. forces. Time and again he led us up the hill of possibilities and dropped us off on the other side with the practical equivalent of a "No can do." After hearing this for the umpteenth time, I asked in exasperation, "What are we saving this superb military for, Colin, if we can't use it?"

While it was understandable that Powell would want clarity about mission and certainty about success before committing forces, Albright argued, "no more quagmires" did not amount to a strategy in a "messy and complex" world: "With careful planning, limited force could be used effectively to achieve limited objectives. There was an urgent need to do that in Bosnia, but Powell did not want the American military to do the job."[49]

If Powell was dubious about intervention in the Balkans, it was because the enterprise was sold as an open-ended humanitarian measure to protect lives and communities. Just as important was his belief that the main objective was left unstated: the Clinton administration needed the expedition to prove, to its European allies, the usefulness of NATO after the Cold War and thus retain U.S. military hegemony in Europe. According to Bacevich, the Bosnian conflict of the early 1990s, as well as the Kosovo crisis, put NATO's credibility on the line: "For the United States, the interests at stake were not merely humanitarian. Bosnia called into question the relevance of NATO and, by extension, U.S. claims to leadership in Europe."[50] If it had not successfully managed the Serbian strongman Slobodan Milosevic, the United States could not have supported its drive for NATO expansion. For the Clinton administration, such expansion would fill the security vacuum in Eastern Europe and institutionalize U.S. leadership in Europe. In Washington's view,

> NATO enlargement would provide an institutional framework to lock in the domestic transitions under way in Eastern and Central Europe. The prospect of alliance membership would itself be an "incentive" for these countries to pursue domestic reforms. Subsequent integration into the alliance was predicted to lock in those institutional reforms. Membership would entail a wide array of organizational adaptations, such as standardization of military procedures, steps toward interoperability with NATO forces, and joint planning and training. By enmeshing new members in the wider alliance institutions and participation in its operations, NATO would reduce their ability to revert to the old ways and reinforce the liberalization of transitional governments. As one NATO official remarked: "We're enmeshing them in the NATO culture, both politically and militarily, so they begin to think like us and—over time—act like us."[51]

The Powell doctrine became a straitjacket that Clinton administration officials tried to shed. Airpower technologies that had been developed during the Gulf War seemed to offer a solution. The fact that aircraft alone would not make the difference militarily was conventional wisdom, certainly from the Army's perspective. But in the eyes of some Navy and Air Force officials, the application of information technology to airpower would permit bombing that was both massive and precise, via cruise missiles, the B-1 Stealth bomber, or the older B-52s. Airpower could become the decisive factor in war; instead of providing support for ground troops, it would make the infantry largely superfluous, thus drastically lowering U.S. casualties.

Clinton, Kosovo, and Airpower. The air war to break the deadlock in Bosnia in 1995 and the much bigger air campaign against Milosevic in 1999 were the result of an alliance among Clinton administration advocates—including Albright, NATO supreme commander Mark Clark, and General Mike Short, Clark's air commander—of the use of flexible force. As one account put it, "What American airpower had done in the Gulf War, Short and other airmen believed, was just a beginning. The effectiveness and power of high-precision bombs and the Stealth bombers had increased exponentially in just eight years, and Short was sure that the pressure he could quickly apply to Milosevic would be unbearable and bring him to the table in a short time."[52]

Short and others argued that information technology had greatly increased the accuracy of bombing, a claim supported by the fact that "today, 70 to 80 per cent of guided munitions fall within 10 meters of their targets, even at night, with overcast skies, or in moderate winds . . . compared to World War II, when only 18 per cent of U.S. bombs fell within 1,000 feet of their targets, and only 20 per cent of British bombs dropped at night fell within 5 miles of theirs."[53]

This new kind of war, in which the object is to pummel ground targets without incurring injuries and fatalities, is vividly described by David Halberstam:

> What was taking place in the struggle over Kosovo was something new, virtual war from fifteen thousand feet or above. It was an antiseptic war waged by remote control, without casualties, if at all possible, or at least without casualties for the side with the higher level of technology. It was, thought those who were its witnesses and fortunate or unfortunate enough to be near any of the bombing sites, truly surrealistic. The NATO planes flew so

high that they were never seen, although on rare occasions there might be a brief glimpse of the bombs themselves falling and then the sound of the explosions. The B-2 bomber pilots flying the missions were based in Missouri, and the question for some of the crews was whether they would get back in time to watch their children's soccer and baseball games. It was war as envisioned by George Orwell or H. G. Wells: invisible planes sent on their missions from scientifically advanced bases elsewhere to pick out unseen targets from high-tech screens and to launch laser-guided or photo-guided weapons of destruction at them. The war, amazingly futuristic in the eyes of men who had fought in other wars, was obviously worthy of a science fiction novel.[54]

Milosevic gave up after seventy-eight days of bombing. The prominent British military specialist John Keegan declared: "There are certain dates in the history of warfare that mark real turning points. . . . Now there is a new turning point to fix on the calendar: June 3, 1999, when the capitulation of President Milosevic proved that a war can be won by airpower alone."[55] Others were not so sure. According to the University of Chicago military analyst Robert Pape, high-level bombing did not inflict great damage to either infrastructure or civilian morale, and the most likely reason why Milosevic sued for peace was his fear that a ground invasion of Kosovo by NATO was imminent "with the devastating help of precision air power."[56]

But whatever the real cause of Milosevic's surrender, precision bombing, to advocates of military intervention, seemed to enable a combatant to be successful without incurring too many casualties and without having to resort to the massive application of ground troops demanded by the Powell doctrine. While it lasted, the NATO air campaign, for most Americans, indeed dropped below the radar screen, allowing the civilian and military elites maximum flexibility in carrying on the war. Albright seemed vindicated in her argument that "with careful planning, limited force could be used effectively to achieve limited objectives."

But what were those objectives? What national interest was served by the Kosovo air campaign? The answer was no longer obvious. If humanitarian intervention was defined as being in the national interest, then there was a yawning gulf between the aim of the bombing and its consequences, as became evident early on. The bombing provoked the Serbs in Kosovo to accelerate their murder and displacement of Albanian Kosovars, while doing "considerable indirect damage" to the people of Serbia, including the targeting of electrical grids, bridges, and water facilities, acts that violated Article 14 of the 1977 Protocol to the 1949 Geneva Convention, which prohibits attacks on "objects indispensable to the survival of the civilian population."[57]

Bacevich argues that if humanitarian relief of the Muslim Kosovars was the object, "effective diplomacy would have precluded NATO action."[58] But military action was what Washington wanted, he argues, because it would serve as a

> demonstration of what a new, more muscular alliance under U.S. direction could accomplish in thwarting "creeping instability." The intent of Operation Allied Force was to provide an object lesson to any European state fancying that it was exempt from the rules of the post–Cold War era. It was not Kosovo that counted, but affirming the dominant position of the United States in a Europe that was unified, integrated, and open. As Clinton himself explained on March 23, 1999, just before the start of the bombing campaign, "if we're going to have a strong economic relationship that includes our ability to sell around the world, Europe has got to be key. . . . That's what this Kosovo thing is all about."[59]

The Clinton administration acted according to a loose, shifting, and oftentimes cavalier interpretation of what was in the national interest. The White House began by enunciating a pacific, economic framework for foreign policy. But it left office, ironically, with a record number of deployments, from show-the-flag exercises to full-scale war. As former secretary of state Alexander Haig observed: "Since 1990 we deployed forces about 45 times. . . . During the entire 50-year span of the Cold War we had only 16 deployments."[60]

Clinton's Legacy to Bush II

To the incoming Bush administration, the Clinton presidency bequeathed a number of dangerous practices. One was an overly elastic definition of national interest that nonetheless might be supported by the force of arms, if necessary. Another was its penchant for identifying the national interest with the promotion of Western-style democracy abroad. As one Republican admirer saw it, Bush, in invading Iraq, simply took the "doctrine of 'democratic engagement' of the first Bush administration, and that of 'democratic enlargement' of the Clinton administration, one step further. It might be called 'democratic transformation.' "[61]

Still another legacy of the Clinton years was the practice of unilaterally identifying the conditions under which state sovereignty could be overturned without multilateral agreement or sanction in international law. The same writer saw the Clinton administration's actions in Kosovo and Haiti as "precedents" that "strengthen the emerging rule that regimes that repudiate the popular basis of sovereignty—by overturning democratic institutions, by denying even the most basic human rights and practicing mass terror against their own people, by preparing and launching unprovoked assaults against their neighbors—jeopardize the rights of sovereignty, including the inherent right to seek whatever weapons a regime may choose."[62] What came to be known as the Bush doctrine, in other words, was simply an extension of what some have called the Clinton doctrine of "humanitarian intervention."[63]

The Clinton presidency passed on to its successor another worrisome notion: that with the use of precision bombing, victory could be effected fairly quickly, and with minimum casualties, thus winning acceptance from a public not prepared to be inconvenienced.

The Clintonites ended up junking any major effort to reform and streamline the military for post–Cold War conditions. What emerged, instead, was the military's "major theater wars" standard, which required that U.S. forces "be constantly ready to fight two major regional conflicts (MRCs) in two widely separated theaters and overlapping time frames."[64] In fact, the MTW standard responded to the Pentagon's desire to maintain a force that was similar to the one that prevailed during the Cold War.

During the 2000 presidential campaign, George W. Bush accused Clinton of underfunding the military and of failing to develop the new technologies of warfare. In fact, writes Lawrence Korb, none of Bush's claims were true: "Clinton had actually increased the size of the defense budget over and above the program he inherited from the outgoing administration of George Bush Senior. . . . Moreover, during the Clinton years, the military was gradually building precisely the systems Bush named. Between 1993 and 2000, the Pentagon increased its stocks of smart bombs ninefold, developed lighter, more agile tanks and armored personnel carriers, and began producing unmanned aircraft like the Predator."[65]

Reflecting the military's satisfaction with Clinton, two prominent analysts at the Pentagon's National Defense University wrote that the two-MTW standard endorsed by the administration "had a positive effect on the U.S. policy process [by setting] limits on post–Cold War reductions while creating a credible rationale for today's posture of 13 active Army and Marine divisions, 20 Air Force active and Reserve fighter wings, and 12 Navy carrier battle groups."[66]

In the end, the grand strategy of the Clinton administration was qualitatively different from that of its successor. But continuities and precedents were established during the 1990s, particularly regarding the employment of force, that would prove to be severely destabilizing to the global order when George W. Bush took over.

BUSH II AND ROLLBACK-PLUS

"If we're an arrogant nation, they'll resent us," George W. Bush declared, referring to the attitudes of other countries, during his foreign policy debate with Al Gore in 2000. "If we're a humble nation but strong, they'll welcome us."[67]

The Main Event

Immediately on assuming power in 2001, Bush and the new team in Washington seemed to set out to contradict those words. "Ten days in, and it was about Iraq," recalled Secretary of the Treasury Paul O'Neill of a meeting on January 30 of the National Security Council, shortly after Bush assumed office:

> The hour almost up, Bush had assignments for everyone. Powell and his team would look to draw up a new sanctions regime. Rumsfeld and [General] Shelton, he said, "should examine our military options." That included rebuilding the military coalition

from the 1991 Gulf War, examining "how it might look" to use US ground forces in the north and south of Iraq and how the armed forces could support groups inside the country who could help challenge Saddam Hussein. [CIA director] Tenet would report on improving our current intelligence. O'Neill would investigate how to financially squeeze the regime.[68]

Crossing swords with other key states in the world, instead of dealing with the terrorist threat, appeared to be the Bush priority in 2001. The president poured cold water on visiting South Korean president Kim Dae Jung's "Sunshine Policy" toward North Korea. China was recategorized: once a "strategic partner" under Clinton, now a "strategic competitor." And Washington announced its intent to withdraw from the Anti-Ballistic Missile (ABM) Treaty. Along with the denunciation of the Kyoto Protocol and the International Criminal Court, these moves were meant to warn the world that a more muscular foreign policy was in the offing.

September 11, 2001, made the war against terrorism a domestic and foreign policy priority. But even the invasion of Afghanistan was seen as a warmup to the main event, the invasion of Iraq. The attacks on the World Trade Center and the Pentagon appeared to reinvigorate multilateralism, and the combination of goodwill toward the United States and the need for allies in a far-flung war against terror persuaded the Bush administration to focus on building coalitions and alliances. But the relapse into multilateralism proved momentary. Washington's attention shifted from attacking the Al Qaeda/Taliban forces in Afghanistan to dealing with its bête noire: Saddam Hussein. The United States grudgingly went to the United Nations to seek approval for an invasion, even as a secret military plan—one that the secretary of state, Colin Powell, did not know about—moved into high gear. Facing a veto at the Security Council by former allies Germany and France as well as by smaller countries like Chile and Syria, the United States abandoned the multilateral pretense and launched its invasion of Iraq on March 20, 2003. Our task here is to understand the source of the destructive dynamic that John Newhouse has characterized as Bush's "assault on world order."[69]

Return of the Reaganites

First of all, Bush's policy registered the return to the White House of the right-wing coalition that had dominated Reagan's administration. Indeed, the new president assumed power "courtesy of Reagan-era Supreme Court appointees" that set aside the ballot verification process in Florida.[70] A group of veterans from the Reagan years took charge of foreign policy, united on two fundamental points: the hard-line rollback policies had led to the collapse of the Soviet Union; and the demise of the Soviet Union provided a golden opportunity for the sole remaining superpower to achieve a level of military supremacy that would ensure that it would never again be threatened. This supremacist view was outlined in the famous (or notorious) draft *Defense Planning Guidance*, drawn up in 1992 under the supervision of Paul Wolfowitz, then a Pentagon senior official in the Bush I administration:

> Our first objective is to prevent the re-emergence of a new rival. This is the dominant consideration underlying the new regional defense strategy and requires that we endeavor to prevent any hostile power from dominating a region whose resources would, under consolidated control, be sufficient to generate global power.
>
> There are three additional aspects to this objective. First, the US must show the leadership necessary to establish and protect a new order that holds the promise of convincing potential competitors that they need not aspire to a greater role or pursue an aggressive posture to protect their legitimate interests. Second, in the non-defense areas, we must account sufficiently for the interests of the advanced industrial nations to discourage them from challenging our leadership or seeking to overturn the established political and economic order. Finally, we must maintain the mechanisms for deterring competitors from even aspiring to a larger regional or global role.[71]

This document, which was rejected by the Bush I administration, essentially proposed Rollback II. It rejected the potential peace dividend that would result from the anticipated drop in defense spending now that the Cold War was over. Instead, it opted for greater spending and a more powerful military.

The Strategic Elite

In 2001, after twelve years in the wilderness, the Rollback II proponents were back in the saddle with George W. Bush. Two major factions quickly came to dominate military and foreign policy. One was represented by the Rumsfeld-Cheney partnership. Donald Rumsfeld, who served as chief of staff and as secretary of defense in the administration of Gerald Ford, succeeded in preventing any movement on the proposed SALT II treaty with the Soviet Union.[72] While still a member of Congress from Illinois, Rumsfeld earned a 100 percent approval rating from right-wing groups.[73] During the Clinton administration, Rumsfeld chaired a commission of the Republican-controlled Congress that recommended that the country develop a missile defense system.[74]

Dick Cheney, a longtime colleague of Rumsfeld's on the Republican Party's hard right, took over as Ford's chief of staff when Rumsfeld moved to the Defense Department, and Cheney himself served as secretary of defense under Bush I, where he cut a "relatively isolated figure" in an administration dominated by conservative pragmatists.[75] With the ascension of Bush II, Cheney emerged as probably the most powerful individual in the national security establishment, one who was "not dependent on the President's National Security Council staff, since his own foreign-policy staff is just as strong."[76] Cheney and Rumsfeld have been termed "aggressive realists," their trademark a "skepticism about the effectiveness of international institutions, treaties, and diplomacy."[77]

Neoconservatives made up the second major force in Bush's foreign policy apparatus. The neocons were a group of disillusioned liberals who split from the Democratic Party in the late 1970s because of differences mainly on military and foreign policy issues. The most prominent neocon in the Bush II administration was Wolfowitz, the deputy secretary of defense, widely regarded as the architect of both the Iraq invasion and of Bush's vision for the Middle East. His former partner "Scooter" Libby headed up an influential policy-intelligence center lodged in the vice president's office. Wolfowitz was said to run a "shadow government centered in the Pentagon with its own intelligence capability independent of the CIA."[78]

At the center of the neoconservative network was Richard Perle, who served as a staff member of Democratic senator Henry "Scoop" Jackson's aggressively anti-Communist entourage before becoming assistant secretary of defense for policy in the Reagan administration.[79] While working under Reagan, Perle earned the sobriquet "Prince of Darkness" for opposing arms control agreements.[80]

Other leading neoconservatives included former CIA director James Woolsey; Douglas Feith, the undersecretary of defense for policy; John Bolton, in charge of arms control and international affairs at the State Department (a case of putting the fox in charge of the chicken coop); and Stephen Hadley, the deputy national security adviser.[81] Outside of government, neocon views were articulated by Robert Kagan, senior associate at the Carnegie Endowment for International Peace; Robert Kaplan, a correspondent for *The Atlantic Monthly;* and Charles Krauthammer, the *Washington Post* columnist who coined the term "the unipolar moment." Key intellectual influences on the more prominent neocons, like Perle and Wolfowitz, were the late University of Chicago professor Albert Wohlstetter, who had argued that the United States "had to fight a nuclear war in order to deter it,"[82] and another Chicago professor, the late Leo Strauss, an émigré intellectual described by political analyst Alex Callinicos as "a conservative critic of modernity and a sceptic about democracy who conceived philosophy as an esoteric wisdom to be concealed from the vulgar masses."[83]

Bush and His Base

And where did the president fit in all this? Paul O'Neill, the former Treasury secretary, paints him as a man of limited intelligence with little originality and with no access to fresh ideas except those that a small "praetorian guard" led by Cheney would allow.[84] But there is another view, articulated by Ivo Daalder and James Lindsey, who argue that the conventional view of Bush—that his foreign policy choices reflect expedience or the pressures of aggressive presidential advisers—is mistaken: ". . . Bush, like Ronald Reagan, brought to the Oval Office a deeply felt and coherent foreign policy worldview. Bush's critics missed it at the time—and continue to miss it—because they focus on how little he knows rather than how intensely he believes. It is a worldview that emphasizes the need to act, disparages the counsel of the cautious and promises that events will vindicate those willing to stand alone."[85]

There is, indeed, a world of difference between the elder Bush and the younger one, with "Bush *fils*," as Callinicos points out, modeling "his personal style on that of Reagan—the folksy great communicator who concentrated on getting . . . the big issues right."[86] According to another analyst, Bush came to Washington already a convinced unilateralist.[87] In John Newhouse's view, the younger Bush is neither a stupid man nor putty in the hands of advisers like Cheney and Karl Rove but a "skillful politician and a relentless campaigner, as much of one perhaps as Bill Clinton, who defined the state of the art."[88] If Bush trusts Cheney and Rove (Bush's chief political guru), it is because he shares their perspective and can leave the details to them while he focuses on communicating the vision.

Bush anchored his foreign and domestic policies on the radical right while skillfully tweaking his image so as to come across as a moderate, even a "compassionate conservative." He sought to attract traditional conservatives and sectors of the middle class that had prospered during the Clinton boom years. And he cultivated a folksy, NASCAR-dad image to attract the so-called Reagan Democrats of the working classes who found Al Gore too "soft" and an intellectual to boot. Once in power, however, Bush showed his true colors. He excluded the old-line conservatives who had served his father, like Lawrence Eagleburger and Brent Scowcroft, and surrounded himself with radical right figures, including Cheney, Rove, and Karen Hughes, a senior White House adviser who counseled the president from Texas after she and her family returned to their home state.

Bush consolidated the Reagan base in the white South and Southwest and the Christian right. Moreover, most of corporate America backed him, as did many voters in the affluent upper middle class. Within the corporate elite, Bush was especially popular among interests tied to the energy industry and the military-industrial complex. Before running for vice president, Cheney had been head of Halliburton, the biggest manufacturer of oil-related equipment.[89] Once a key executive of Harken Oil, a Dallas company, Bush had roots deep in the Texas oil industry; his efforts to loosen regulation of offshore drilling, and power production and distribution, won him the support of oil interests as well as energy traders like Enron.[90]

Despite the fact that defense-related production dropped to 4 percent of the gross domestic product, the military-industrial complex continued to exercise tremendous influence—in part because it has distributed defense production facilities throughout the states, securing, in the process, a popular base as well as a bipartisan network in Congress in favor of high levels of defense spending. With his plan to increase defense spending aggressively and to introduce programs such as antimissile defense, Bush nailed down the support of a powerful bloc of corporate interests and attracted large numbers of voters.

Furthermore, defense contracts are a lucrative source of income for firms, such as General Electric, AT&T, and General Motors, that operate mainly in the civilian sector. Aircraft manufacturers Lockheed and Boeing are "dependent on military orders to sustain their non-military operations."[91] Hi-tech Motorola is tied tightly to the Pentagon by defense contracts. Then there are the innovators that have their feet in both economies. Halliburton, once led by Cheney, for instance, not only manufactures oil equipment but has subsidiaries that provide services to the military—everything from erecting tent cities to transporting supplies to feeding the troops. Halliburton is one of several corporations that benefit from the privatization of services once provided by military support units.[92] And security for high-profile political figures supported by the United States are increasingly parceled out to the private sector.[93]

Bush depends, as well, on a segment of the Jewish community closely identified with the state of Israel. Some Jews viewed the Clinton-sponsored Oslo peace process as a sellout of Israel's interests in favor of the Palestinians. And Bush and Rove were "eager to win more of the Jewish vote in 2004 than Bush in 2000 and to maintain the support of the Christian right, whose members are also strong supporters of Israel."[94] Several of the leading neoconservatives are Jewish and rabid backers of Ariel Sharon, the Israeli prime minister, and his Likud Party. Indeed, as Newhouse notes, the "pro-Sharon-Netanyahu cohort in the Pentagon has operated, in effect, like an extension of the Likud leadership."[95] A strategy document prepared in 1996, when Benjamin Netanyahu was prime minister, recommended the "removal of Mr. [Saddam] Hussein as a means of foiling Syria's regional ambitions" and was drawn up with the participation of Perle and Feith.[96] Thus the neocons have played a key mediating role between the pro-Zionist community and Bush.

A Truly Grandiose Strategy

The Bush administration's grand strategy was indeed grandiose in its objective: to attain such overwhelming military superiority that any

country or coalition of countries could not even dream of catching up. The
project would be achieved not only by massive spending for defense to fund
innovation in military technology but also through the acquisition of "bases
and stations within and beyond Western Europe and Northeast Asia, as well
as temporary access arrangements for the long-distance deployment of US
forces."[97] Treaties and multilateral institutions were to be used only when
they advanced U.S. interests and sidestepped when they didn't. Bolton, head
of the arms control office of the State Department, justified this practice in a
1997 opinion piece: "[T]reaties are simply 'political' obligations [that] can
be unilaterally modified or terminated by congressional action [since]
America's constitutional requirements override 'international law.' "[98]

Special emphasis would be placed on destroying terrorist networks and
on the states that sheltered them, and on preventing rogue states from
developing weapons of mass destruction. "The overlap between states that
sponsor terror and those that pursue WMD compels us to action," asserted
the National Security Strategy Paper issued by Bush on September 17,
2002.[99] The United States would extend the right to attack other states
beyond the self-defense rationale contained in the UN Charter's Article 51.
It would strike preemptively against those that had the capability to
develop WMDs. As the National Security Strategy Paper put it:

> The United States has long maintained the option of preemptive
> actions to counter a sufficient threat to our national security. The
> greater the threat, the greater is the risk of inaction—and the
> more compelling the case for taking anticipatory action to
> defend ourselves, even if uncertainty remains as to the time and
> place of the enemy's attack. To forestall or prevent such hostile
> acts by our adversaries, the United States will, if necessary, act
> preemptively.[100]

Security would be ensured not only by knocking out or isolating rogue
regimes but by replacing them with democratic ones, on the grounds that
rogue states are threats to both their neighbors and to their people and
have thus "lost sovereignty." For the neoconservative writer Max Boot,
global leadership was partly about "imposing the rule of law, property
rights, free speech and other guarantees, at gunpoint if need be."[101]

Underlying and fortifying these currents, Tom Barry points out, is the language of antiterrorism, which has replaced anti-Communism as the strategy's core organizing and unifying principle.[102]

The grand strategy of the Bush II administration certainly differed from that of its predecessor. The Clinton administration promoted economic globalization as the mechanism of imperial consolidation while selectively engaging in intervention to keep perceived threats to the imperial order off balance. The Bush policy, on the other hand, which had its roots in the rollback tradition of strategic thinking, is the extension of rollback into the post–Cold War period, where it sought to take advantage of America's military supremacy. The rollback approach, however, was profoundly hubristic. It ignored the problem of matching goals to resources, a consideration that acted as a restraint on Reagan's strategic policy—as the U.S. withdrawal from Lebanon and the enunciation of the Weinberger doctrine, following the killing of 241 marines by a suicide bomber in 1983, demonstrated.

Unilateralism, preemption, and an extraordinary sense of omnipotence created an agenda that was less conservative than radical. It destabilized long-standing arrangements with allies and neutral parties and threatened both old and new foes of the United States.[103]

CHAPTER 2

Imperial Hubris/Imperial Overextension

One more such victory, and I am lost.

KING PYRRHUS, 280 BC

[Iraq] is going to suck the oxygen out of everything.

SECRETARY OF STATE COLIN POWELL

*What's the point of being the greatest, the most powerful nation
in the world and not having an imperial role? It's unheard of
in human history. The most powerful nation always had
an imperial role.*

IRVING KRISTOL

When George W. Bush landed on the aircraft carrier USS *Abraham Lincoln*,
off the California coast, on May 1, 2003, to mark the end of hostilities in
Iraq, Washington seemed to be at the zenith of its power. Many commentators called the city, with a mixture of awe and disgust, the "New Rome." The
carrier landing, as the Canadian scholar Anthony Hall points out, was a cel-
ebration of power—a spectacle that was masterfully choreographed along
the lines of the American sci-fi thriller *Independence Day*. According to
Hall, the Bush extravaganza also evoked the memory of *Triumph of the
Will*, by the Nazi propagandist and filmmaker Leni Riefenstahl:

In the opening scene of *Triumph*, Adolf Hitler is pictured approaching from the air the Nazi Party rally at Nuremberg in 1934. President Bush began his big spectacle on board the *Abraham Lincoln* by touching down on the vessel's deck in a S-3B Viking jet. Emblazoned on the windshield of the aircraft were the words "Commander in Chief." The U.S. president then emerged in full fighter garb, invoking the imagery of the dramatic concluding scenes in *Independence Day*. In those scenes, an American president leads a global coalition from the cockpit of a small jet fighter. The aim of this U.S.-led operation is to defend the planet from the attack of outer-space aliens.[1]

But fortune is fickle, particularly in wartime. A year later, Bush and his advisers must have wished they'd never staged the May 1 spectacle. For the scene in Iraq was anything but triumphant. In the face of world opinion that condemned the American occupation as a colonial venture and a majority of Americans who said the war was not worth the cost, the United States engineered a transfer of power, on June 28, 2004, to an Iraqi government that was anything but genuine.

The world was not taken in by Washington's "handing over" sovereignty to Iraqi leaders it handpicked. Washington made it clear that it reserved the right to control its occupying army of 130,000-plus troops and to maintain them there indefinitely. Secretary of State Colin Powell's qualification that the United States would leave if the new government requested it seemed disingenuous, since the regime would never ask for the elimination of the military might on which its own existence depended.[2] The American empire was suffering a serious crisis of overextension. Armed with a grand strategy that ignored constraints on American power, the Bush administration had dragged the nation into a quagmire that weakened its position everywhere else. The causes, dynamics, and consequences of overextension constitute the focus of this chapter.

STRETCHED THIN

An overstretched military was the most obvious symbol of imperial overextension. As Deputy Secretary of State Richard Armitage saw it, "The Army, in particular, [is] stretched too thin . . . fighting three wars—Afghanistan still, Iraq, and the global war on terrorism."[3] According to the analyst James Fallows, it was "only a slight exaggeration to say that today the entire U.S. military is either in Iraq, returning from Iraq, or getting ready to go."[4]

Most of the Army's maneuverable brigades were overseas, and those left in the United States were "too few to maintain the contingency reserve or the training base necessary."[5] Lack of human resources—in part the consequence of efforts by Clinton and Bush to downsize the regular Army—led the command to call on the Reserves and the National Guard. As might be expected, morale plummeted, especially as duty tours were extended and casualities mounted in a land to which these part-time soldiers had never expected to be assigned.

Even the famed Special Forces, praised for their actions in Afghanistan and Iraq, were severely understrength. Actual numbers in the field came to "hundreds at the most."[6] Nor could the shortfall be remedied quickly, since, as one expert pointed out, "[I]ncreasing the size of Special Operations Forces is a long-term effort; it takes six years to train a Navy SEAL and the majority of sailors and marines who sign up do not complete the course."[7]

IRAQ: THE REASONS WHY

Iraq reversed the fortunes of the empire. Why did the Bush administration commit a serious crime against international law: the unprovoked invasion of another country? How did events unravel so quickly? What has been the impact of Iraq on the overall strategic position of the United States? In trying to discern the real rationale for the invasion of Iraq in 2003, many analysts fix on one motivation or another. This approach represents a futile quest, because the invasion of Iraq seems to have been overdetermined— various circles within the Bush administration had their own particular reasons to pursue the war.

Securing Israel's Flank

"Regime change" in Iraq was central to the administration's view of how to treat the Middle East, which it identified as the most problematic region, the source of terrorism and global instability. Under Clinton, the Bush team felt the nation had expended too much political capital, with little to show for its efforts, in trying to gain a peaceful solution to the Palestinian–Israeli conflict. To Bush and the neoconservatives, that conflict had reached a stalemate mainly because of Palestinian intransigence. The tilt toward Israel became pronounced in 2002, as Ariel Sharon responded to suicide bombings, according to the *Washington Post*, "by systematically destroying the infrastructure and institutions of the Palestinian Authority, all the while insisting that his intention was to pressure the very forces he targeted into cracking down on the terrorist groups."[8]

Philip Gordon provided a cogent summary of the Bush position:

> By standing resolutely behind Israeli Prime Minister Ariel Sharon, Bush believes he will convince the Palestinians that they will get nowhere with violence, a message the administration wants the entire world to understand as part of the war on terrorism. The Bush team, like many Israelis on the right of the political spectrum, believes that, particularly in the Middle East, signs of strength are respected but weakness is punished—thus they believe that Israel's withdrawal from Lebanon in 2001 did not entice the Arab world toward compromise but, rather, incited it to further violence, with Palestinians attempting to implement the Hizbollah model [i.e., Islamic forces become the center of gravity of the resistance]. Bush apparently believes that Palestinians will eventually recognize that their *intifada* has been a disaster not only for Israel but for themselves: thousands of Palestinians dead, the Palestinian economy devastated, the Palestinian Authority undermined, Arafat marginalized, the Israelis back in West Bank cities and the link between suicide bombings and Palestinians embedded in the minds of people around the world.[9]

A change in Palestinian leadership was necessary. If it should happen and the new leadership cracked down on terrorism, then Washington would recognize and support a Palestinian state.[10]

The Palestinian-Israeli relationship would remain frozen in conflict, in the view of Bush and the neoconservatives, until there occurred a democratic transformation in the region. The intended shift would start with regime change in Iraq. As Paul Wolfowitz and others put it before the invasion, "the road to peace in the Middle East goes through Baghdad."[11] To critics of the neoconservatives, however, this assertion was not so much principle as it was politics. Elizabeth Drew noted that "their aim to 'democratize' the region [was] driven by their desire to surround Israel with more sympathetic neighbors."[12] The targets for democratization were mainly enemies of Israel and the United States, particularly Iraq, Syria, and (already democratic but not liberal) Iran—and certainly not Saudi Arabia, Egypt, and the Persian Gulf monarchies that were soft on Israel and allied to Washington. Moreover, the democratic rhetoric quickly disappeared when it came to dealing with strongman regimes in Uzbekistan, Kazakhstan, and Pakistan, which the administration eagerly incorporated into its strategic alliance system.[13]

Indeed, one of the immediate consequences of the invasion appeared to be highly beneficial to Israel: "The Iraq war helped bolster Israel's strategic position by the fact that a radical regime has disappeared, the weakness of the Arab world has been exposed, and there is greater American pressure on states like Syria and Iran."[14] Since the end of hostilities, it is claimed, Syria has put out peace feelers to Israel, Iran has been under international pressure over its nuclear program, and Libya has unveiled and promised to end its secret weapons projects—leading some critics of the war to charge that it "was fought principally on Israel's behalf."[15] As we shall show later, Israel's gains were illusory.

"Kicking Ass"

Yet the dynamics of the decision making on Iraq were a response as well, to forces, issues, and developments outside the Middle East. Analysts like Stephen Kinzer argue that the invasion originated in a desire to "kick ass"—to satisfy the need "for revenge against *someone* for the losses of September 11."[16] Interestingly, this view is shared by Richard Clarke, the administration's former antiterrorism point man, who says that, for Bush, "there was a felt need to 'do something big' to respond to the events of September 11." Alternatives, such as stabilizing Afghanistan or assisting other nations in dealing with Islamic extremism, were not "the big, fast, bold, simple move that would send a signal at home and abroad, a signal that said 'don't mess with Texas, or America.' "[17] Given the subliminal macho streak that the more prominent Bush people scarcely conceal, this motivation is not to be underestimated.

Oil and Strategic Power

Oil was central to the invasion, although the administration consistently denied the link at first. Perhaps this explanation was best articulated by Jeffrey Sachs, an opponent of the invasion, who credited the influence of Vice President Cheney in the implementation of the policy. Iraq sat atop 10 percent of the world's oil, and, in Cheney's view, it was vital to eliminate Saddam's control over the petroleum reserves, to prevent him from using the oil as political blackmail against America and its allies. But to critics of the war, Saddam's ability to blackmail had been crippled by the UN sanctions in effect since the end of the Gulf War. More important was what Sachs regarded as the "core strategy of stationing troops in Iraq to secure long-term access to Middle East oil."[18] Sachs alleged that a major reason for moving into Iraq was to get U.S. troops out of oil-rich but politically volatile Saudi Arabia, where their presence was becoming acutely provocative.[19] This motivation was, in fact, confirmed by Wolfowitz after the invasion, when he admitted to *Vanity Fair* magazine that "an almost unnoticed but huge" rationale was the prospect of "lifting the burden from the Saudis" by redeploying U.S. troops from Saudi Arabia to Iraq.[20]

In fact, Wolfowitz affirmed the centrality of oil on yet another occasion, a few weeks after the occupation of Baghdad, when he was asked why the United States was treating North Korea differently from Iraq, where no weapons of mass destruction had been found. The deputy defense secretary responded, "Let's look at it simply. The most important difference between North Korea and Iraq is that economically, we had no choice in Iraq. The country swims on a sea of oil."[21]

But probably more central than direct control of Middle Eastern oil was the intention of limiting the access of Europe and China to it. Controlling access to oil was the key motivation for the establishment of bases and access agreements in Afghanistan and the former Soviet states of Kyrgyzstan and Uzbekistan, overflight arrangements with Azerbaijan and Kazakhstan, and plans for basing rights in Tajikistan.[22] As Chalmers Johnson notes, these bases were not so much intended to support military operations in Afghanistan as to project U.S. power into energy-rich Central Asia.[23]

Oil is the element that has led some analysts to argue that the Iraq war was directed principally at a power outside the region: although relations between the United States and China improved somewhat because of

America's need for allies after September 11, the Bush regime saw China as the nation's main strategic competitor. Summing up the thinking of this group, Patrick Seale writes that the underlying rivalry continues and is unlikely to vanish, a point buttressed by the harsh criticisms of China contained in Bush's National Security Strategy Paper of September 2002. "To contain China, the U.S. needs to take sole control of the strategic Gulf area, which contains more than 25 percent of the world's oil reserves, a resource China desperately needs as it seeks to consolidate and expand its already formidable economic power."[24]

Assuring U.S. control over the oil spigot, muscle flexing, improving Israel's strategic posture, bringing about regime change, preemptively containing China, staging an exercise to "kick ass"—all these motivations, advanced by different factions of the Bush administration, came together to make Iraq the perfect opportunity, the perfect target. What served as the chief pretext for invasion turned out to be the least credible rationale, according to those in the know, but the most potent for winning public approval. As Wolfowitz revealed to *Vanity Fair*, most of the White House strategists had a pet reason to move against Saddam, but the one uniting them all was Saddam's alleged possession of WMDs: "For bureaucratic reasons we settled on one issue, weapons of mass destruction, because it was the one reason we could agree on."[25]

The Strategic Imperative

Iraq may have been targeted for all these reasons, but perhaps the overriding objective was a strategic one. Iraq was invaded mainly to reshape the political environment in the post–Cold War era along the lines laid out in the September 2002 National Security Strategy Paper. The occupation of Iraq was the centerpiece of an imperial hubris. For the Bush inner circle, it was step 1 in a démarche that would go on to eliminate so-called rogue states, compel greater loyalty from dependent states or supplant them with stronger allies, and put strategic competitors like China on notice that they should not even think of vying with the United States. Iraq was then an "exemplary war," whose purposes reached far into the future. In Ellen Meiksins Wood's view, such a policy leads to a "state of permanent war."[26] The Bush doctrine might more appropriately be called a strategy of permanent intimidation or aggressiveness designed to make future applications of force unnecessary because of the fear they would engender among friends and foes alike.

As events in 2003 and 2004 would show, the strategy would backfire badly, very badly.

IRAQ: AN IMPERIAL EXPEDITION UNRAVELS

As soon as U.S. troops entered Baghdad in the early spring of 2003, when widespread looting of government agencies and other establishments took place, the occupation began to go awry. Two subsequent events spelled disaster for the American enterprise: the resistance in the city of Falluja and the scandal that erupted over the sexual abuse of prisoners at the main military prison of Abu Ghraib in Baghdad.

Falluja: The Turning Point

In April 2004, Falluja became the turning point of the war in Iraq. Located one hour west of Baghdad on Highway 1, Falluja is a resort town of 300,000 on the banks of the Euphrates River. Contrary to U.S. military propaganda, Falluja was never considered a Ba'ath Party stronghold during the days of Saddam Hussein.[27] What turned Falluja into a center of resistance was the indiscriminate firing by American troops on a largely peaceful demonstration against their presence on April 29, 2003, during the U.S. advance to Baghdad. That massacre turned the town decisively against the United States, and over the next year, "under a steady drumbeat of attacks, US troops withdrew from the town," beneath the guise of handing over security functions to Iraqi police and civil defense forces.[28]

In late March 2004, four "civilian" mercenaries connected with the Blackwater security company, who had been recruited from the U.S. military, were attacked by Iraqi resistance fighters and their bodies mutilated. Then their charred remains were strung up on a bridge by a large crowd of townspeople, in full view of television. In what will certainly go down as one of the worst decisions of the occupation authorities, a posse of two thousand troops from the First Marine Expeditionary Force encircled Falluja on April 4, to search out and punish the Iraqis involved in the incident. Earlier, on April 1, Brigadier General Mark Kimmit, deputy director of operations in Iraq, promised "an overwhelming response," saying, "We will pacify that city."[29]

Residents of the city had intoned a defiant slogan during the months of occupation: "Falluja is the graveyard of the Americans." In April the chant become a reality. A significant number of the 102 U.S. combat deaths during that month were accounted for by the fighting in and around the city. But there was a bigger sense in which the slogan was true: Falluja became the graveyard of U.S. policy in Iraq.

The struggle for the city was not yet over on April 9, when American forces declared a "unilateral suspension of offensive operations." But the Iraqi resistance had already won psychologically. Irregular fighters, fueled mainly by spirit and courage, were able to battle the elite of America's colonial legions—the marines—to a standstill on the outer neighborhoods of Falluja. Moreover, so frustrated were the Americans that, in their trademark style of technology-intensive warfare, they unleashed firepower indiscriminately, killing some six hundred people, mainly women and children, according to eyewitness accounts. Captured graphically by Arab television, these incidents produced both inspiration and deep anger, likely to be translated into thousands of recruits for the already burgeoning resistance. U.S. allies as well as Iraqis were repelled by the carnage. General Sir Michael Jackson, the chief of the British general staff, distanced himself from the bloodbath: "We must be able to fight with the Americans. That does not mean we must be able to fight as the Americans," he asserted. "That the British approach to post-conflict is doctrinally different to the U.S. is a fact of life."[30]

The Americans were confronted with an unenviable dilemma: they could stick to the ceasefire, which Iraqis would interpret to mean they couldn't handle Falluja, or they could take the city at a terrible price both to the civilian population and to themselves. There was no doubt the heavily armed marines could pacify Falluja, but the costs were likely to make that victory a Pyrrhic one.

The marines took the less disastrous option, concluding an unusual agreement that created a force, the Fallujah Protective Army, to enter the city and provide security. The new unit would consist of up to 1,100 former Iraqi soldiers led by a former division commander under Saddam.[31] It was unclear how the protective army would function. But members of the Falluja resistance were soon seen patrolling the city's streets. In all likelihood, some of them had participated in the ambush and mutilation of the Blackwater mercenaries.

Late in 2004, U.S. military operations intensified around Fallujah. But even if it fell to U.S. forces, the city had already attained a symbolic and mythical status that was rallying hundreds of thousands of Iraqis to the resistance. At least 55 cities had become no-go zones for U.S. and Coalition troops. The predators became the prey, being either confined to heavily fortified barracks that were subject to mortar attacks or harassed by guerrilla fire or booby traps when they dared to venture out.

In Fallujah and other centers of resistance especially targeted by the Americans, the likely response of the guerrillas to overwhelming U.S. power was, as in Samara, to trade a conventional defense of a city for a guerrilla presence that harasses and pins down the U.S. Army and its Iraqi mercenaries.

For some analysts, the problem lay in miscalculations by Rumsfeld. He had simply underestimated what it would take to carry out a successful occupation of Iraq. Apparently Rumsfeld and his planners thought they'd need no more than 115,000 troops to occupy and pacify the country and had not made plans for a larger force.[32] But even with that number, if one took into consideration unit rotations and replacements, the demands on the military were enormous.

To other observers, it was the ineptitude of Paul Bremer, the American proconsul, that created the crisis. In this view, Bremer made three big mistakes of a political nature, all during his first month in office: removing bureaucrats from Saddam's Ba'ath Party—some thirty thousand of them—from office; dissolving the Iraqi Army, thus throwing a quarter of a million Iraqis, with arms, out of work and prowling the streets; and making the handover of power indefinite and dependent on the writing of a constitution under military occupation.[33] Other risky moves also backfired badly, triggering the uprising of the Shiite cleric Muqtad al-Sadr that began in April 2004. Bremer had closed down a Shiite newspaper critical of the occupation and ordered the arrest of an aide of Muqtad al-Sadr—acts that, the Canadian journalist Naomi Klein contended, were calculated to draw al-Sadr into open confrontation in order to crush him.[34]

Inept, Rumsfeld and Bremer certainly were, but their military and political blunders were inevitable consequences of the collective delusions of George Bush and the reigning neoconservatives at the White House. One element of the distortion was the belief that the Iraqis hated Saddam so much that they would tolerate an indefinite occupation that had the license to blunder at will. A second persistent misreading was that mainly "remnants" of the Saddam regime were behind the spreading insurgency, although everybody else in Baghdad realized that the resistance had grassroots backing. A third misperception considered the divide between the traditionally dominant Sunni Muslims and the majority Shiites so deep that their uniting for a common enterprise against the United States on nationalist and religious grounds was impossible. In other words, the Americans were trapped by a web of false, self-deluding assumptions.

Even outside the regime itself, conservative circles had lost touch with reality. For instance, an influential conservative critic of the administration's policy, Fareed Zakaria, editor of *Newsweek*'s international editions, had this to offer as the way out: "The U.S. must bribe, cajole, and co-opt various Sunni leaders to separate the insurgents from the local population. . . . [T]he tribal sheiks, former low-level Ba'athists, and regional leaders must be courted assiduously. In addition, money must start flowing into Iraqi hands."[35]

The Resistance

The truth is that the neoconservative scenario of quick invasion, pacification of the population with chocolates and cash, installation of a puppet "democracy" dominated by Washington's protégés, then withdrawal to distant military bastions out of reach of the insurgents while an American-trained army and police force took over security in the cities was dead on arrival.

For all the country's many fractures, the cross-ethnic appeal of nationalism and Islam is strong in Iraq. The situation was brought home to me by two incidents when I visited Iraq along with a parliamentary delegation shortly before the American bombing. When we asked a class at Baghdad University what the students thought of the coming invasion, a young woman answered firmly that had George Bush studied his history, he would have known that the Americans would face the same fate as the countless armies that had invaded and pillaged Mesopotamia for the last four thousand years. Leaving Baghdad, we were convinced that the young men and women we talked to would not submit easily to foreign occupation.

Two days later, at the Syrian border, hours before the American bombing, we encountered a group of mujahideen, or Islamic guerrilla fighters, heading in the opposite direction, full of energy and enthusiasm to take on the Americans. They were from Libya, Tunisia, Algeria, Palestine, and Syria, and represented the cutting edge of droves of Islamic volunteers that would stream into Iraq over the next few months to participate in what they welcomed as the decisive battle with the Americans.

As the invasion began, many of us predicted that it would face an urban resistance that would be difficult to pacify in Baghdad and elsewhere in the country.[36] Famously, Scott Ritter, the former UN arms inspector, said that the United States would be forced to exit Iraq "with its tail between its legs, defeated. It is a war we cannot win."[37]

We were wrong, of course, since there was little popular resistance when the Americans entered Baghdad. But we were eventually proved right. Our mistake lay in underestimating the time it would take to transform the population from an unorganized, submissive mass under Saddam to a force inspired by nationalism and Islam. Bush and Bremer constantly talked about their dream of a "new Iraq." Ironically, the new post-Saddam Iraq was being forged in a common struggle against a hated occupation.

The Americans thought they could coerce and bribe the Iraqis into submission. They failed to reckon with the indigenous spirit of resistance to the occupation. Of course, spirit was not enough. The movement experienced a steep learning curve that ran from uncoordinated acts of resistance to a sophisticated repertoire combining the use of improvised explosive devices (IEDs), hit-and-run tactics, stand-your-ground firefights, and ground missile attacks.

Unfortunately, these tactics also included car bombings and kidnappings that harmed civilians along with U.S. and coalition combatants and mercenaries. Unfortunately, too, in the Islamic resistance's effort to sap the will of the enemy, it carried out missions that deliberately targeted civilians, like the March 2004 subway bombing in Madrid that killed hundreds of innocents. Such acts were unjustifiable and deplorable. But to those quick to condemn such tactics, one must point out that the indiscriminate killing of an estimated ten thousand Iraqi civilians by U.S. troops in the first year of the occupation and the targeting of civilians in the siege of Falluja occupy the same moral plane as the methods used by the Iraqi and Islamic resistance. Indeed, the American way of war has always involved the killing and punishing of the civilian population. The firebombings of Dresden and Tokyo, the atomic bombing of Hiroshima and Nagasaki, Operation Phoenix in Vietnam—all deliberately targeted civilians.

Falluja did not decisively shift the balance of forces in favor of the

Iraqi resistance. For the war was being waged on many fronts, including that of worldwide public opinion and, most significant, in the hearts and minds of the American people. While the United States was largely isolated internationally—its actions in Iraq drawing more and more criticism because of the large numbers of civilian deaths in Falluja—there was still backing for the war in a large section of the U.S. population, although the support was softening. A University of Pennsylvania poll conducted in April 2004 found that 51 percent believed that it had not been worth going to war, while 43 percent said that it was.[38] True, antiwar protests were picking up in the United States, but a massive antiwar movement that could sustain its actions across the country, like the ones that occurred before and after the Tet Offensive in Vietnam, had yet to develop.

Abu Ghraib and the Crisis of the U.S. Army

Then in early May 2004, American popular support for the war received a massive psychological shock. Stunning evidence of systematic sexual abuse of prisoners at Abu Ghraib prison, Saddam's old detention and torture center outside Baghdad, horrified millions. The combination of Abu Ghraib and Falluja constituted the Iraqi equivalent of Tet.

The investigative report of abuses at Abu Ghraib concentration camp by Major General Antonio Taguba spoke of "extremely graphic photographic evidence," some of which covered the following acts: forcibly arranging detainees in various sexually explicit positions for photographing; forcing naked male detainees to wear women's underwear; demanding that groups of male detainees masturbate while being photographed and videotaped; placing a dog chain or strap around a naked detainee's neck and having a female soldier pose for a picture; positioning a naked detainee with a sandbag on his head, and attaching wires to his fingers, toes, and penis to simulate electric torture; encouraging a male MP guard to have sex with a female detainee; using unmuzzled military dogs to frighten and bite detainees; and "sodomizing a detainee with a chemical light and possibly a broomstick."[39]

The Taguba report highlighted several facts that shocked Americans (though not Iraqis): that the American jailers thought that the Geneva Conventions on the treatment of prisoners did not apply to their Iraqi captives; that the jailers either thought there were no standard operating procedures or felt that humiliation, blows, sexual abuse, and dog attacks were part of

SOPs to soften detainees for interrogation; that the abuse was systemic rather than the uncoordinated acts of individuals.[40]

Later revelations showed that, at the very least, directives from the top did not clearly distinguish legitimate methods of information extraction from abuse and torture. Indeed, the tendency was to blur the two and render unclear the application of the Geneva Conventions, the Torture Convention, and the Torture Statute to "enemy combatants," a category invented by Rumsfeld precisely to avoid giving captives the category of "prisoners of war," which would clearly make them subject to the conventions.[41]

The Abu Ghraib horrors angered the Arab world and probably shamed most people in the United States, where popular approval for Bush's handling of Iraq eroded more rapidly. Yet, in the short term, the impact on the U.S. Army was the most threatening to Washington.

Most of those accused of sexual abuse and torture at the Abu Ghraib prison were from the Army—ironically, the service whose leaders had been most reluctant to take part in the planned Iraq intervention. In the lead-up to the invasion, General Eric Shinseki, the Army chief of staff, told a congressional committee that at least 200,000 troops would be necessary to invade and pacify Iraq. He was publicly contradicted by Rumsfeld, who projected that the number of troops needed to garrison Iraq would dwindle to 30,000 by the end of the summer of 2003.[42] Relying on precision bombing and airpower to blow Saddam's Republican Guards to smithereens, Rumsfeld felt confident that the Army need concern itself only with mopping-up operations and a largely peaceable occupation.

The planned deployment violated the key tenets of the Powell doctrine, which held that interventions had to be massive and have clear objectives, significant public support, and a well-defined exit strategy. Otherwise, nothing doing. But in Iraq the objective was open-ended, the force of 150,000 was too small, and planning for the occupation was inadequate. There was no exit strategy and little appreciation for the urban insurgency to follow. Warned retired general Joseph Hoar, former chief of the Central Command: "In urban warfare, you could run through battalions a day at a time. . . . All our advantages of command and control, technology—all those things are, in part, given up and you are working with corporals and sergeants and young men fighting street to street."[43]

By the time U.S. troops reached Baghdad, it was clear that the force committed to Iraq was too small. American soldiers were helpless to prevent the widespread looting of government buildings, including the National Museum, where antiquities of great value were stored. What Powell and many in the Army high command had feared transpired in the following months: the U.S. Army found itself fighting a frustrating and ultimately unwinnable war against guerrillas.

The Army paid the price for the massive miscalculation by Rumsfeld and other civilian leaders at the Pentagon. Some 135,000 troops remained in Iraq as of March 2004. The Army had to draw on the Reserves and the National Guard to garrison Iraq. Already, nearly 40 percent of the military contingent in Iraq, noted James Fallows, came from the Reserves and the National Guard, popularly referred to as "weekend warriors" because they usually held down civilian jobs.[44] As the resistance stepped up its activity in April, 20,000 troops scheduled to return home that month had their rotations extended until June. Replacements would be hard to find, given the Bush administration's limits on the size of the Army.[45] A scenario that many studies had warned about transpired: the Army was reduced to skimming soldiers from its divisions at the volatile Thirty-eighth Parallel in Korea.

Morale had been sinking fast even before Abu Ghraib. Now, extended service would disrupt "the lives of tens of thousands who counted on their civilian jobs to pay mortgages and other family expenses."[46] A replay of what happened to the Army during the Vietnam War seemed imminent. The troops knew that the problem lay at the top, where officers tried to curry favor with their civilian bosses in Washington. As one soldier wrote to *The New Yorker* magazine contributor George Packer:

> The reason why morale sucks is because of the senior leadership, the brigade and division commanders, and probably the generals at the Pentagon and Central Command too, all of whom seem to be insulated from what is going on at the ground level. Either that or they are unwilling to hear the truth of things or (and this is most likely), they do know what is going on, but they want to get promoted so badly that they're willing to screw over soldiers by being unwilling to face the problem of morale, so they continue pushing the soldiers to do more with less because Rummy [Rumsfeld] wants them to get us out of here quickly. These people are like serious alcoholics unwilling to admit there is even a problem.[47]

The administration's handling of the Abu Ghraib scandal threatened to worsen the morale problem. The apparent game plan of the Bush people was to limit those charged, disciplined, and punished in connection with the abuses to a few enlisted men and women and maybe a handful of officers. The abuse would be attributed to these few bad eggs and would not be regarded as systemic. Guilt would come to rest far down the chain of command and leave untouched the civilian leadership that had planned the criminal invasion that spawned the conditions that led to the abuses in the first place. When some high-level officers had to be sacrificed, as was the case with Lieutenant General Ricardo Sanchez, the strategy was apparently to cashier them, then quickly remove them from public view instead of prosecuting them.

This approach might save the high military and civilian command, but it would be devastating to morale at the lower levels. What Colin Powell and his generation of Vietnam-era junior officers had tried so hard to avoid—the unraveling of the morale of the U.S. Army a second time—now stared them in the face. Thus nobody was surprised when, in mid-October 2004, a number of army reservists refused an order to deliver fuel to a town north of Baghdad because they considered their vehicles "extremely unsafe." The question in many people's minds: Was this the beginning of the end?

AFGHANISTAN: AN EPHEMERAL VICTORY

The war in Afghanistan is said to be one of the casualties of the war in Iraq. Perhaps it would be more appropriate to characterize it as a perilous imperial enterprise from the start, one whose unraveling was accelerated by the developments in Iraq.

The invasion of Afghanistan shortly after September 11, 2001, was the first real exercise of the Bush doctrine. But this was not clear at the time, since the UN Security Council had recognized the right of the United States to respond in self-defense to the September 11 events. Moreover, the General Assembly, in its Resolution 56/1, condemned the World Trade Center attacks and called for "international cooperation to bring to justice the perpetrators, organizers, and sponsors of the outrages."[48] The Al Qaeda terrorist group of Osama bin Laden was alleged to run terrorist training camps in Afghanistan that were protected by the ruling Taliban regime.

In military terms, what the Afghan invasion did was to provide an opportunity for the United States to perfect the precision bombing and mercenary strategy that had been employed in Bosnia. In Afghanistan, one analyst notes, "precision American airpower was undoubtedly a precondition for . . . victory—together with its SOF [Special Operations Forces] spotters, it turned a stalemated civil war into a dramatic battlefield victory for America and its allies." Although precision bombing was necessary, however, it was not sufficient:

> It could annihilate poorly prepared fighting positions, and it could inflict heavy losses on even well-disposed defenses. But it could not destroy the entirety of properly prepared positions by itself. And unless such positions are all but annihilated, even a handful of surviving, actively resisting defenders with modern automatic weapons can slaughter unsophisticated indigenous allies whose idea of tactics is to walk forward bunched up in the open. To overcome skilled, resolute defenders who have adopted the standard countermeasures to high-firepower air strikes still requires close combat by friendly ground forces whose own skills enable them to use local cover and their own suppressive fire to advance against hostile survivors with modern weapons.

The Northern Alliance and the main indigenous allies of the United States were said to have "either enjoyed such fundamental skills or profited from accidentally tight coordination of their movement and American firepower, or both."[49]

The problem with this and similar assessments is that while airpower was critical in winning the battle, it did not contribute to postwar stability because it was not really that precise and it created deep resentment among the local population. While the United States did not appear to target civilians deliberately, its bombs, in many cases, could not distinguish between military and civilian targets. The result was an unacceptably high level of civilian casualties; one estimate, by Marc Herold, placed the figure at between 3,125 and 3,620, from October 7, 2001, to July 31, 2002.[50] Comparing the rates of civilian casualties per bomb delivered in Afghanistan and in Kosovo and Serbia in the 1999 NATO campaign, Michael Mann, in fact, claims that U.S. bombing had become "less smart."[51] So-called collateral damage to civilians is not just a peripheral issue, for its intensity affects the outcome of the postwar pacification—a notable failure in Afghanistan.

But there was an even bigger issue: If terrorism was the principal enemy, was invading Afghanistan the solution? In the view of some, the Afghan war was a conflict fought on the wrong premises, and would ultimately fail in its declared objective. As one analyst noted, "Afghanistan has been substituted for terrorism because Afghanistan is accessible to military power, and terrorism is not. The employment of high-tech munitions against irrelevant targets is a distraction from measures that actually deal with the threat."[52] This charge would resonate even more widely in 2002, as the Bush administration made known its intentions to invade Iraq.

Afghanistan was, indeed, a distraction for the Bush administration, as was the war on terror. Waging them was important, especially in the context of September 11, but not at the expense of deflecting attention from the strategic goal of the White House—to bring down the Saddam Hussein government. To the Bush administration, Afghanistan was "a military and political backwater—a detour along the road to Iraq," according to Richard Clarke, formerly its top antiterrorism official.[53] But it was a significant detour, since Secretary of Defense Rumsfeld "wanted to have a laboratory to prove his theory about the ability of small numbers of ground troops, coupled with air power, to win decisive battles."[54] Afghanistan, in short, would demonstrate that the Powell doctrine's dictum about the need for a massive commitment of troops was obsolete—an idea that skeptics had to be persuaded to accept before they could be convinced to take on Iraq.

Afghanistan turned out to be an ephemeral victory. Three years after the toppling of the Taliban, the U.S. commitment of 13,500 troops in Afghanistan and support units totaling 35,000 personnel outside the country failed to bring it any nearer to stability and peace.

According to a report of the Center for Strategic and International Studies, "security has actually deteriorated since the beginning of the reconstruction in December 2001, particularly over the summer and fall of 2003."[55] With attacks on personnel representing the United Nations and various nongovernmental organizations (NGOs) increasing, one-third of the country was declared off-limits to UN staff.[56] Washington's handpicked head of state, Hamid Karzai, didn't really have authority outside Kabul and two or three other cities, according to Clarke.[57] In fact, a report from the UN secretary general's office noted that "Kabul itself is not invulnerable. Sophisticated attacks were directed against the International Security Assistance Force (ISAF) on 27 and 28 January [2004], when successive suicide carbomb attacks struck a Canadian and United Kingdom patrol, killing two soldiers, injuring seven, and killing three Afghan civilians. This suggests that . . . the risk of suicide attacks against well-protected international military targets remains of concern."[58] And according to a Dutch parliamentarian who visited the Netherlands' contingent of NATO's 5,000-person International Security Assistance Force in December 2003, security outside Kabul was so bad that instead of providing security for NGOs, the Dutch troops, for their own safety and for political reasons, spent most of the time holed up in their camp and rarely ventured outside.[59]

U.S. troops have been staging highly publicized raids into mountainous areas seeking to nail Osama bin Laden, his deputy Ayman Zawahiri, and Taliban leader Mullah Omar, with a singular lack of success. At the same time, the Taliban regrouped both militarily and politically. In October 2003, there were an estimated fifteen attacks a day on American soldiers, as well as a "resurgence of Taliban and Al Qaeda activity in southeastern Afghanistan along the border with Pakistan."[60] Meantime, the warlords, many allied to and receiving money from the United States, ruled much of the country, engaged in extortion, and controlled the resurgent production and sale of heroin. In Afghanistan, which accounted for 76 percent of the world's heroin, poppy production in 2002 had increased eighteen-fold since the last year of Taliban rule.[61] One by-product of the easy availability of heroin was a growing drug problem among U.S. troops, something that the military leadership has approached with a "head-in-the-sand" attitude.[62]

The focus on Iraq created a major problem for the Afghan campaign. The priority assigned to Iraq prevented Washington from providing a military force large enough to stabilize Afghanistan. Moreover, the shift in focus led to a deterioration of both the political and the military situation, as many Special Forces units and CIA paramilitary teams were shifted to Iraq.[63] Even more problematic was the lack of a viable political and economic reconstruction plan. The United States was stuck with an unworkable arrangement uniting a weak central government it had set up in Kabul and powerful independent warlords who engaged in extortion and drug dealing. For them, "insecurity," as Kofi Annan put it, was a "business" and extortion "a way of life."[64] Despite U.S.-sponsored elections, Annan noted, "without functional state institutions able to serve the basic needs of the population throughout the country, the authority and legitimacy of the new government will be short-lived."[65]

Not surprisingly, Washington had created a failed state, one that could not provide even minimum security. A number of people compared the present unfavorably to Taliban times, when, many Afghanis argued, at least they enjoyed some security. And as in Iraq, there was little chance that the United States would leave—unless, of course, it was pushed out.

STRATEGIC SETBACK FOR TEL AVIV AND WASHINGTON

In the Near East, the United States found itself in a worse position after the Iraq invasion. The invasion, the full backing of Ariel Sharon, and the push to democratize the Arab countries were supposed to serve as a catalyst for a more sober Palestinian leadership, one that would sue for peace with Israel.

Instead, the invasion heightened an already acute pan-Arab and pan-Islamic consciousness, translating it into fierce opposition to the U.S. presence in Iraq and Washington's alliance with Israel. While provoking Arab opposition, the U.S. coddling of Sharon stoked Israeli right-wing aggressiveness, including the dramatic emergence of seventy new settler outposts in Palestinian areas under the Sharon-Bush dispensation.[66] With no weapons of mass destruction found in Iraq, Israel's so-called strategic gain was largely illusory. Instead, it faced the prospect of an unstable Iraq, where militantly anti-Israel Shiite Islamists might come to power and open up new fronts against the Jewish state.

That state was already under severe strain dealing with one front, the Palestinian *intifada* or insurrection. Much as Israel denied it, suicide bombings carried out by the Islamic group Hamas and other Palestinian groups forced the Sharon government to undertake a unilateral withdrawal from all of the Gaza strip and part of the West Bank because it could not provide effective security for Israeli settlements in these areas. The Palestinian side saw the withdrawal as a partial victory, though they promised to intensify their struggle for more territory and rights. [67] The majority of the voters in Sharon's Likud Party saw it as a setback for their project of settler colonialism, leading to their rejection of it in a referendum in June 2004.

This severely weakened not only the position of Sharon but also that of the United States, which had tied its flag to the prime minister's project. Both Sharon and Bush were further isolated when, in July 2004, the International Court of Justice in the Hague ruled illegal the miles-long "wall" that the Israelis were constructing as a barrier against Palestinians.

For several reasons, Middle East democratization never got off the ground. First, it was endorsed by pro-Likud neoconservatives in the United States whose interest was never in genuine representation but, rather, in surrounding Israel with weak pluralist governments. Second, the United States itself feared that Islamists would use democratic elections to come to power. And third, democratization was never meant to apply to repressive regimes that were allies of the United States, like Saudi Arabia, the Gulf states, Egypt, and Tunisia. Indeed, U.S. policy actually undermined democratization, since Washington opposed elections in Iraq before a handover of power—the voting might bring Shiite or Sunni Islamists to power.[68]

In sum, by tying its fortunes to Sharon and invading Iraq, Washington undermined its strategy to create a more pliable, or moderate, Palestinian leadership. As the occupation marked its first year in Iraq in the spring of 2004, the Middle East was even more polarized, and the United States had lost whatever credibility it had as an honest broker from the Clinton era.

ADVANTAGE AL QAEDA

Al Qaeda and Al Qaeda–linked groups were not severely damaged, either by the Bush administration's war on terror or by the war on Iraq. Certainly, they demonstrated vitality in carrying out several attacks on residential estates housing U.S. citizens in Riyadh, Saudi Arabia, on May 12, 2003, in which 35 people died; the Bali bombing on October 12, 2002, which took nearly 201 lives; and the bombing of the Madrid railway on March 11, 2004, which killed 200 people. Such attacks were evidence of a network or networks that had survived the U.S. antiterror war and the Iraq invasion.

That invasion, according to Richard Clarke, represented a massive diversion of resources and attention from the antiterror war, especially since there were no links between Al Qaeda and Saddam Hussein.[69] And Clarke was probably right that "nothing America could have done would have

provided al Qaeda and its new generation of cloned groups a better recruit-
ment device than our unprovoked invasion of an oil-rich Arab country. . . .
It was as if Usama bin Laden, hidden in some high mountain redoubt, were
engaging in long-range mind control of George Bush, chanting 'invade
Iraq, you must invade Iraq.' "[70]

The invasion, say some, has doubly backfired. Not only did it radicalize
Muslim youth; it showed them that the United States can be defeated or at
least stalemated in war. As one private intelligence provider put it:

> One of the purposes of the war was to disprove al Qaeda's asser-
> tion that the United States was actually militarily weak and that
> it could not engage in close combat in the Islamist world, cer-
> tainly not in the face of a mass uprising. An American with-
> drawal would prove al Qaeda's claims and would energize
> Islamists not only with hatred of the United States, but also—
> and worse—with contempt for American power. It would create
> the worst of all possible worlds for the United States.[71]

What many critics of Bush's policies failed to realize, however, was that
even if the Bush administration had not invaded Iraq but treated terrorism as mainly a matter of smart police and intelligence work, such a
response would not have been sufficient to undercut terrorism. Indeed,
U.S. intelligence and police work were backfiring in many places. In
southern Thailand, for example, the aggressive police identification of foreigners, including Islamic missionaries—encouraged by a U.S.-sponsored
regional counterterrorism center—was said to have created resentment
among Muslims and contributed to the tragic events of April 28, 2004,
when more than one hundred Muslim youth were killed.[72]

To combat terrorism, one must address its roots in poverty, social and
economic injustice, and Western attitudes of cultural superiority. Two
other political and strategic issues cannot be ignored: the continuing
Israeli domination of Palestinians and the occupation of Arab countries to
secure Middle East oil. Unless there is progress in resolving these issues,
there will be no progress in the war on terror.

THE END OF THE ATLANTIC ALLIANCE

One of the biggest casualties of the war on Iraq was the Atlantic alliance. Even before the Iraq invasion, to be sure, there were major issues dividing Europe and the United States. Trade, Palestine, multilateralism, and other questions generated serious frictions. However, the Bush administration and, especially, its war in Iraq aggravated the differences.

To analysts like Robert Kagan, the problem was with the Europeans, who thought that there could be a world based on the rule of law and multilateralism. The United States, though, knew better, and it was American power that—Europeans had forgotten—made possible the rule of law and fended off the forces of anarchy so that Europeans could have "their world of laws and rules and transnational negotiation and cooperation."[73] In short, "Americans are from Mars and Europeans are from Venus."[74]

In the neoconservative view, the bias for multilateralism among the European elites and the peace-at-any-price mood of the European public created the chasm over Iraq. In the European view, American unilateralism squandered the European public's feelings of solidarity with Americans' grief after September 11. But the tension in the Atlantic community was not just a question of values. Franco-German opposition to the United States over Iraq represented the return of balance-of-power diplomacy in reaction to the Bush administration's siege mentality.

John Mearsheimer, in *The Tragedy of Great Power Politics,* says that among balance-of-power systems, "bipolar" arrangements, such as the U.S.-Soviet faceoff that dictated the dynamics of the Cold War period, are more stable and less likely to break down than "multipolar" systems, like the pre–World War II situation, which was marked by relative equality among a number of powerful states.[75] What he fails to tell us is that the situation most likely to generate conflict and instability is one in which a single, overwhelmingly dominant power is surrounded by midget powers—today's world.

Instability and unchallenged hegemony have often gone hand in hand. Even when backed up by overwhelming force, unchallenged hegemony is a transient state. As was the case in Napoleonic Europe, lesser powers may calculate that a posture of compliance might be necessary in the short term, but they know that it is disastrous as a long-term strategy. Sub-servience is simply an invitation to more aggression.

Such reasoning was what the standoff at the UN Security Council over Iraq, in the months before the invasion, was all about. The real debate was less about Saddam's compliance and more about the containment of a hege-mon that thought it had a blank check to threaten, intervene, and depose anywhere in the world whenever it felt its security threatened. If France and Germany went the distance in refusing to legitimize the invasion, it was not simply because of the antiwar sentiments of their citizens. It was to discour-age future U.S. moves that might pose a more direct threat to their own national security. As Ivo Daalder observed, Bush's aggressive unilateralism led many observers among Europe's elites, as well as among the public at large, to "no longer see a common basis for action—and not a few now fear the United States more than what, objectively, constitute the principal threats to their security."[76] Cultural bonds, or a sense of appreciation for being liber-ated from Nazism more than half a century ago, was a weak rationale when compared to the fear of ambitions that could translate into economic bully-ing in the short term and military blackmail in the long term.

Even before the Iraq invasion, in fact, France grew less shy about describing its foreign policy as a matter of balancing American power. This view, not confined to France,

> begins with an assertion that unipolarity is by definition both undesirable and dangerous. It then proceeds to the suggestion that the world is naturally structuring itself around a small num-ber of "poles," based on regional power-bases (China, India), regimes (Mercosur) or communities (the EU), which exemplify different political and cultural approaches to world politics. From this, it is argued that the "international community" can derive its greatest legitimacy from structured dialogue among the poles leading to some form of universal consensus around agreed norms of international behavior.[77]

So, too, the Germans framed their opposition to the invasion in terms of interest and realpolitik. As German foreign minister Joschka Fischer put it, "A world order in which the national interests of the strongest power is the criterion for military action simply cannot work."[78] The same calculations were made by the other members of the Security Council, including countries like Chile, which had even more to lose by refusing to give their vote to the United States in the run-up to the second resolution, which the United States eventually abandoned for lack of votes.*

Thus Washington managed not only to kill the Atlantic alliance but to rekindle balance-of-power politics, as the midget powers moved into active cooperation to contain U.S. aggression. Joining France and Germany in what was becoming this era's version of the pre–World War I Triple Alliance were China and Russia; even the weightier developing countries like Brazil and India joined in.

No member of the new small-power coalition was willing to provide the superpower with a life saver in the form of a troop commitment. Unwittingly, the United States hastened the end of what, as we noted in Chapter 1, Charles Krauthammer called the "unipolar" era.[79] The sense of a shift in power relations was evident in an article in *Foreign Affairs* (March–April 2004 issue) by the very same Robert Kagan who, just two years earlier, had spoken so disparagingly of Europeans. "To address today's global dangers," he claimed in the more recent work, "Americans will need the legitimacy that Europe can provide, but Europeans may well fail to grant it."[80]

BACKYARD REBELLION

Focused on the Middle East, the United States could not pay much attention to what was happening in its backyard. In Venezuela, Hugo Chávez came to power in an election in 1998 and started to shake up the country with a populist reform program. Chávez's plans were mild enough, as John Pilger points out: "a modest agrarian reform program that allows the state to expropriate and redistribute idle land; and a law that limits the exploitation of oil reserves, reinforcing a constitutional ban on the privatization of the state oil company."[81] What enraged the middle class and the traditionally pro-American upper class were his efforts to mobilize the impoverished with his anti-elite, nationalistic appeals.

---

*The first resolution, which passed 15–0, required Saddam to submit a detailed declaration of Iraqi programs to develop weapons of mass destruction. The second resolution would have been an authorization to go to war with Saddam.

The opposition carried out a coup against Chávez on April 11, 2002, and briefly held him prisoner. In that short period, the United States endorsed the coup. Bush's spokesman Ari Fleischer told the press: "We know that the action encouraged by the Chávez government provoked the crisis . . . now the situation is one of tranquility and democracy."[82] In less than two days, however, massive demonstrations by the urban poor and loyal military units restored Chávez to power. Washington, meanwhile, came under attack from Latin American countries, from the European Union, and from other governments for supporting the unseating of a democratically elected government. The diplomatic debacle was resounding.

The Venezuela affair was, however, just one of a number of setbacks that Washington and U.S.-backed neoliberal governments suffered in Latin America. In November 2002, a progressive nationalist colonel, Lucio Gutiérrez, won the Ecuadoran presidential elections, on a leftist nationalist platform and with firm backing from the marginalized indigenous people of the country. Although his government began conciliating the IMF and Washington after his victory, the results of the election reflected a broader continental trend against U.S.-supported neoliberal programs.

More momentous in its implications was the victory at the polls that same month of Luis Inácio da Silva, better known as Lula, the longtime Brazilian industrial worker and the candidate of the progressive Workers' Party. While Lula's hands were tied by his promise to respect the terms of a harsh stabilization program he inherited from his neoliberal predecessor, he was central in forging a South American front that successfully prevented the United States from imposing the comprehensive, mandatory trade liberalization program inscribed in the Free Trade Area of the Americas (FTAA) treaty.[83]

The election, in the spring of 2003, of the Argentine progressive populist Néstor Kirchner dealt yet another blow to Washington. He came to power promising a hard line against the IMF, refusing to make full payment of Argentina's current debt. But perhaps the biggest shock to the Americans was the popular overthrow, in mid-October 2003, of the president of Bolivia, Gonzalo Sánchez de Lozada, a free marketer who supported a plan to export gas to the United States as well as a U.S.-backed drive to eliminate coca crops, the raw material for cocaine.[84] While a potentially powerful bloc of anti-U.S., antineoliberal governments south of the equator had emerged, Washington remained almost totally focused on the unfolding debacle in Iraq. As Hugo Chávez saw it, "If Argentina, Brazil, and Venezuela could act together as a bloc, then they would pose a significant counterweight to the United States."[85]

Iraq not only deflected Washington's attention from developments in Latin America. It was a key factor radicalizing the continent against the United States. As Jorge Castañeda, former foreign minister of Mexico and one of America's closest allies on the continent, put it, many Latin American governments had "high expectations for the team that moved into the White House in 2001" but "Iraq changed all of this. The invasion, the absence of any weapons of mass destruction or any link between Saddam Hussein and Al Qaeda, the pictures of Iraq civilian casualties, and the subsequent scenes of humiliating mistreatment or torture of Iraqi prisoners and detainees have all contributed to a wide, deep, and probably lasting collapse of sympathy for the U.S. in the region."[86]

CREDIBILITY GAP

The erosion of U.S. power was perhaps most dramatically illustrated in Washington's relations with states that Bush regarded either as part of the "axis of evil" or as prime candidates for that distinction.

The immediate aftermath of the invasion of Iraq in March 2003 elicited noises from the neoconservatives that other "failed states" would be next. Even before the invasion, for example, John Bolton, the undersecretary of state, told Ariel Sharon that "America would attack Iraq and . . . afterward it would be necessary to deal with threats from Syria, Iran, and North Korea."[87] By October, with Washington's hands full trying to contain a burgeoning Iraqi resistance, Bolton's threat was no longer credible. Indeed Bush was talking about giving a "security pledge" to North Korea—whose aggressive isolation had been one of the hallmarks of his first year in office—in return for Pyongyang's dismantling of its nuclear energy program. By the beginning of the six-party talks on the Korean peninsula's nuclear crisis, deft North Korean diplomacy combined with U.S. difficulties in Iraq weakened Washington's negotiating position.[88]

The Bush grand strategy had brought the United States to the nadir of its influence and credibility in the post-Vietnam period.

ROMAN RUMINATIONS

The United States currently spends about $400 billion a year on defense, more than the next twenty-three countries combined.[89] It enjoys absolute superiority in nuclear and conventional arms. But as Afghanistan and Iraq have shown, these advantages count for little in fighting wars of national liberation, in much the same way a sledgehammer is useless in swatting flies. In both urban and rural contexts, the often-touted uses of airpower and precision bombing were nullified by the conditions of guerrilla warfare. To make any headway in guerrilla warfare, the Pentagon would have to increase the number of ground troops.[90] But there is no way that the American people would tolerate a much larger commitment of troops to a war that more than half of those polled said was not worth it.[91]

At the global level, sheer military force without legitimacy and without political alliances is a hollow reed for the empire to rest on. The debacles in Iraq and Afghanistan have proved that coalition building and consensus are more critical than military force in holding an empire together. When Washington launched two demonstration wars, it ended up teaching two valuable lessons to the global South: that it is possible to stand up to empire, and that effective resistance in one part of the empire weakens the empire as a whole. One thing is certain: if the Romans were around today, they would say that this is no way to run an empire.

CHAPTER 3

Contemporary Capitalism's Classic Crisis

The real barrier *of capitalist production is capital itself.... The means—unconditional development of the productive forces—comes continually into conflict with the limited purpose, the self-expansion of existing capital.*

KARL MARX, *CAPITAL*

Around the world, Washington was experiencing a crisis of military overextension and political legitimacy. At home, stagnation plagued the American economy. This chapter focuses on the crisis of overproduction and overcapacity,* which afflicts not only the United States but all other central capitalist economies. This historic dilemma consists of certain salient features:

- Speculative finance has replaced industrial and manufacturing activity as the primary source of profitability. This is profoundly destabilizing.
- China has entered the world market and plays a critical role in aggravating the crisis of overproduction.

Overproduction, overaccumulation, overcapacity, and *excess capacity* refer to related dimensions of the same phenomenon. Although academic analysts distinguish the terms, they will be used interchangeably here.

• Recent recessions in the central economies and the phenomenon of anemic, jobless growth in the United States suggest that
the global economy is at the tail end of the fifty-year wave of
capitalist expansion and decline.

Five years into the new millennium, there is hardly anymore talk about a
New Economy, the one pundits not long ago proclaimed had transcended
the boom and bust cycle of the Old Economy.

"Jobless growth," the oxymoron of our times, describes a condition in
which gross domestic product grows slowly while jobs vanish, morph into
poverty-level work, or reappear abroad at similarly miserable levels of
remuneration. In early 2004, an uptick in job creation appeared to mark
the beginning of a genuine recovery after a dismal three years. However,
unemployment remained at 5.6 percent of the workforce, in contrast to 3.8
percent in early 2000. This meant that 8.2 million Americans were still out
of work. Moreover, despite a pickup in corporate investment, capacity utilization remained low, at around 75 percent. And the recovery itself seemed
artificial. It was fueled mainly by military-related production; a sector that
represented only around 4 percent of the total economy accounted for 14
percent of the GDP growth for 2003. American imperial power and ambition depend heavily on the robustness of the economy. But all signs pointed
to stormy weather ahead.

STAGNATION SETS IN

Short-term cycles of boom and bust have marked the U.S. economy and its
international counterpart since the early 1970s. The cycles punctuate a long-
term trend of markedly slower growth. In the global North, the postwar
boom ended, giving way to extended downturns and hesitant recoveries. In
the global South, the industrialization of countries by means of import-
substitution strategies—creating industrial capacity by producing for domestic markets protected from competing imports—came to an end, and in the
two decades after 1980, the developing economies lost ground, were stagnant,
or grew erratically. This condition of relative stagnation varied only in East
Asia, where full-scale incorporation into the global capitalist economy by
state-assisted regimes—that is, capitalist systems marked by strong inter-

vention and direction by the government to achieve rapid development—
produced growth rates of 8–10 percent. Given the preponderant weight of the
central capitalist economies, however, the distinctive mark of the period from
the early 1970s to the early 1990s was what Robert Brenner and others have
called "the long downturn."[1]

The trend toward global stagnation is difficult to dispute. The work of
Angus Maddison, writing for the Organization for Economic Cooperation
and Development (OECD), is the most widely accepted version. According
to Maddison's calculations, the annual rate of growth of real global GDP
fell from 4.9 percent in what is now regarded as the golden age of the
post–World War II system, 1950–73, to 3 percent in 1973–89, a drop of 39
percent.[2] The United Nations, confirming this trend, said that world GDP
grew at an annual rate of 5.4 percent in the 1960s, 4.1 percent in the 1970s,
3 percent in the 1980s, and 2.3 percent in the 1990s.[3]

The fundamental cause of the long downturn was a crisis of profitability.
It stemmed from downward pressure on prices, the result mainly of the
conjunction of stagnant demand and excess industrial capacity, which in
turn triggered intense competition among the center economies.[4] In the
immediate postwar period, the United States helped revive the economies
of Europe and Japan, by providing massive aid as well as by serving as a
market for their goods. By the late 1970s, however, the center economies
became less complementary and more competitive. The United States, Europe, and Japan built up huge industrial capacity that was not matched by
available markets, at a time when many parts of the world were too poor to
absorb the output of the industrialized world.

In the 1980s the excess capacity, or the difference between potential and
actual output, was exacerbated by the massive expansion of industrial and
manufacturing plants in the newly industrializing countries (NICs) of East
Asia, particularly those of South Korea and Taiwan. As Brenner notes:

> Whereas Japan had increased its share of world exports from 0.9
> per cent to 6.0 per cent between 1950 and 1975, the four Asian
> NICs [Singapore, Hong Kong, Taiwan, and South Korea]
> increased their combined share from 1.2 per cent to 6.4 per cent
> between 1965 and 1990. By 1990, the share of world exports of
> goods held at this point by all of non-OPEC, non-Japanese Asia
> had risen to 13.1 per cent, higher than that of the US (11.7 per

cent), Germany (12.7 per cent), or Japan (8.5 per cent). In the immediately preceding years, the four Asian NICs had not only stepped up their export of heavy industrial, capital-intensive outputs, but also begun to venture into technology-intensive lines.[5]

Since these economies followed export-oriented industrialization strategies, deliberately targeting increased market share, particularly in the United States, they posed a rising competitive threat to U.S. industry. Dealing with them was not seen as urgent as confronting the Japanese juggernaut, however.

To counter the fall in profitability, U.S. capital led the drive to restructure the global economy. First, Washington compelled its competitors to bear the burden of adjustment by allowing their currencies to appreciate. Second, it led the way in liberating business from domestic regulatory constraints and in doing away with the barriers that limited capital and goods from moving freely across national borders.

FROM WEAK TO STRONG DOLLAR

Economies such as Japan's and South Korea's pursued high-speed-growth policies in the 1960s to the mid-1980s by keeping their currencies undervalued relative to the dollar and other hard currencies. As a result, their exports remained cheap, allowing deeper penetration into the markets of the wealthiest countries. The Reagan administration borrowed this tactic of exchange-rate manipulation from its Asian competitors, but in a world increasingly marked by industrial overcapacity, this policy translated into a zero-sum game of cornering growth while exporting recession to one's competitors. Under the Reagan administration, as Brenner has pointed out in *The Boom and the Bubble*, the United States engineered the famous Plaza Accord of 1985. By drastically pushing up the value of the Japanese yen and setting the stage for the "relentless rise" of the German mark, the pact made the Japanese and German manufacturing sectors bear the lion's share of adjustment. The eventual recession into which both Japan and Germany fell paved the way for greater U.S. competitiveness and profitability in the late 1980s and early 1990s.[6]

The effect was, however, two-edged. Even as U.S. manufacturing regained profitability, it was threatened by the prolonged recession that settled over Japan and Germany and degraded the capacity of these economies to absorb exports. In an increasingly integrated global economy, Brenner points out, "the fact remains that while the U.S. economic revival took place largely at the expense of its leading rivals, that it had to do so was ultimately at the cost of the U.S. economy itself."[7] Consequently, the Clinton administration engineered what Brenner calls the "reverse Plaza Accord" in the mid-1990s, when the value of the dollar was allowed to rise relative to the yen, in an effort to spark an export-led recovery in Japan. Just as the Plaza Accord had essentially been a rescue operation of U.S. industry by Japan and Germany, the reversal of the rising dollar, engineered by Clinton and his Treasury secretary Robert Rubin, was a bailout of Japan's crisis-bound manufacturing sector and stagnant European economies.

The effort to revive Japan and Europe was costly. It significantly decreased the competitiveness of U.S. goods both in the domestic market and in export markets. By 2003, there was a current account deficit of about $500 billion that needed to be financed by foreign capital inflows and an escalating foreign debt totaling some $7.1 trillion. But there was an upside to the strong dollar. As Robert Blecker notes:

> A high dollar helped to keep inflation low during the boom of the 1990's by keeping import prices down. Low prices of imported goods benefited U.S. consumers. Low inflation in turn induced the Fed to keep interest rates lower than it would have otherwise. The capital inflows that pushed the dollar ever higher also helped to finance the U.S. trade deficit and domestic investment in the face of a growing shortfall of domestic saving. U.S. financial markets gained from the inflows of foreign funds that helped push up asset values, while U.S. investors benefited from the inflated purchasing power of the dollar in foreign countries.[8]

Moreover, the liberalized global rules governing the flow of goods and capital proved a boon to some American firms. By moving their production facilities to countries with low exchange rates, or by outsourcing some portion of the production process to foreign contractors, U.S. multinationals "could actually profit from the high dollar, although American workers (and those companies that did not move abroad, such as in the steel industry) did not share in those gains."[9]

The strong dollar, however, failed to spark sustained economic revival in Japan and had a limited impact in Europe. Japan could not sidestep two massive problems inherited from the era of rapid growth, problems exacerbated by the forced appreciation of the yen in the late 1980s. Banks were burdened with so much debt that they were inoperative, and the economy still shouldered massive surplus industrial capacity. As one report underlined, "Japan has a staggering overcapacity in a vast array of industries, dotting the landscape with more bank branches, gas stations, construction companies, and automakers than the nation and its global customers can support profitably."[10] Thus despite some growth in 2003 and 2004, the result of demand from China, there was still too little demand to activate installed capacity profitably. Recession continued to characterize the domestic market, with income growth static and a 5.1 percent unemployment rate, just 0.3 percent off its all-time high; prices continued to fall, squeezing corporate profit margins and exacerbating the existing debt burden of borrowers.[11]

But even as it failed to reactivate the Japanese economy, the strong-dollar policy played a key role in undermining the competitiveness of the Northeast Asian and Southeast Asian economies. Since their currencies were tied to the dollar, the rise of the dollar made their exports increasingly noncompetitive in global markets. When these economies experienced massive capital flight during the Asian financial crisis, one result was a recession and a severe decline in domestic demand. Like the constriction of Japanese demand during the long recession of the 1990s, the collapse of mass purchasing power in the East Asian tiger economies, later in that decade, contributed to an even bigger gap between industrial capacity and demand at the global level.

The recessions in Japan and East and Southeast Asia could have been an opportunity to shed capacity by shutting down factories as firms went bankrupt. What happened, however, was that the capacity overhang remained, since many of the factories of insolvent Asian conglomerates were simply purchased cheaply by European and American conglomerates. In the car industry, for instance, Isuzu's capacity, Mitsubishi's factories, and Nissan's plants were simply added to those of Ford, Daimler Benz, and Renault, respectively.[12]

NEOLIBERAL REFORM GUTS GLOBAL DEMAND

The depressive effects of recessions in Japan and East Asia fed into the demand-reducing impacts of ongoing economic reforms taking place globally during the 1990s. Labeled "free-market" or "neoliberal" reforms in the North and "structural adjustment" in the South, these programs were designed by their proponents to liberate the market from the constraints imposed by the political economy of managed capitalism of the post–World War II period.

By the late 1970s, Keynesian-managed capitalism was widely blamed for the conjunction of stagnation and inflation. Riding a wave of middle-class disillusionment, Ronald Reagan and Margaret Thatcher came to power in the United States and the United Kingdom, promising to roll back the state and expand the realm of the free market.

The process of neoliberal reform, however, was marked by destabilizing contradictions, in the North and in the South. Liberating capital from the constraints of governments that had imposed a compromise between labor and capital and a modus vivendi between northern capital and developing-country elites entailed (1) bringing down wages, which meant cutting the engine of demand that capital needed in order to reproduce itself profitably, and (2) adding to the ranks of the global unemployed, as the penetration of goods and capital into the less competitive and less developed economies bankrupted local firms and farms, eliminating millions from the market.

In the North, sloughing off labor, enacting tight budgets, and instituting social security cuts stunted the rise of mass purchasing power. The statistics are telling: Between 1979 and 1989 in the United States, the hourly wages of 80 percent of the workforce declined, with the wage of the typical (or median) worker falling by nearly 5 percent in real terms.[13] By the end of the Bush I administration, in 1992, the bottom 60 percent of the population had the lowest share, and the top 20 percent had the highest share, of total income ever recorded. And indeed, among the wealthiest 20 percent, gains were concentrated at the top 1 percent, which captured 53 percent of the total income growth among all families.

These trends continued during the reign of the Democratic Party in the 1990s. Wages stagnated or declined for most workers over most of the Clinton years.[14] On the other hand, after-tax corporate profits reached a forty-year peak of 5.6 percent in 1997:[15] The 1990s were said to have been driven by consumption, but this was not the case for 60 percent of households, which actually reduced their consumption as a proportion of disposable income.[16] As Robert Pollin noted, the overall rise in spending during the Clinton era "was driven almost entirely by the enormous increase in consumption by the country's richest households, tied to the similarly formidable increase in wealth for these households."[17]

In the South, neoliberal policies in Latin America and Africa were central to producing what many later termed the "lost decade" of the 1980s. In Latin America, income inequality shot up, while people living in poverty rose from 130 million in 1980 to 180 million at the beginning of the 1990s.[18] In Africa, structural adjustment or programs of trade liberalization, deregulation, and privatization combined with lower commodity prices and civil war to depress per capita income by 2.2 percent a year in the 1980s, so that by the early 1990s, some 200 million of the region's 690 million people were classified as poor.[19]

These trends accelerated in the 1990s. The number of people living in extreme poverty increased, globally, by 28 million. According to the UN Development Program, per capita income growth was less than 3 percent in 125 developing and transition economies, and in 54 of them average per capita income fell. The number of poor increased in Latin America and the Caribbean, Central and Eastern Europe, the Arab states, and sub-Saharan Africa. Instead of becoming a new frontier for exploitation, Central and Eastern Europe exacerbated the problem as the number of people living in poverty tripled, to 100 million in the 1990s.[20]

Only in East Asia, where integration into the world capitalist market was managed by strong states that pursued protectionism at home and mercantilism abroad, was there a sharp reduction in poverty rates in the 1980s and early 1990s. In China, some 128 million people emerged from poverty. However, the East Asian financial crisis in 1997–99 drove more than 1 million Thais and more than 21 million Indonesians below the poverty line.[21] Then the U.S. Treasury Department and the IMF took advantage of the crisis. These institutions had long criticized East Asian governments for their protectionist trade policies and state-assisted economic development. Now the IMF compelled them to adopt free-market remedies that exacerbated the contraction of mass purchasing power.

Even as neoliberal policies of structural adjustment reduced or limited global demand, policies removing restrictions on the movement of goods and capital meant intensified competition in this limited global market. By the 1990s, the U.S. automobile and steel industries, for instance, did not have to contend just with European and Japanese products but with cars and steel from Korea. The competitors from the newly developing countries had become formidable firms, oftentimes with state support, in protected markets. Now the old oligopolies could no longer avoid unrestricted competition. This situation only aggravated the crisis of massive overcapacity and of reduced profitability.[22]

EXCESS CAPACITY AND COERCED COMPETITION

After 1997, corporate profits in the United States stopped growing, largely because of the deadly combination of overcapacity and demand-repressive neoliberal policies. No comprehensive statistics on capacity exist, but a variety of sources have agreed that "large excess capacity has plagued almost all globally contested industries for almost two decades."[23] By the 1990s, the indicators were stark. In the United States, the computer industry's capacity was rising at 40 percent annually, far above projected increases in demand.[24] The world auto industry was selling just 74 percent of the 70.1 million cars it built each year. There was so much investment in worldwide telecommunications infrastructure that traffic carried over fiber-optic networks was reported to take up only 2.5 percent of capacity. In steel, excess capacity neared 20 percent.[25] It was estimated, in volume terms, to be an astounding 200 million tons, so that plans by steel-producing countries to reduce capacity by 100 million tons by 2005 would still leave "a sizeable amount of capacity which . . . would not be viable."[26] And according to the former General Electric chairman Jack Welch, "there was excess capacity in almost every industry."[27] Indeed, by the end of the decade, the gap between capacity and sales was, the *Economist* said, the largest since the Great Depression.[28]

If the combination of excess capacity and limited demand was making production unprofitable, why didn't firms simply liquidate their investments and cut their losses? Because, as James Crotty asserts, *"established firms have good reason not to exit quickly from unprofitable core industries."* He continues:

They have huge illiquid physical, human, and organizational assets that will suffer considerable loss of value if they are forced to pull out of the industry. But consider the firm's prospects if it decides not to exit. The outcome of the intra-industry wars for survival unleashed by neoliberalism is unpredictable. If it were known in advance which firms would lose the struggle for survival, the losers would exit early to cut their losses. . . . But given the major loss entailed in exit, most competitors try to "stay in the game" even as competition intensifies. Firms that survive the current struggle will reap the secure, above-average profits that are expected to emerge when the eventual winners are in a position to eliminate excess capacity and get the industry under oligopolistic control once again. [Thus] *refusal to exit is often a rational choice.*[29]

In the meantime, diminishing profits resulting from overproduction led to a wave of mergers, whose main purpose was the elimination of competition. The most prominent were the Daimler Benz-Chrysler-Mitsubishi union, the Renault takeover of Nissan, the Mobil-Exxon merger, the BP-Amoco-Arco deal, and the blockbuster "Star Alliance," a passenger-sharing network composed of United Airlines, Lufthansa, Thai International, Varig, and several other international airlines. In 2000, global merger and alliance deals were worth $3.5 trillion, about six times their value in 1994. The $1.1 trillion worth of cross-border mergers in 2000 was thirteen times the figure for 1991, signifying a "merger and alliance wave of historic proportions."[30]

Nevertheless, the UN *World Investment Report* noted that, despite the increase in merger-and-acquisition activity in recent years, "many M&A's have not delivered the anticipated positive results to the acquiring firms in terms of both share prices and 'real' economic effects such as profits and productivity."[31] This conclusion is not surprising, for the elimination of competition did not mean the elimination of excess capacity. In fact, as one analyst observed in the case of the car industry, "placing weak automakers into the hands of stronger companies only means that the auto industry is institutionalizing excess capacity on a scale never seen before."[32] Again, Crotty's insights are valuable. Firms that remain in competition, he argues, have no choice but to invest, even under deteriorating conditions of profitability, in order to have a chance of surviving, and much of that investment adds to capacity.

> To stay in the game, firms must invest to take advantage of the ever larger returns to scale made possible by rapid technical change and global market integration. Investment is also needed to shed labor through downsizing and reengineering and, with attacks on labor the order of the day, to increase direct monitoring and control of workers. Firms must invest to acquire best-practice technology for both cost reduction and quality reasons. In core markets such as autos and semiconductors, the acquisition of best-practice technology requires investment of ever increasing size. . . . *Many of these investments increase capacity*—even though this is not the reason firms undertake them.[33]

"Coerced competition"—a phenomenon that adds rather than eliminates capacity and thus further reduces profitability until only the firms with the deepest pockets remain—is the term that Crotty applies to the struggle among firms in core industries such as automobile, electronics, steel, aircraft, and energy. In the auto industry,

> even though firms faced excess capacity, losses or minuscule profit margins, and excessive debt, they continued to pour investment capital into the industry. Investment to take advantage of rapidly rising economies of scale is mandatory. Estimates of current minimum efficient production scale range from 2 million to an astounding 4 million cars per year. Ford, GM, and Daimler-Chrysler are again investing heavily in Asia, even though sales are not expected to return to 1996 levels until 2004. According to the *Wall Street Journal,* "Asia has turned into a war of attrition, with the Big Three aiming to be among the winners." Meanwhile, Honda and Toyota have increased capacity in the United States by 50 per cent since 1996. GM recently invested $1.5 billion in Saturn to try to maintain its competitiveness and thereby avoid losing the $5 billion it had previously invested. DaimlerChrysler, Volkswagen, and Renault plan to collectively invest $5 billion in production facilities in Mexico in the immediate future. The *Wall*

Street Journal observed that "many experts warn of vast overcapacity in Asia and South America if auto makers complete even a fraction of already announced plans for new plants." All the large auto makers are investing heavily in the development of new models, an expensive undertaking thought to be required to maintain market share.[34]

FINANCE-DRIVEN GROWTH

Because, in the core global industries, mergers did not alleviate the problem of diminishing profitability, they forced capital to seek investment elsewhere. With manufacturing and the rest of the "real economy" ceasing to be profitable, capital migrated to the speculative sector, where a period of hyperactive growth in high-technology stocks was carefully nursed by the low-interest-rate policy and New Economy talk of Federal Reserve chairman Alan Greenspan. One major source of this capital was the 20 percent of the population that benefited from the regressive redistribution of income that accompanied the U.S. boom of the 1990s. Another was foreign investors who sought high returns without incurring the risks of sinking their money in unpredictable economies like those of Mexico and East Asia.

While the more established sectors of the economy operated according to "real capitalism," the finance-driven information technology and telecommunications sectors functioned under "virtual capitalism," whose dynamics were based on the expectation of future profitability rather than on current performance. The workings of virtual capitalism were exemplified by the rapid rise in the stock values of Internet firms such as Amazon.com, which by 2001 had not yet turned a profit. Once future profitability rather than actual performance became the driving force of investment decisions, Wall Street operations were indistinguishable from high-stakes gambling in Las Vegas.

The dot.com phenomenon probably extended the boom of the 1990s in the United States about two years. "Never before in U.S. history," Brenner contends, "had the stock market played such a direct, and decisive, role in financing non-financial corporations, thereby powering the growth of capital expenditures and in this way the real economy. Never before had a U.S.

economic expansion become so dependent upon the stock market's ascent."[35]

Yet as early as 1998 there were danger signs, indications that the Wall Street–driven economy was bound to unravel. Long Term Capital Management was an exemplary hedge fund that many thought had perfected the art of the "casino economy." Backed up by computer models of stock market behavior devised by Nobel Prize winners, LTCM at its height did well. It managed over a trillion dollars worth of leveraged funds, resulting in an average profit of 34 percent annually for its investors.[36]

In the wake of the Asian, Russian, and Brazilian financial crises of 1997–98, however, investor behavior began to depart from the computer simulations. Instead, players in the global casino panicked or became conservative. As massive losses accumulated, LTCM verged on bankruptcy in the fall of 1998. But it couldn't be allowed to fail. As Clyde Prestowitz notes, "LTCM had borrowed so much money and placed such risky bets that it if collapsed, it threatened to take major banks and perhaps the system with it." Faced with that prospect, Alan Greenspan, who had previously argued against regulating hedge funds like LTCM, gave the New York Federal Reserve the green light to bail it out.[37]

The LTCM experience did not pour cold water on the speculative frenzy, however, nor did it push the federal authorities to enact and enforce tighter regulatory rules. In fact, Greenspan suggested that, with a little help from the Federal Reserve in the form of clever manipulation of the prime rate, the New Economy could leave behind the limitations of the Old Economy.

In the telecom industry, aggressive Wall Street financial intermediaries linked capital-flush investors with capital-hungry techno-entrepreneurs, all three interests united by a naive faith in a high-tech boom that they expected would go on and on. The supply of capital rather than real demand was driving investment decisions, and the telecom firms "were soon laying tens of millions of miles of fiber-optic cable across the [United States] and under the oceans."[38] By the spring of 2000, the market capitalization of telecom firms had reached $2.7 trillion, close to 15 percent of the total for nonfinancial corporations. But as Brenner points out, the picture was less than rosy:

> The problem, of course, was that thanks to the unregulated
> product and financial markets, everyone was doing it. In 2000 no

fewer than six U.S. companies were building new, mutually competitive fiber-optic networks. Hundreds more were laying down
local lines and several were also competing on sub-oceanic links.
All told, 39 million miles of fiber-optic line now criss-cross the
U.S., enough to circle the globe 1566 times. The unavoidable by-
product has been a mountainous glut: the utilization rate of telecom networks hovers today at a disastrously low 2.5–3 percent,
that of undersea cable at just 13 percent.[39]

Not surprisingly, profits plunged drastically from a peak of $35.2 billion
in 1996, the year the industry was deregulated, to $6.1 billion in 1999, and
then to minus $5.5 billion in 2000. As Brenner notes, "There could hardly
be clearer evidence that the market—and especially the market for
finance—does not know best."[40] Once the darlings of deal makers like
Salomon Smith Barney and Merrill Lynch, the telecom firms led the way to
high-profile bankruptcy: Global Crossing, Qwest, and Worldcom.

The problem, however, was systemic. With the profitability of the sector
dependent on the actual profitability of the manufacturing sector, the
finance-driven growth ultimately had to run out of steam. The dizzying
rise in market capitalization of nonfinancial corporations, from $4.8 tril-
lion in 1994 to $15.6 trillion in the first months of 2000, represented an
"absurd disconnect between the rise of paper wealth and the growth of
actual output, and particularly of profits, in the underlying economy."[41] A
few months after the stock market began to collapse in March 2001, the
$4.6 trillion in investor wealth that was wiped out, *Business Week* pointed
out, was half of the gross domestic product and four times the wealth
wiped out in the 1987 Wall Street crash.[42] A year after the downspin
started, that figure had risen to $7 trillion.

The massive loss of paper wealth represented the rude reassertion of the
reality of a global economy crippled by overcapacity, overproduction, and
lack of profitability. With the mechanism of "stock market Keynesianism"—
that is, reliance on speculative activity in the financial sector to drive
growth—broken and perhaps beyond repair,[43] the ability of the economy to
avoid a serious, prolonged downturn seemed greatly eroded.

CAPITALISM AND CORRUPTION

It was during this downward spiral that the Enron scandal broke, in the summer of 2001, followed in 2002 by similar scandals among the pillars of the Wall Street establishment, including the accounting giant Arthur Andersen and the investment bank Merrill Lynch, as well as upstart operators like Tyco International, Rite Aid, Global Crossing, Martha Stewart Living Omnimedia, Adelphia Communications, and Worldcom.

Enron underlined the deep corruption at the heart of American capitalism. Crony capitalism—a label that U.S. officials had once used to stigmatize the Asian economies, following the outbreak of the 1997 financial crisis—now reared its ugly head back home. The spectacular collapse of Enron and other corporate high rollers also demonstrated that trading on illusions could get you only so far. In the end, there was no getting around the fact that a firm's balance sheet had to show an excess of revenue over costs if it was to continue to attract investors. This was the simple but harsh reality that led to the proliferation of fancy accounting techniques such as that of Enron finance officer Andrew Fastow's "partnerships," which were mechanisms to keep major costs and liabilities off the balance sheet, as well as cruder methods, like Worldcom's masking of current costs as capital expenditures.

In the context of deregulation, it was easy for such pressure to erode the so-called firewalls—between management and board, stock analyst and stockbroker, auditor and audited. Faced with the specter of an economy on the downspin and slimmer pickings for all, the watchdogs and the watched abandoned the pretence that they were governed by a system of checks and balances. All had an interest in promoting the illusion of prosperity—and in maintaining their financial lifeline to unsuspecting investors—as long as possible.

This united front could not be maintained for long, however, since those who knew the real score were easily tempted to sell before the mass of investors got wise to what was happening. In the end, business acumen was reduced to figuring out when to sell, take the money, and run—and avoid prosecution. Enron CEO Jeffrey Skilling read the handwriting on the wall, resigned, and made off with $112 million from the sale of his stock options a few months before the fall. Less nimble was Tyco's Dennis Kozlowski, who was not content with raking off $240 million. He was still trying to milk his cash cow when his company went under.

THE BUSH RECESSION AND THE RETURN OF THE WEAK DOLLAR

The bitter fruits of excess capacity, neoliberal policies, and finance-driven growth were harvested during the Bush administration. They took the form of the stock market collapse, recession, and jobless growth. Burdened with what *New York Times* reporter and columnist Louis Uchitelle described as "a glut of boom-era investment that continues to litter the economy with underused factories,"[44] firms held back on significant new outlays on equipment, machinery, and technology. To counter the decline in profits, businesses shed workers and forced the survivors to increase their output. Making more with less: this was the essence of the productivity boom that marked the period 2001–2004, when productivity rose despite a dramatic fall in business investments in technology, traditionally the source of rises in productivity.[45] Not surprisingly, GDP grew, although in a tepid fashion, but so did the unemployment rate, peaking at 6.0 percent. By February 2003, according to the Bureau of Labor Statistics, the economy had lost about 3 million jobs.[46]

One response of the Bush administration was to cut taxes, which, in fact, did little to stimulate mass demand. About 42 percent of the overall gains from the immediate tax cuts that kicked in in 2001 went to the richest 20 percent of families. The cuts that would go into effect after 2001 were even more regressive in their impact: the richest 20 percent would get over 84 percent of the benefits, with the top 1 percent raking in more than half the overall benefits![47]

Probably more effective for countering the economic downspin was the weak dollar policy. By early 2003, it became clear that the strong dollar policy of the Clinton years was a thing of the past. A slow depreciation of the dollar vis-à-vis the euro could be interpreted as the result of market-based adjustments, but the 25 percent fall in value within a relatively short period was surely the outcome of a conscious policy. What was happening, in fact, was a repeat of the Reagan strategy of devaluing the dollar to gain competitive advantage. While the Bush administration issued denials that this was a beggar-thy-neighbor policy, the U.S. business press saw it for what it was: an effort to revive the American economy at the expense of the European Union and other center economies marked by stagnant demand. U.S. goods were now competitively priced in the domestic market, while U.S. exporters enjoyed a field day in foreign markets. In an election year, a weak dollar was an important mechanism for reviving the economy. Moreover, there were geopolitical reasons why the Bush administration was not willing to curb the dollar's free fall. As one report noted, "[A]fter the bust-up with France and Germany over Iraq, Washington is in no mood to do the Europeans any favors."[48]

The weak dollar certainly contributed to the pickup in the growth rate in early 2004. How sustained this would be, however, was open to question. Capacity utilization remained at 74.6 percent—well below the long-term average of 80 percent.[49] This situation was not unrelated to the fact that as Bush neared the end of his term in office, at least half the population was still experiencing the effects of recession. Real wages were barely growing. Production and supervisory workers continued to see a fall in their hourly wages. Moreover, as *Business Week* observed, "The share of the economic pie going to wages and salaries has plummeted to just over 50 percent, its lowest level in at least the past 50 years, and perhaps longer."[50] When one looked at the inequality of personal holdings, the picture was even worse: "The top 1 percent of families, as measured by net worth, receive about 15 percent of income but own 30 percent of the nation's assets—including stocks and bonds, homes, and closely held businesses. . . . The top 10 percent of families, as measured by net wealth, own 65 percent of assets, and the top 50 percent own a stunning 95 percent of assets. That means the gains from rising wealth have effectively left out half the population."[51]

THE CHINESE CONUNDRUM

At the beginning of the twenty-first century, China cast both light and shadow over the U.S. economy. For American investors, China was a nirvana of cheap labor and higher profitability. U.S. investors increasingly outsourced not only traditional manufacturing jobs but high-skilled computer and service jobs as well. Today, China attracts $53 billion in global investment a year, second only to the United States.[52] For the same reason, China was the bane of the American labor movement, because its wage levels were only one-fiftieth of those of the United States and Japan. Even if the productivity of labor was low in China, locating there remained competitive: in terms of per dollar output value, the average U.S. wage was still one-third higher than that of China.[53]

Since 2000, American manufacturing has lost 2.8 million jobs—3 million in some estimates—more than four times the loss during all of the 1990s.[54] Another 3 million jobs, representing $136 billion in wages, will likely move offshore.[55] The destination of most of these jobs is China. For many observers who felt that industrial jobs represented the heart of the economy, "the loss of manufacturing capacity across the board" was a strategic disaster.[56] The downward slide in manufacturing was at the center of a structural crisis that also saw the decline of related industries like mining and raw-material processing, a dwindling of the U.S. share of world exports, and stagnant spending for research and development.[57]

Ambivalence marked the Bush administration's posture toward China. The White House probably looked with approval at the massive flow of dollars into China, since, as U.S. investors argued, they could not compete with their European and Japanese counterparts unless they moved to China. Perhaps their reasoning was best expressed by one corporate executive: "We don't do it just to eviscerate United States jobs. We do it to be competitive."[58] Following this logic of preemptive investment, about 80 percent of the Fortune 500 corporations set up shop in China.[59] But the Bush administration also feared that Chinese economic growth would serve as the basis for the country's eventual strategic challenge to the United States. In the wake of September 11, however, as the nation sought allies for its war against terror, the administration's posture shifted from confrontation to accommodation. The Chinese, after all, backed Washington's antiterror campaign, at least rhetorically.

Nonetheless, it is in the area of the structural dynamics of global capitalism that China posed a powerful contradiction. On the one hand, China's 8–10 percent growth rate was probably the principal stimulus of what little growth occurred in the world economy. In the case of Japan, for instance, a decade-long stagnation was broken in 2003 by the country's first sustained recovery, fueled by exports to slake China's thirst for capital and technology-intensive goods; the exports shot up by a record 44 percent, or

$60 billion.[60] Indeed, China displaced Japan as the main destination for Asia's exports, accounting for 31 percent while recession-plagued Japan's share dropped from 20 percent to 10 percent. As one account pointed out, "In country-by-country profiles, China is now the overwhelming driver of export growth in Taiwan and the Philippines, and the majority buyer of products from Japan, South Korea, Malaysia, and Australia."[61]

On the other hand, China became an important contributor to the crisis of global overcapacity. Investment in China was not just the obverse of disinvestment elsewhere, although the shutting down of facilities and sloughing off of labor was significant not only in Japan and the United States but in the countries on China's periphery, like the Philippines, Thailand, and Malaysia. China itself was beefing up its capacity, at the same time that the ability of the Chinese market to absorb the output was limited.

Originally, when transnational corporations moved to China in the late 1980s and the 1990s, they saw it as the last frontier, the unlimited market that could endlessly absorb investment and endlessly throw off profitable returns. However, investment, in many cases, turned into excess investment because of China's restrictive rules on trade and investment, which forced the transnationals to locate most of their production processes in the country instead of outsourcing some of their needs. This is what analysts termed the "excessive internalization" of production activities by transnationals.[62]

By the turn of the millennium, the dream of exploiting a limitless market had vanished. Foreign companies headed for China not so much to sell to millions of newly prosperous Chinese customers, as to make China a manufacturing base for global markets, taking advantage of its inexhaustible supply of cheap labor. Typical of companies that found themselves in this quandary was Philips, the Dutch electronics manufacturer. Philips operates twenty-three factories in China and produces about $5 billion worth of goods, but two-thirds of their production is exported to other countries (not consumed in China).[63]

Excess capacity could have been rapidly overcome had the Chinese government focused on expanding individual income. Doing so would have meant a slower process of growth but a more stable one. China's authorities, however, chose a strategy of dominating world markets precisely by exploiting its cheap labor. As one account noted, although China's population is 1.3 billion, 700 million people—or over half—live in the countryside, earning an average of just $285 a year. Because of this reserve army of rural poor, manufacturers have been able to keep the wages down. But the same policy has effectively led to the dumping of cheap Chinese goods on an international market constrained by slow growth.

As the UNDP's *Human Development Report* has noted, China's "spectacular achievement of lifting 150 million out of income poverty" in the 1990s was concentrated in the coastal regions, while the western and northwestern provinces were left behind.[64] According to one observer,

> China is already troubled by problems arising from perceived inequities between the new classes of "haves" and "have nots." These problems exist at macro (regional) and micro (neighborhood) levels. Efforts to meet WTO requirements could worsen geographic and urban/rural frictions, widen an already growing gulf between rich and poor, and generally make China more ungovernable. WTO-mandated reforms will almost certainly worsen existing problems with massive unemployment, increases in uncontrolled migrant populations, major public safety and public health issues, and rapid degradation of social welfare infrastructure.[65]

For global capitalism, China thus posed both an opportunity and a challenge. On the one hand, it was the locomotive pulling the rest of the world out of the doldrums of the early 1990s. On the other hand, it was a time bomb, burdening a limited global market with massive capacity that could translate into overproduction, deflation, and recession. Two accounts cogently captured the two sides of the Chinese coin. Here's the bright outlook:

> The Chinese economy's share of global output has doubled, to 4 percent in the last decade. China is devouring 7 percent of the world's oil supply, a quarter of its aluminum, 30 percent of iron-ore output, 31 percent of the world's coal, and 27 percent of all steel products. Last year[2003], China-linked exports and industrial production accounted for a third of the recent rebound in Japan's gross domestic product. China is the top destination for South Korean exports: Trade with China kept the Korean economy from slipping into outright recession last year. Emerging-market companies in Brazil, Russia, and elsewhere have benefited

from the heavily China-influenced rise in global commodity markets. And China profits are coming in too. U.S. multinationals such as Motorola now rely on China for up to 10 percent of sales.[66]

But then there's the dark side:

China is producing so fast that it may be impossible for the population to absorb it all. Already there are price wars in industries like autos, mobile phone, and auto parts. Excess capacity first. Price wars next. Then a drop in investments. China's growth could slow sharply next year [2004], damaging the mainland itself and neighboring countries increasingly dependent on China. And it could hurt manufacturers worldwide if those excess goods get exported.[67]

END OF THE LONG WAVE?

Survey the current global economic terrain: An illusory recovery in the United States. Stagnation in Western Europe. Stagnation in Eastern Europe and most of the developing world. China racing, but toward an overcapacity that could severely disrupt Asian economies now dependent on it. According to Gary Shilling and a number of other pessimists, current macroeconomic imbalances are working themselves out in what is likely to be a prolonged period of jobless recovery, stagnant growth, deflation, and perhaps even a depression. What the world is undergoing, they say, is more than the usual business cycle.[68]

Their reasoning is that we are now at the downward curve of the so-called Kondratieff cycle. The cycle is named after the Russian economist Nikolai Kondratieff, who argued that the progress of global capitalism is characterized not only by short-term business cycles but by long-term "supercycles," roughly fifty- to sixty-year-long waves. The upward curve of the Kondratieff cycle is marked by the intensive exploitation of new technologies, followed by a crest as the exploitation matures, then a downward curve as the old technologies produce diminishing returns and developing technologies, still in an experimental stage, are not ready for profitable exploitation, and, finally, a trough, or prolonged deflationary period.

The trough of the last wave was in the 1930s and 1940s, the period of the Great Depression and World War II. The ascent of the current wave began in the 1950s, and the crest was reached in the late 1970s. The profitable exploitation of postwar advances in the key energy, automobile, petrochemical, and manufacturing industries slackened, while that of information technology was still at a relatively early stage. From this perspective, the New Economy of the late 1990s, which was based on developments in information technology, did not represent a transcendence of the business cycle, as many economists believed, but the last phase of the current supercycle.

Contrary to forecasts by analysts who see information technology at the core of a long-wave upswing in the first decade of the twenty-first century, the productivity gains from information and communications technology have been disappointing and certainly are insufficient to propel an upswing. Phillip O'Hara, following David Gordon, for instance, has argued that the much vaunted information revolution of the 1980s and 1990s was actually "a pale imitation of a major technological revolution compared with the applications of electricity, the automobile, the airplane, chemicals, telephone, radio, television, sanitation, and plumbing in previous phases of capitalist development."[69] The jobless growth of the recent recovery, in which productivity gains have come not from new applications of information and communications technology but from the shedding of labor, would seem to support this claim. The contradictory trends of the last few years may be the prelude to deflation, a deeper recession, and perhaps even a depression, as we enter the tail end of the current long wave of capitalist expansion.

CONCLUSION

Overcapacity and overproduction significantly decreased profitability in basic industry. Instead, finance capital emerged as the dynamo of both the U.S. and the global economies. On the one hand, financial institutions represent the chief source of corporate funding. Their power has grown enormously while the leverage of manufacturing and other industrial corporations has correspondingly diminished. On the other hand, financial transactions and speculative activity have become the chief sources of profit. Finance capital has gutted the regulations constraining its activities within the United States and other center economies. It has done the same abroad, whittling away international constraints on its movement in the global economy.

The financial integration of the center economies and the penetration of the global South by speculative capital has left the world exquisitely vulnerable to financial perturbations, generating crisis after crisis. The impact of this financial destabilization is felt most acutely in the South. It is to this particular dilemma of domination which has accompanied the rise of finance capital that we now turn.

CHAPTER 4

The Ascendancy of Finance

Future financial crises are almost surely inevitable and could be even more severe.

ROBERT RUBIN, FORMER SECRETARY OF THE TREASURY, 2003

Financial speculation increasingly drives global economic activity, even in developing countries. The mobility of capital, facilitated by the elimination of capital and foreign exchange controls, has proven to be largely a boon for the United States, although the situation can turn into its opposite quickly enough. For developing countries, however, capital flows can be extremely destabilizing. Financial crises have become more frequent and more serious, and most of them have occurred in the South. Thus the costs of international upheavals are borne largely by the peoples of the Third World. In contrast, the IMF and the U.S. Treasury have consistently intervened to minimize the impact of these disruptions on powerful corporate and financial interests in the North. But these are stopgap measures. Meanwhile, the economic promise of the free market seems increasingly threadbare, further aggravating America's imperial dilemma. The ascendancy of finance capital is a rolling disaster.

SPECULATION AND GLOBAL CAPITALISM

If there are three words that best describe the dynamics of global capitalism in the last twenty years, they are the "ascendancy of finance."

In the ideal capitalist system taught in Economics 101, financial institutions are said to intermediate between those who have the capital to lend and those who lack the capital to produce or to consume. Production and consumption drive the system, with the financial sector passively providing the wherewithal for producers and consumers.

The reverse is true today. Speculation drives the process, with the dynamics of global production and consumption increasingly subordinated to those of global finance. The situation stems from the crisis of overproduction, or excess capacity, analyzed in Chapter 3: With key industrial sectors no longer profitable, capital seeking high returns has increasingly resorted to speculative activity—an unstable, artificial process that, in essence, tries to squeeze more value out of already created value. In other words, the difference between financial indicators and actual values—for instance, between the momentary price of a stock and its real worth—cannot diverge too much before reality bites back. The assertion of true value triggers financial crises, and as speculative activity has become more and more the source of profitability, crises have multiplied.

The ascendancy of finance in today's global system is perhaps best illustrated in the case of the United States. As noted in Chapter 3, speculative activity raised stock prices of high-tech and other corporations to unrealistic highs, inviting new investment funds that prolonged the lives of unprofitable firms and extended the boom of the 1990s by about two years. Then followed the Wall Street crash of 2001, a year in which the economy was officially defined to be in recession, then two years of de facto recession, or jobless growth. Today, the economy, by a number of indicators, is in serious trouble. In 2003, the United States was $2.4 trillion in debt, a figure that came to 23 percent of the 2003 gross domestic product; had a record trade deficit of $489 billion; and ran a federal budget deficit of $370 billion.

Yet, at least for now, the economy has escaped a true disaster, thanks to the inflow of foreign speculative capital. It allows the nation to live beyond its means and to avoid stabilization measures that other governments in a similar state would by now have been forced to take. The multiple ways in which the United States benefits from the divergence between its real conditions and the rosy prospects that foreign speculative investors see in it are captured in the following account:

> [G]lobalization means the market for assets is now worldwide. That's good news for the [United States]. . . . The influx of foreign money has the effect of holding down interest rates and pushing up asset values, both of which have supported strong consumer spending despite the weak jobs performance. Over the past three years, foreigners have grabbed over $500 billion in U.S. corporate bonds, more than $400 billion in Treasury securities, and $225 billion more in agency securities, primarily mortgage-backed securities. In this last case, foreigners are effectively lending Americans money, using the appreciated values of their homes as collateral. This cash flows, eventually, into the pockets of U.S. homeowners, providing an enormous amount of financing for the housing boom and (indirectly) for consumer spending. The foreign inflow of money is the major reason why the interest rate on 10-year Treasuries is as low as 4.2 percent, despite the big budget deficits and the rebounding economy.[1]

Also, with equity markets becoming global, high-priced stocks sold to foreigners have helped finance the consumption of imports. As the stock market rose foreign speculative investors snapped up $84 billion in U.S. corporate equities in the fourth quarter of 2003—an inflow that was sufficient to finance much of the current account deficit for that quarter.[2] Thus the money needed to cover the gap between the value of U.S. exports and imports of goods and services was provided by foreign speculators.

The situation can change, pessimists point out, in response not only to economic factors but also to political ones, like a worsening of the Iraq war. Then, as a result of the same global reforms that facilitated its entry, foreign capital could exit quickly, leading to a debacle like the collapse of the stock market in mid-2001, which inaugurated a recession.

Much more exposed to the volatility of speculative capital, however, was the rest of the world, particularly the developing countries. For them, speculative capital, which both Wall Street and their own technocrats initially heralded as a blessing, as providing the wherewithal for development, has turned out to be a curse.

THE LIBERATION OF FINANCE CAPITAL

In the financial sector, as a World Bank study noted, "as recently as the early 1970's, few countries, whether industrial or developing, were without restrictions on capital movements."[3] Indeed, capital controls were maintained in Europe well into the 1970s. The IMF's articles of agreement (Article VI, Section 3) allowed members to "exercise such controls as are necessary to regulate international capital movements."[4] By the late 1990s, in contrast, finance was thoroughly liberated, and, more than industry or trade, it had become the driving force of the global economy. By the middle of the decade, in fact, the volume of transactions per day in foreign exchange markets came to over $1.2 trillion—a figure equal to the value of world trade in goods and services in an entire quarter.[5]

Several factors led to the liberalization of financial flows, Vietnam first of all. U.S. transactions to finance the war produced a massive dollar surplus overseas. It formed the basis of the Eurodollar or Eurocurrency market, centered in London, which the big commercial banks and other financial institutions tapped to expand their international and domestic activities—an option that freed them from dependence on profits from their retail banking activities that serviced consumers.[6]

Second, Eurocurrency liquidity was vastly increased by the recycling of OPEC money following the oil price rise of the 1970s. By 1981, the Organization of Petroleum Exporting Countries had piled up a surplus of $475 billion, waiting to be profitably invested; $400 billion of this amount was placed in the industrial countries[7]—an enormous supply of funds in search of high return. Pressure for greater liberalization came from the big commercial banks, which sought to recycle many of these funds by way of cross-border lending—primarily in the Third World, because of the relatively unattractive opportunities in the North during that decade. The preference for offshore lending also contributed to greater domestic deregulation, as governments made tax and other concessions to entice finance capital back onshore.[8]

We'll take closer look, a little later in the chapter, at the amazing journey of OPEC money.

The third key factor was the rise of free-market, neoliberal ideology, which fostered the liberalization of trade and of capital flows. Margaret Thatcher's removal of foreign exchange controls in Britain was a big first step.[9]

And, fourth, technology played a critical role in igniting what the *Financial Times* called the global bang, which swept away geographic, institutional, and regulatory boundaries within the financial services industry. The technology of financial services underwent an electronic revolution, and governments, for reasons of necessity, scrapped, rewrote, or ignored the rules that had controlled and compartmentalized the industry since the Great Depression. The lines of demarcation that distinguished the international Eurocurrency markets from the national domestic markets also blurred or disappeared altogether.

KEY FEATURES OF CONTEMPORARY FINANCE CAPITAL

The wave of liberalization in the 1980s exhibited several significant traits.

First, the flow of private capital to the South increased dramatically, rising more than six times—according to one account, from $24 billion to $148 billion.[10]

Second, the commercial banks, fearing their overexposure in the Third World, pulled back from international lending. Other major players emerged as key conduits for cross-border flows of capital. The most important were investment banks like Goldman Sachs, Salomon Brothers, Smith Barney, and Merrill Lynch, as well as mutual funds, pension funds, and hedge funds.

Third, the role of banks in raising funds was eclipsed by "securitization," or the transfer of capital through the sale of stocks and bonds—that is, corporations and governments increasingly raised money by selling equity or certificates redeemable in the future at fixed interest rates. In 1976–80, loans accounted for $59.4 billion of lending on international capital markets and securities for $36.2 billion; by 1993 the situation had seesawed, with securities accounting for $521.7 billion and loans for $136.7 billion.[11]

Fourth, there was an explosion in both old and new activities and financial instruments, such as arbitrage and derivatives. In arbitrage, the investor takes advantage of foreign-exchange or interest-rate differentials to turn a profit. Trading in derivatives is the practice of buying and selling "all the risk of an underlying asset without trading the asset itself."[12] Derivatives are, as one description had it, "very esoteric instruments, which are difficult to understand, monitor, or control."[13]

Fifth, a great many transactions, including those involving derivatives, were increasingly hard to monitor because they were made "over the counter," not on the floor of an exchange but among a few parties communicating by telephone and computer. Monitoring was all the more difficult by the fact that many of these transactions, such as forward contracts or agreements to fix exchange rates at a certain level so as to avoid losses resulting from exchange-rate fluctuations, were "off balance sheet." Since these transactions were not reflected in a company's record of assets and liabilities, the true financial condition of many institutions was hard to ascertain.

GLOBALIZATION'S VOLATILE ENGINE

The globalization of finance happened so fast and was so massive that, more than foreign direct investment or trade, finance capital had become, by the 1990s, the force driving the world economy. Indeed, as early as 1991, the UN Conference on Trade and Development (UNCTAD) warned of the "ascendancy of finance over industry"[14]—in other words, of speculation over production.

The ascendancy of finance has been coupled with its almost complete lack of regulation. Deregulation at the national level has not been replaced by reregulation at the global level, so that, as one analyst points out, "international financial transactions are carried out in a realm that is close to anarchy. Numerous committees and organizations attempt to coordinate domestic regulatory policies and negotiate international standards but they have no enforcement powers. The Cayman Islands and Bermuda offer not only beautiful beaches but also harbors that are safe from financial regulation and international agreements."[15] As might be expected, lack of regulation has been a major cause of the volatility of international finance. Another is the fact that a great deal of international finance is a game of worldwide arbitrage, in which capital moves from one financial market to another, seeking to exploit the imperfections of globalized markets.

And why has there been so little regulation? The answer is finance capital's tremendous political clout. Efforts at even minimal control—such as the Tobin tax, a small fee collected from capital transactions at strategic points in the world economy and intended to serve as a speed bump to slow down global capital flows—have faced opposition from a strong lobby in key northern governments, especially in Washington. Christened the "Wall Street–Treasury Complex" by the free-trade economist Jagdish Bhagwati (who does not support the unregulated movement of capital),[16] the lobby includes former Treasury secretary Robert Rubin, who was one of the mainstays of the investment bank Goldman Sachs, and Federal Reserve chairman Alan Greenspan.

FINANCE CAPITAL TARGETS THE SOUTH

Variations in exchange rates, interest rates, and stock prices among capital markets in the North tend to be relatively small. The big differentials are found in the emerging markets of Asia and elsewhere. Movements of capital from North to South have therefore been particularly volatile.

Northern Commercial Banks Recycle OPEC Money, 1973–82

The integration of the global South into world capital markets began in the nineteenth century, but the process was slowed down considerably by the Great Depression and World War II. After the war and up until the 1970s, the main conduits of capital into the South were foreign direct investment and multilateral assistance provided by the World Bank, the IMF, and the regional development banks. Integration speeded up, as we noted earlier, with the massive recycling of OPEC money to the South following the oil price hikes of the 1970s.

The changing pattern of capital flows was illustrated sharply in the case of Latin America. In 1961–65, official sources (i.e., governments, multilateral agencies) supplied 59.8 percent of the average annual inflow from abroad; that dropped to 40.4 percent in 1966–70; 25.3 percent in 1971–75; and to only 12.1 percent in 1976–78. Foreign investment as a percentage of capital inflow likewise dropped, from 33.7 in the second half of the 1960s to 15.9 percent in the second half of the 1970s. On the other hand, the share of foreign bank and bond finance rose sharply, from 7.2 percent in the early 1960s to 46 percent in the early 1970s, and to 64.6 percent in the late 1970s.[17]

In the same way that "irresponsible" Asian banks and companies were later made the scapegoat for the East Asian crisis in 1997–98, "profligate" governments were blamed for the crisis that broke out in 1982, an upheaval that cost Latin America a decade of growth. The hundreds of billions of dollars deposited by the OPEC nations in American commercial banks sought outlets for profitable investment. Citibank chairman Walter Wriston succinctly formulated the rationale for shipping dollars down south: "Countries don't go bankrupt."[18]

The supply-driven dynamics of commercial bank lending was underlined by Karin Lissakers's comprehensive account of the process. For all intents and purposes, such lending to developing countries had stopped during the Great Depression. But four decades later,

> awash in oil money, with credit demand depressed in the home market, commercial banks resumed large-scale lending to developing countries and their governments. For U.S. banks, international borrowing and lending was transformed from a limited adjunct of domestic business to an activity that dominated the balance sheet. While their domestic business languished, international activities exploded, accounting for 95 percent of the earnings growth of the nation's ten largest banks during the first half of the decade and probably more than half their total earnings in the late 1970's.[19]

Long lines of senior managers from New York banks trooped to the suites of finance ministers from developing countries during the annual World Bank–IMF meetings in Washington. Meanwhile, their field representatives in those countries "competed for the nod from the same cluster of state corporations and agencies."[20]

On the eve of the Mexican default in 1982, some $400 billion in OPEC money had found its way into the coffers of northern banks. The bulk had been recycled to Third World and Eastern European governments, leaving them $700 billion in debt. Because loans had been contracted at high floating rates, the debt was unsustainable. In the summer of 1982, Mexico led the way to a disastrous decade when it declared it could not make its quarterly payments on its $100 billion debt. Brazil, Argentina, Venezuela, the Philippines, and many other debtors soon followed Mexico into de facto insolvency.

Debt Crisis and Structural Adjustment, 1983–91

It took Mexico seven years to reenter world capital markets. It would take longer for many of the other nations.

In the intervening period, Mexico and some seventy other developing countries underwent structural adjustment programs (SAPs) managed by the IMF and the World Bank, the details of which will be discussed in Chapter 5. What is important to note here is that these programs, which were supposed to discipline profligate governments, had the paradoxical effect of making the developing countries even more open to capital flows from the North and thus more vulnerable to global financial perturbations. As SAPs imposed tight fiscal and monetary policies on the government, foreign-exchange controls were lifted and capital accounts liberalized. The role of the state as a mediator between the domestic private sector and foreign capital was dramatically reduced. At the same time, the government was forced to serve as the ultimate guarantor of private-sector borrowing, as Chile's dictator Augusto Pinochet was rudely reminded by Wall Street when he tried to abjure state responsibility for the losses by Chilean private banks during the financial crisis of 1983.[21]

Speculative Capital Floods the South Anew, 1992–97

The accumulation of finance capital in the North with no place to go remained troubling in the early 1980s. Federal Reserve chairman Paul Volcker's anti-inflationary high-interest policy dampened economic activity, not only in the United States but in the rest of the now financially integrated Group of 7 nations as well. That the economies of the Third World were growing weaker was not perceived as a critical barrier to further capital flows from the North. After squeezing nearly $220 billion from the region in debt service between 1982 and 1990, international capital markets, suddenly and spectacularly, started pouring money into

Latin America. Following years of net outflows, net inflow into the region came to $7 billion in 1991, then rose to $31 billion in 1992 and $32 billion in 1993.[22]

Mexico, in particular, was a star performer, attracting $4.5 billion in foreign investment in 1990, $15 billion in 1991, $18 billion in 1992, and $32 billion in 1993. Yet Mexican GDP declined from 4.5 percent in 1990 to 3.6 percent in 1991, to 2.8 percent in 1992, to 0.4 percent in 1993.[23] As Timothy Kessler pointed out, "The vast majority of foreign capital was invested in Mexico for the unambiguous purpose of extracting financial rents, while a decreasing proportion went to direct investment."[24]

If Mexico and Latin America suddenly became the darlings of foreign speculators in the early 1990s, no small part of the credit goes to the IMF and the World Bank. The bank, in particular, came to the conclusion that portfolio investing might be a better way than foreign aid or foreign direct investment of channeling capital into developing countries. The result was the public relations transformation of Latin American countries deep in debt into "big emerging markets"—a phrase coined by a World Bank official.[25]

In addition, the World Bank, through its private investment arm, the International Finance Corporation (IFC), set up mechanisms to channel capital from the North to the South; in 1986 it put up seed money for the first emerging markets fund, or a capital pool designed to attract investment to markets considered the most attractive in the developing world.[26] The Capital Group, a money management giant based in Los Angeles that ran this fund, did very well, with total returns to investors of 24 percent in 1987, 42 percent in 1988, and 94 percent in 1989.[27] "Those numbers," according to Justin Fox, "drew in more and more money managers, which set the stage for the mad rush of 1993."[28] As the Asian Development Bank put it, "The declining returns in the stock market of industrial countries and the low real interest rates compelled investors to seek higher returns on their capital elsewhere."[29] In any event, the mad rush of foreign capital to the Third World in 1993 was unlike anything since the late 1970s.

SPECULATIVE CRISES: THREE CASE STUDIES

Crises are endemic to this system of global finance, and they have their roots in the volatility of capital seeking to exploit evanescent fluctuations in interest rates, currency values, and stock prices. Since the early 1970s, at least eight upheavals were triggered by speculative capital movements, largely in the financial markets of developing or newly industrializing countries. A close study of three cases—the crises in Mexico, East Asia (focusing on Thailand and Korea), and Argentina—reveals some common dynamics of what UNCTAD has called the "post-Bretton Woods financial system."

Mexico: From Crisis to Crisis

The financial crisis that hit Mexico in late 1994 was the second in twelve years.

There were two striking characteristics of the Mexican financial scene in the early 1990s. First was the rapid, massive buildup in foreign capital into the region. The country received $91 billion in just four years, a figure that amounted to 20 percent of all net capital inflows to developing countries.[30]

Second, this surge was mainly a supply-driven phenomenon. It had little basis in the actual prospects of the real economy, which experienced a decline in the GDP growth rate during the financial boom years, a 40 percent unemployment rate, and poverty that engulfed around half the population— all were a legacy of the structural adjustment imposed on the economy after the debt debacle of the 1980s.[31] The lack of correlation between the sorry prospects for the real economy and the rosy view of investors was captured in the World Bank's observation that the "rapidity and magnitude of the resurgence of private flows [to Mexico and other highly indebted countries] in the 1990s surprised many observers." According to one Mexican scholar, speculative gain rather than strategic investment in a promising economy was the key motive of foreign investors, as indicated by the fact that only one-fourth of capital inflows actually went into investment in plants; the remaining funds were put into financial markets and speculation.[32]

But the process was not only supply-driven. The country's technocrats formulated measures that would attract money. Interest rates were maintained at a much higher rate than in the northern money centers, so that an investor borrowing in New York's money market "could capture the spread between returns of five to six percent in America and twelve to fourteen percent in Mexico."[33] Informally fixing the rate of exchange between the dollar and the peso through government buying and selling in the currency market was a policy calculated to assure foreign investors that they would not be blindsided by devaluations. As Jeffrey Sachs has pointed out, the role of external actors in promoting this policy was not insignificant: financial authorities "fell under the influence of money managers who championed the cause of pegged exchange rates" by arguing that "only a stable exchange rate could underpin the confidence needed for large capital inflows."[34]

Finally, there was the policy of financial and capital account liberalization; here again, the role of external institutions was central. The structural adjustment programs imposed by the IMF and the World Bank in the 1980s targeted liberalization not only of the trade account but also of the capital account. However, it was the country's entry into the Organization for Economic Cooperation and Development (OECD) in 1993 that was decisive, for it required Mexico's complete elimination of all restrictions on capital movements.[35]

Much foreign investment went to purchase government debt instruments that were denominated in dollars, with speculators, according to Rubin, not "paying sufficient attention to the danger that the central bank's currency reserves might not be sufficient to maintain their promised convertibility into dollars.[36]

The inflow of a huge mass of foreign capital into the country created a real appreciation of the currency, and Mexico's exports become less competitive in world markets. Another consequence was a consumption boom that drove up the nation's imports, since the deindustrialization resulting from structural adjustment ensured that much of the demand for light and durable consumer goods could no longer be met by domestic manufacturing. The upshot was a current account deficit that stood at 8 to 8.5 percent of GDP by 1994, a development that began to make foreign investors nervous. Ariel Buira noted the paradox:

> As inflows eventually translate into a growing current account deficit, the very same investors who were eager to bring in their capital will look at the size of the deficit and become nervous. Investors may overreact to any unfavorable development by withdrawing their funds and in this way may contribute to the emergence of a payment crisis. Thus, as capital inflows—a symbol of success—give rise to a current account deficit, ironically, they become the country's weakness.[37]

Worried about an unstable macroeconomic landscape they had collectively contributed to, individual investors started pulling out in 1994. The yawning current account gap served as another source of instability as currency speculators, local investors, and foreign investors, expecting or betting on a government "correction"—a devaluation that would reduce the deficit—subjected the peso to a massive assault beginning in mid-November 1994. It subsided only when the peso was allowed to float in late December and promptly lost half its nominal value. The combined attack by speculators and panicky investors, seeking to change their pesos for dollars and get the hell out before the expected devaluation, was simply too strong for the government to repel. On December 21, the Central Bank spent $4.5 billion of its already depleted reserves in a futile defense of the peso.[38] A massive devaluation and financial crisis was inevitable. The Clinton administration orchestrated a $50 billion package to stabilize the situation in Mexico, and a great deal of that money was spent bailing out, *in full*, holders of Mexican government securities.[39] Some $20 billion of the total amount came from a U.S. government facility known as the Exchange Stabilization Fund (ESF), drawing howls of protest from Congress that the White House was circumventing legislative authority. Another $17.8 billion came from the IMF. This massive sum was, in the words of Michel Camdessus, the fund's managing director, "the largest ever approved for a member country, both in absolute amount and in relation to the country's quota [capital subscriptions] [700 per cent] in the Fund."[40] Its role in the rescue operation triggered criticism from various powerful members of the IMF.

From the standpoint of the European industrial powers, IMF drawings on this scale amounted to a U.S. raid on the fund's piggy bank. In effect, the United States was bending the rules—that IMF loans not exceed 300 percent of quota—for its own purposes. In a rare show of discord, several European executive directors abstained in the vote on the Mexican loan.[41]

The price exacted from Mexico was a program of economic contraction. The high interest rates that restored the confidence of foreign capital inevitably triggered a recession. Stability achieved through high interest rates, admitted Rubin—who as Treasury secretary managed the bailout—led to growing unemployment, a significant drop in real wages, and severe impairment of bank balance sheets.[42] Despite his recognition of Mexico's troubles, Rubin proudly claimed that the success of the program, as proven by that nation's repayment of the bailout money more than three years ahead of schedule, provided the United States with $1.4 billion in interest and left the ESF with a profit of $580 million.[43] That record was achieved, however, at the cost of a full-blown depression that lasted several years and entailed widespread unemployment and social disintegration, including the proliferation of criminal activities, like drug dealing, which became one of the few growth sectors of the economy.

Southeast Asia: Speculative Capital Supplants Foreign Direct Investment

In the case of Southeast Asia, the surge in the inflow of portfolio investment and short-term private bank credit in the early 1990s followed an earlier steep rise in foreign direct investment beginning in the mid-1980s. This sudden arrival of investment lifted the region out of the recession of the mid-1980s. A significant portion of the capital came from Japan and was a direct consequence of the Plaza Accord of 1985, which drastically revalued the yen relative to the dollar and other major currencies, forcing Japanese manufacturers to relocate a major part of their labor-intensive operations from Japan to Southeast Asia.

Between 1985 and 1990, some $15 billion worth of Japanese direct investment flowed into the region in one of the largest, swiftest movements of capital to the developing world in recent history.[44] The direct investment was accompanied by billions of dollars more in bilateral aid and bank loans from Tokyo. Moreover, it provoked an ancillary flow of billions of dollars in direct investment from the newly industrialized economies of Taiwan, Hong Kong, and South Korea.

It was this prosperity that attracted portfolio investors and banks and, with the collapse of Mexico in 1995, fund managers, who channeled the biggest chunk of their investments and loans for Third World markets to the East Asian region. The interests of speculators seeking better climes than the relatively low-yield capital markets of the North and the risky markets of Latin America coincided with the search by Asian technocrats for alternative sources of foreign capital as infusions of the yen leveled off in the early 1990s.

With the advice of fund managers and the IMF, Thailand followed Mexico's example and formulated a three-pronged strategy. It liberalized the capital account and the financial sector as a whole; maintained high domestic interest rates relative to those in northern money centers, to lure portfolio investment and bank capital; and fixed the local currency at a stable rate relative to the dollar, to insure foreign investors against currency risk.

Portfolio investments in both equities and bonds rose, and so did credit from international banks to Thai financial institutions and enterprises, which sought to take advantage of the large differential between the relatively low rates at which they borrowed from northern money-center banks and the high rates at which they could relend the funds to local borrowers.

In the short term, the formula was wildly successful in attracting foreign capital. Net portfolio investment came to around $24 billion in the three years before the crisis erupted in 1997, while at least another $50 billion entered in the form of loans to Thai banks and enterprises. These results encouraged finance ministries and central banks in Kuala Lumpur, Jakarta, and Manila to copy the Thai formula, with equally spectacular results. According to Washington's Institute of International Finance, net private capital flows to Malaysia, Indonesia, the Philippines, Thailand, and Korea shot up from $37.9 billion in 1994, to $79.2 billion in 1995, to $97.1 billion in 1996.[45]

In retrospect, Thailand illustrated the fatal flaws of a development model based on huge, rapid infusions of foreign capital. First, just as in Mexico, there was a basic contradiction between encouraging foreign capital inflows and keeping an exchange rate that would make the country's exports competitive in world markets. The former demanded a currency pegged to the dollar at a stable rate, in order to draw in foreign investors. With the dollar appreciating in 1995 and 1996, so did the pegged Southeast Asian currencies. Consequently, the international prices of Southeast Asian exports rose.

The second problem was that the bulk of the funds coming in consisted of speculative capital seeking high, quick returns. With little regulation of its movements, foreign capital did not gravitate to the domestic manufacturing sector or to agriculture, which were considered low-yield sectors that would provide a decent rate of return only after a long gestation period. The high-yield sectors with a quick turnaround time to which foreign investment and foreign credit inevitably gravitated were the stock market, consumer finance, and, in particular, real estate development. In

Bangkok, at the height of the boom in the early 1990s, land values were higher than in urban California.

Not surprisingly, a glut in real estate developed rapidly. Bangkok led the way with $20 billion worth of new commercial and residential space unsold by 1996. Foreign banks had competed to push loans on to Thai banks, finance companies, and enterprises in the boom years of the early 1990s. By the middle of the decade, lenders woke up to the realization that their borrowers were loaded with nonperforming loans.

Alarm bells began to sound. The flat export growth rates for 1996 (an astonishing zero growth in both Malaysia and Thailand) and burgeoning current account deficits were worrisome. Since a foreign-exchange surplus earned through the consistently rising exports of goods and services was the ultimate guarantee that the foreign debt contracted by the private sector would be repaid, the slowing of exports was a blow to investor confidence. What the investors failed to realize was that the very policy of maintaining a strong currency, calculated to draw them in, was also the cause of the export collapse. Many also failed to realize that the upgrading of the quality of exports, which could have counteracted the rise in export prices, had been undermined by the easy flow of foreign money into the speculative sectors of the economy. Manufacturers had channeled their investments there in order to harvest quick profits, instead of pouring them into the long, slow process of research and development and of improving the skills of the workforce.[46]

By 1997, it was time to get out. Because of the liberalization of the capital account, there were no mechanisms to slow down the exit of funds. With hundreds of billions of Thai baht chasing a limited number of dollars, the outflow of capital could be highly destabilizing. Many big institutional players and banks began to leave, but what converted a nervous departure into a catastrophic stampede was the speculative activity of the hedge funds and other arbitrageurs. Gambling on the authorities' eventual devaluation of the overvalued baht, they accelerated the process by unloading huge quantities of the Thai currency in search of dollars.

In the Thai debacle, hedge funds played a key role. Essentially they are investment partnerships that are limited to the very wealthy, are often based offshore, and are little regulated. Specializing in combining short and long positions in different currencies, bonds, and stocks in order to net a profit from the combined transactions, the funds had been attacking the baht occasionally since 1995. But the most spectacular assault occurred on May 10, 1997, when in just one day, hedge funds are said to have "bet U.S. $10 billion against the baht in a global attack."[47] Of the Bank of Thailand's $28 billion forward book (money tied to contracts for currency exchange for the future, based on less attractive rates for the local currency than the current rate) at the end of July, according to an IMF report, approximately $7 billion "is thought by market participants to represent transactions taken directly with hedge funds. Hedge funds may have also sold the baht forward [that is, at less attractive terms for the local currency than the current rate] through offshore counterparties, onshore foreign banks, and onshore domestic banks, which then off-loaded their positions to the central bank."[48]

Under such massive attacks, the Bank of Thailand lost practically all its $38.7 billion of foreign-exchange reserves between the end of 1996 and mid-1997. On July 2, the decade-long peg of 25 baht to the dollar was abandoned, and the Thai currency lost over 50 percent of its value in a few months.

Jakarta and Kuala Lumpur experienced the same conjunction of massive capital flow, property glut, and rise in the current account deficit. The nervousness had existed there, too, but the baht collapse was what triggered the severe anxiety among foreign investors. Jeffrey Winters describes the deadly dynamics of mass panic:

> Suddenly, you receive disturbing news that Thailand is in serious trouble, and you must decide immediately what to do with your Malaysian investments. It is in this moment that the escape psychology and syndrome begins. First, you immediately wonder if the disturbing new information leaking out about Thailand applies to Malaysia as well. You think it does not, but you are not sure. Second, you must instantly begin to think strategically about how other EMFMs [emerging market financial managers] and independent investors are going to react, and of course they are thinking simultaneously about how you are going to react. And third, you are fully aware, as are all the other managers, that the first ones who sell as a market turns negative will be hurt the least, and the ones in the middle and the end will lose most value in their portfolio—and likely to be fired from their position as

an EMFM as well. In a situation of low systemic transparency, the sensible reaction will be to sell and escape. Notice that even if you use good connections in the Malaysian government and business community to receive highly reliable information that the country is healthy and is not suffering from the same problems as Thailand, you will still sell and escape. Why? Because you cannot ignore the likely behavior of all the other investors. And since they do not have access to the reliable information you have, there is a high probability that their uncertainty will lead them to choose the escape. If you hesitate while they rush to sell their shares, the market will drop rapidly, and the value of your portfolio will start to evaporate before your eyes.[49]

Winters comes to a radically different conclusion from Adam Smith, who believed that the invisible hand of the market should bring about the greatest good for the greatest number. "The chain reaction," Winters writes, "was set in motion by currency traders and managers of large pools of portfolio capital who will operate under intense competitive pressures that cause them to behave in such a manner that is objectively irrational and destructive for the whole system, especially for the countries involved, but subjectively both rational and necessary for any hope of individual survival."[50]

Speculative Capital Fells a Tiger Economy

Unlike Southeast Asia, Korea's development had not been based principally on foreign investment. Instead, it rested on capital amassed through monopoly of a domestic market by local capital and on an aggressive mercantilist policy promoted by the state.

A close working relationship between the private sector and the state fostered high-speed industrialization. By "picking winners," providing them with subsidized credit through a government-directed banking system, and protecting them from competition from transnationals in the domestic market, the state nurtured *chaebol*, or industrial conglomerates that it later encouraged to enter the international market.

In the 1980s, the state-*chaebol* combine appeared to be unstoppable in international markets, as the deep pockets of the commercial banks were extremely responsive to government wishes and provided the wherewithal for Hyundai, Samsung, LG Electronics, and other conglomerates to carve out market shares in Europe, Asia, and North America.

It did not take very long, however, for the tide to turn against the Koreans. Several factors contributed to this development, among them overinvestment resulting in overcapacity, which led to declining profitability. Easy credit by government-controlled banks had been a central reason for the so-called Korean miracle, but by the early 1990s, the credit demands of the *chaebol* to support investment and expansion had become voracious. At the same time, foreign banks and foreign funds were eager to lend to Korea and pressed Washington, the World Bank, and the IMF, in turn, to pressure the Koreans to open up their financial sector. Korea then entered the OECD, which required it to liberalize its capital account, financial sector, and foreign investment regime.[51] Although Korea formally adopted a gradualist strategy embodied in the so-called Reform of the Foreign Exchange System, the inflow of foreign funds was, in fact, anything but gradual. In 1993, the Kim Young Sam government relaxed its controls over cross-border capital flows, allowing both conglomerates and newly created banks greater liberty to borrow abroad. As Ravi Arvind Palat has pointed out, the 1993 financial liberalization signified the weakening of the state as a buffer between the local economy and the international economy, on the one hand, and the rise of an uncontrolled private sector as the principal mediator between the two arenas, on the other.[52]

The results were disastrous. Korean banks plunged gleefully into the interbank market, "taking advantage of lower interest rates overseas and passing the funds on to their domestic customers.... [T]his was hardly prudent banking practice since it meant that Korea Inc. was borrowing short-term money abroad—money that had to be repaid in hard currency—and lending it long-term to the expansion-crazed *chaebol.*"[53] But, as always, it took two to tango, and "foreign banks rushed into this promising new market, led by the Europeans and the Japanese."[54] South Korea's foreign debt promptly trebled, from $44 billion in 1993 to $120 billion in September 1997, and went on to reach $153 billion in February 1998.[55] Most aggressive among the borrowers of short-term foreign funds were the thirty new merchant banks, which accounted for $20 billion of the $153 billion debt.[56]

The high-profile collapse of some severely indebted *chaebol* early in 1997 and the financial panic in Southeast Asia in the summer of 1997 combined to make the Korean economy a sitting duck. Exhibiting much the same herd mentality demonstrated by fund managers during the Southeast Asian crisis a few months earlier, the banks began pulling out, paying little attention to the fact that Korea was a more advanced, solid industrial economy—in fact, a member of the OECD—than Thailand or Indonesia. As one IMF staffer recalled:

> I was being called by a lot of banks in October and November, and it was amazing how little they knew about Korea. They'd ask, "Has Korea ever defaulted?" Well, the answer is no. They'd ask, "How recent is Korea's miracle? Isn't it all driven by foreign capital flows?" Well, it's not. I remember one indignant guy in New York saying, "We're a responsible bank; we cannot roll over our claims in a nontransparent country." And I thought, "Well, you certainly seem to have been able to *lend* to them!" In a panic situation, once something becomes an issue, no bank wants to be left out on a limb.[57]

When fund managers began to dump the local currency, the *won*, in early November 1997, the Korean government tried to defend the exchange rate by using its reserves. It promptly lost about $10 billion, or over one third of its foreign currency reserves. The *won* was devalued on November 17, resulting in a 24 percent loss in value against the dollar by early December, or a 24 percent hike in the cost of servicing dollar-denominated loans by local borrowers. With Korean banks and firms facing bankruptcy, the IMF negotiated a record $57 billion rescue to enable Korean borrowers to repay their international creditors. This funding did not, however, halt the flight from the *won* by foreign banks—nor did an additional $10 billion ponied up by the United States and other governments during Christmas week.

Only the looming threat of a bankruptcy that would disrupt the global financial system compelled Washington to pressure bankers to roll over their loans to Korea, and the bleeding stopped.[58] On January 29, 1998, a consortium of thirteen international banks agreed not to take any more money out of the country and to restructure $24 billion of the short-term debt scheduled to come due in 1998: they would swap these short-term

loans for new debt coming due in one to three years.[59] In his acco
those tense days, Paul Blustein remarked: "In a sense, the international
banks got away with murder. They had foolishly injected billions of dollars
of short-term loans into a country with a shaky financial system, yet they
were suffering no losses."[60] Indeed, as the key architect of the bailout
admitted (Robert Rubin, again), not only did the banks emerge unscathed
but they "were paid back in full and ended up receiving a higher rate of
interest in the interim."[61]

In both Mexico and East Asia, creditors and speculative investors got off
pretty lightly, thanks to rescue packages put together by the IMF. Yet the
price was high for the peoples in these countries. In exchange for rescue
funds, governments were forced to adopt IMF policies that emphasized
stabilization, which included cutting government expenditures and raising
interest rates. Instead of playing a countercyclical role to offset the collaps-
ing private sector, government policy speeded up contraction of the economy. In 1998 the economies affected by the crisis plunged into recession or
registered zero growth. Joseph Stiglitz, former chief economist of the
World Bank, noted, "[A]usterity, the Fund's leader said, would restore confidence in the Thai economy. . . . [E]ven as evidence of policy failure
mounted, the Fund barely blinked, delivering the same medicine to each
ailing nation that showed up on its doorstep."[62] But as over 1 million people in Thailand and 22 million in Indonesia sank beneath the poverty line
in a few weeks' time, not even the IMF could deny the devastating results of
its policy. Indeed, the IMF, in a mid-1999 paper, issued what amounted to
a mea culpa. It admitted that in the East Asian countries it advised during
the crisis, "the thrust of fiscal policy . . . turned out to be substantially different . . . because the original assumptions for economic growth, capital
flows, and exchange rates . . . were proved drastically wrong."[63]

But the price paid by the affected countries was not just their people's
suffering. They were forced to yield large tracts of their sovereign authority
over their own economies. Chalmers Johnson has argued that a good case
can be made that Washington's opportunistic behavior during the Asian
financial crisis reflected the fact that "having defeated the fascists and the
communists, the United States now sought to defeat its last remaining
rivals for global dominance: the nations of East Asia that had used the conditions of the Cold War to enrich themselves."[64]

In Thailand, local authorities agreed to remove all limitations on foreign ownership of Thai financial firms, accelerate the privatization of state enterprises, and revise bankruptcy laws along lines demanded by foreign creditors. As the U.S. trade representative Charlene Barshefsky told Congress, the Thai government's "commitments to restructure public enterprises and accelerate privatization of certain key sectors—including energy, transportation, utilities, and communications—which will enhance market-driven competition and deregulation—[are expected] to create new business opportunities for U.S. firms."[65]

In Indonesia, Barshefsky emphasized that "the IMF's conditions for granting a massive stabilization package addressed practices that have long been the subject of this [Clinton] Administration's bilateral trade policy. . . . Most notable in this respect is the commitment by Indonesia to eliminate the tax, tariff, and credit privileges provided to the national car project. Additionally, the IMF program seeks broad reform of Indonesian trade and investment policy, like the aircraft project, monopolies and domestic trade restrictive practices, that stifle competition by limiting access for foreign goods and services."[66] The national car project and the plan to set up a passenger jet aircraft industry had elicited the strong disapproval of Detroit and Boeing, respectively.

In the case of Korea, the U.S. Treasury and the IMF did not conceal their close working relationship, and the fund clearly played a subordinate role. Not surprisingly, the concessions made by the Koreans—including raising the limit on foreign ownership of corporate stocks to 55 percent, permitting the establishment of foreign financial institutions, fully liberalizing the financial and capital market, abolishing a restrictive classification system for automobile import, and agreeing to end government-directed lending for industrial policy goals—had a one-to-one correspondence with Washington's bilateral policy toward Korea before the crisis. As Barshefsky candidly told members of Congress:

> Policy-driven, rather than market-driven, economic activity meant that U.S. industry encountered many specific structural barriers to trade, investment, and competition in Korea. For example, Korea maintained restrictions on foreign ownership and operations, and had a list of market access impediments. . . . The Korea stabilization package, negotiated with the IMF in December 1997, should help open and expand competition in

Korea by creating a more market-driven economy. . . . [I]f it
continues on the path to reform there will be important benefits
not only for Korea but also the United States.[67]

Summing up Washington's strategic goal, Jeff Garten, undersecretary of
commerce during President Bill Clinton's first term, said, "Most of these
countries are going through a dark and deep tunnel. . . . But on the other
end there is going to be a significantly different Asia in which American
firms have achieved a much deeper market penetration, much greater
access"[68] By 1998, transnationals and U.S. financial firms were buying up
Asian assets, from Seoul to Bangkok, at fire-sale prices.

Argentina: End of a Neoliberal Disneyland

Argentina is the most tragic example of what can happen to a country that
takes seriously the IMF and the U.S. Treasury Department's advice to liberalize its financial sector.

Argentina's financial liberalization was part and parcel of a broader program of economic reform. Argentina had been the poster child of globalization, Latin-style. It brought down its trade barriers faster than most
other countries in Latin America, liberalized its capital account more radically, and offered a comprehensive privatization program involving the sale
of some four hundred state enterprises creating about 7 percent of the
nation's annual domestic product—a complex including airlines, oil companies, steel, insurance companies, telecommunications, postal services,
and petrochemicals.[69]

In the most touching gesture of neoliberal faith, Buenos Aires voluntarily
gave up any meaningful control over the domestic impact of a volatile
global economy by adopting a currency board. This system tied the quantity
of pesos in circulation to the quantity of dollars coming in. Paul Blustein
observes that, "in adopting a currency board, a government essentially
admits that it has lost all credibility with financial markets, so to restore
faith in its currency, it hands over its monetary controls to a credibility-
laden foreigner (in Argentina's case, Alan Greenspan, the man in charge of
the world's supply of dollars)."[70] Pleased at the prospect of Argentina
accepting external discipline, the IMF endorsed the arrangement.

Moreover, some technocrats promised that dollarization, or the abandonment of the peso as the national currency, was right around the corner. When that happened, the last buffers between the local economy and the global market would disappear and the nation would enter the nirvana of permanent prosperity.

All of these measures were taken either at the urging of, or with the approval of, the Treasury Department and its surrogate, the International Monetary Fund. In fact, in the wake of the Asian financial crisis, when capital account liberalization was increasingly seen by most observers as the villain of the piece, Lawrence Summers, then secretary of the Treasury, extolled Argentina's selling off of its banking sector as a model for the developing world: "Today, fully 50 percent of the banking sector, 70 percent of private banks, in Argentina are foreign-controlled, up from 30 percent in 1994. The result is a deeper, more efficient market, and external investors with a greater stake in staying put."[71]

As the dollar rose in value in the mid-1990s, so did the peso, making Argentine goods uncompetitive both globally and locally. Raising tariff barriers against imports was regarded as a no-no. Instead, borrowing heavily to fund the dangerously widening trade gap, Argentina spiraled into debt, and the more it borrowed, the higher the interest rates rose as creditors grew increasingly alarmed.

Not surprisingly, Argentina got hit by significant speculative outflows in the wake of the Mexican financial crisis in 1994 and the Brazilian crisis in 1998, forcing it to go to its mentor, the IMF, for emergency credits to assure skittish speculators. On both occasions, the IMF came to the rescue, providing credits of $14 billion in 2000. As soon as things quieted down a bit, however, the speculators returned, pouring money into the country, ignoring the deteriorating macroeconomic profile.[72]

When neighboring Brazil allowed its currency, the real, to float in 1998, things got hairy, since one result was a flood of now cheap tariff-free Brazilian exports to its Mercosur (Market of the South) neighbor and a collapse of demand for expensive Argentine goods in Rio de Janeiro. But with the approval of the IMF, Argentina kept the peso-dollar peg. The nation's economics minister, Domingo Cavallo, notes George Soros, "sacrificed practically everything on the altar of maintaining the currency board and meeting international obligations."[73] With the peso hostage to capital movements, the banking system and the pension system came unglued.

Contrary to the so-called Summers doctrine, foreign control of the banking system was no panacea. In fact, foreign control simply facilitated the outflow of much-needed capital by banks that became increasingly reluctant to lend, both to governments and to local businesses. With no credit, small and medium enterprises, and not a few big ones, closed down, throwing thousands out of work.

The crisis unfolded with frightening speed in December 2001. Cap in hand, Argentina went to the IMF for a multibillion-dollar loan to meet payments on its $140 billion external debt. This time the loan was not forthcoming. Riots erupted and toppled one government after another. Argentina defaulted on $100 billion of its debt, the biggest sum of any country in history; already in recession, the economy went into a further downspin. By the first quarter of 2002, GDP had declined at an annual rate of 16.3 percent; unemployment stood at 21.5 percent of the workforce; 53 percent of Argentines lived below the poverty line, with 25 percent defined as "indigent."[74] Once the most prosperous nation in Latin America, Argentina is now near the bottom in terms of per capita income, below Peru and parts of Central America.[75]

The election of a populist, nationalist president, Néstor Kirchner, in 2003, along with the beginning of economic recovery, emboldened the new government. It offered to repay its massive foreign debt at a steep discount. On an estimated $88 billion to $100 billion in defaulted government bonds, Argentina would write off 75 to 90 percent. Kirchner told Argentina's debtors that this was a one-time offer that they had to accept or lose the rights to any repayment. Unbudging in his position, Kirchner told creditors he would not tax poverty-ridden Argentines to pay off the debt and invited them to visit the country's slums to "experience that poverty first hand."[76]

Kirchner also played hardball with the IMF, telling the fund, in early March 2004, that it would not repay a $3.3 billion installment due to the IMF unless it approved a similar amount of lending to Buenos Aires. The Argentines appeared to have the upper hand in the diplomacy of brinkmanship, having gotten the fund, in September 2003, to roll over up to $21 billion that Argentina owed it and other multilateral lenders. According to one analysis, the future of the IMF was at stake in the negotiations: "If Argentina walks away from its private and multilateral debts successfully—meaning that it doesn't collapse economically when it is shut out of international markets after repudiating its debt—then other countries might soon take the same path. This could finish what little institutional and geopolitical relevance the IMF has left."[77] The IMF blinked. Kirchner stuck to his guns on his radically devalued payment to foreign bondholders, and the fund came up with a new multibillion-dollar loan for his government.

THE ERA OF FINANCIAL ASCENDANCY: AN ASSESSMENT

The Argentine standoff in 2004 capped a decade, starting with the Mexican debacle of 1994, of financial disaster for the developing world. It was the outcome of a toxic brew of ideology and self-interest. Financial liberalization, like trade liberalization, was a fundamental tenet of the neoliberal doctrine that served as the ideology of corporate-driven globalization. Through financial liberalization, Third World nations were promised, their private sectors would get the capital they needed for development, in exchange for a just return to foreign financial investors. Financial liberalization would gradually supplant official lending institutions, like the World Bank and the U.S. Agency for International Development (AID), as the main source of capital. And this shift was only right, since dealings between private actors were "more efficient" than arrangements between public bodies.

Many nations in the South bought this line. It did not take long for them to realize, however, that speculative investors were not interested in nurturing strategic sectors of the economy, like industry and agriculture. Rather, they were there to play the stock and real estate markets. Nor were they committed for the duration; they would take advantage of local hospitality only as long as the rates of return on their investments in a particular market were higher than in other markets and the political conditions more stable. Governments had liberalized their capital accounts with an eye to facilitating the entry of speculative capital, not recognizing that the same easy road in would be the easy road out once a market fell from favor or, worse, panic took hold. Then they stared disaster in the face.

When the inevitable crisis finally hit, Washington or the IMF was there to bail out speculators, even as capital flight led to the collapse of the local economy. The IMF refused to promote a countercyclical approach, to employ government spending to contain the downturn in the private sector. Instead, it imposed expenditure-cutting programs that simply worsened the recession. The financial crisis cum IMF stabilization program was a one-two punch that led to massive unemployment. Worse, it resulted in a loss of sovereignty. Few dared, as did Prime Minister Mohamad Mahathir in Malaysia, to defy the U.S. Treasury and the IMF, and to impose capital controls to prevent speculative funds from leaving the country.

In his memoirs of his years in the Clinton administration, Robert Rubin, the ex-Wall Street investment banker, finally admitted what he had refused to admit then—that a large part of the blame "should go to private investors and creditors."

> They systematically underweighted the risks of investing in and lending to underdeveloped markets over a number of years, and consequently supplied capital greatly in excess of what would have been sound and sensible. And that excess capital, in time, fueled the extremes—overvalued exchange rates, unsound lending by domestic banks, and the rest—that led to the crisis.[78]

That the U.S. Treasury was part of the problem Rubin also conceded, if not in so many words:

> Many faulted the United States for pressing emerging markets to open up to external capital too fast. It is legitimate to ask whether some of the crisis countries deregulated their capital markets too rapidly and, if they did, how much responsibility the industrialized countries should bear. At the Treasury Department, in particular after the Mexican crisis, we emphasized the need for an adequate institutional framework and appropriate policy regimes in emerging markets. However, in hindsight, that emphasis should have been more intense.[79]

Rubin's words are hardly reassuring about the future:

> [F]uture financial crises are almost surely inevitable and could be even more severe. The markets are getting bigger, information is moving faster, flows are larger, and trade and capital markets have continued to integrate. . . . It's also important to point out

that no one can predict in what area—real estate, emerging markets, or whatever else—the next crisis will occur.[80]

This was, of course, hypocrisy of the worse kind, since Rubin, like his Wall Street buddies, continued to oppose any meaningful capital controls.

One of the biggest problems with financial markets is that, unlike elephants, they have very, very short memories. In 2004, stock analysts—the sirens of finance capital—were again listing Thailand and Brazil as "good picks" for speculative investors roaming the world. Indeed, on October 21, 2003, with the real economy still devastated by the economic collapse of 2001 and with Buenos Aires still negotiating repayment on its $140 billion debt, Argentine stock prices hit an all-time high.[81] It seemed only a matter of time before the most tragic victim of financial liberalization would be rehabilitated in the eyes of global finance capital.

CONCLUSION

The liberation of finance capital promised economic development. More often than not, it has delivered severe instability. Recurrent crises plunged economies into recession from which local populations suffered, even as foreign speculators were bailed out by the IMF and the U.S. Treasury.

These disruptions also served to discipline and resubordinate developing countries in the interests of the United States and other center economies. The Third World debt crises of the early 1980s were exemplary in this regard, as was the Asian panic of 1997. The dynamics of domination are not merely financial, however. Imperial efforts to transform the South over the last two decades embrace every aspect of Third World economic life. Moreover, they foreclose any significant development except along lines that favor northern interests. In Chapter 5, then, we'll turn to an examination of that more comprehensive system of antidevelopment economics.

CHAPTER 5

The Economics of Antidevelopment

This [the World Trade Organization] is a precious system,
the jewel in the crown of multilateralism.

MIKE MOORE, FORMER DIRECTOR GENERAL
OF THE WTO, 2003

Financial liberalization was a late development in the broader process of incorporating the former colonies and territories of the South as subordinate members of the global capitalist community.

Managing the South was a central challenge that the United States confronted in the post–World War II period, one that paralleled the challenge posed by the Soviet Union and Communism. Dealing with the South would not be easy. Some of the developing countries came under the leadership of Marxist-oriented parties, while others were in the hands of more moderate, but still anticapitalist, progressive parties. Almost all, including the conservative regimes, envisaged a major (if not central) role for the state in a process of rapid industrialization that would enable the South to catch up with the West. And almost all claimed a sovereign right to protect their markets and impose restrictive rules on foreign investors.

The United States responded to the challenge from southern countries bilaterally. But it also created, over time, a system of multilateral agencies to manage the various dimensions of its relationship with the South: the

International Monetary Fund, in the area of exchange rates and financial flows; the World Bank, for development aid; and, more recently, the World Trade Organization to regulate trade.

The multilateral agencies, which included most nations of the world as members, nevertheless institutionalized decision-making structures and international rules that gave the United States and other wealthy countries de facto control. Thus the global agencies provided the United States with a far more effective mechanism of influence and power than direct pressure from Washington. Multilateral activities in support of U.S. interests had a legitimacy that unilateral government initiatives did not have.

The UN economic agencies were also part of this system. Because their structure of decision making was unwieldy, however, Washington's route to achieving hegemonic influence through them was complex and troublesome. Indeed, these agencies had to be reined in when they moved in directions that the United States felt was inimical to its interests.

Together, the United States and these multilateral organizations pursued a course of action ostensibly aimed at encouraging economic growth in the South. What they actually practiced, though, was an economics of antidevelopment.

COMPLETING THE MULTILATERAL SYSTEM

The World Trade Organization is the newest addition to the multilateral system. When it was established in 1995, the WTO was hailed as the supreme institution of global economic governance in the era of globalization. The product of eight years (1986–94) of painstaking, querulous, off-and-on trade negotiations known as the Uruguay Round, the nearly twenty agreements that underpinned the WTO supposedly eliminated power and coercion from trade relations by subjecting them to a common set of rules backed by an effective enforcement apparatus.

The WTO was a landmark, declared the billionaire George Soros, because it was "the only international institution to which the United States has been willing to subordinate itself."[1] In the WTO, it was claimed, the superpower United States and one of the world's poorest nations, Rwanda, had the same number of votes: one.

The First Ministerial of the WTO, in Singapore in November 1996, sounded a triumphalist note. The WTO, the International Monetary Fund, and the World Bank issued their famous declaration that the challenge of the future was to make their policies on global trade, finance, and development "coherent" so as to lay the basis for global prosperity. The vision was ambitious, even grandiose:

> The interlinkages between the different aspects of economic policy require that the international institutions with responsibilities in each of these areas follow consistent and mutually supportive policies. The World Trade Organization should therefore pursue and develop cooperation with the international organizations responsible for monetary and financial matters, while respecting the mandate, the confidentiality requirements, and the necessary autonomy in decision-making procedures of each institution. . . . Ministers further invite the Director General of the WTO to review with the Managing Director of the International Monetary Fund and the President of the World Bank, the implications of the WTO's responsibilities for its cooperation with the Bretton Woods institutions, as well as the forms such cooperation might take, with a view to achieving greater coherence in global economic policymaking.[2]

Practically speaking, the WTO was meant to preside over the accelerated global integration of capital, production, and markets. Corporate profitability was clearly the engine driving the process. According to the ideologues of globalization, however, the result would be efficiency and "the greatest good for the greatest number," thanks to the wisdom of the market.

However, the creation of the WTO, whose most prominent feature was a dispute-resolution mechanism, was a confession that, far from being a smooth process, globalization generated conflict. While fighting for freedom of entry into other markets, for instance, national capitalist interests often resisted offering free access to their own markets, and they were able to harness the support of their respective states for such defensive strategies.

Moreover, globalization was taking place in a world marked by great disparities in wealth and power. In the global economy, there were a handful of dominant powers. These powers—the European Union, Japan, and the United States—needed each other's markets but sought to maintain privileged access to their own. As the crisis of overcapacity discussed in Chapter 3 deepened, conflicts among these powers became sharper. The role of the WTO was to manage this intensified competition.

Equally central was the WTO's goal to open up southern countries or to complete the process of economic liberalization that had been initiated by World Bank- and IMF-directed structural adjustment programs. In the 1990s, expansion of the market for global capital grew increasingly urgent, aimed as it was at confronting overproduction and stagnation, especially in the North. Not surprisingly, southern elites and governments that were still in the process of developing and of establishing control over their national markets resisted this process.

CHALLENGE FROM THE SOUTH

From the perspective of the southern governments, the founding of the WTO and the acceleration of corporate-driven globalization marked a retreat from efforts at independent national development dating back to the 1970s. At that time, the dominant perspective was "developmentalism," based on the "structuralist" analysis associated with the Argentine economist Raul Prebisch. According to this approach, the Third World could progress only by transforming an unequal relations of international trade, which consigned developing countries to the exporting of low-value-added agricultural and raw materials and to the importing of high-value-added manufactured products from the North. What was needed was not free trade but, in effect, a program of affirmative action for the countries of the global South.

The UN Conference on Trade and Development, with Presbisch as its first secretary general, spearheaded this strategy. UNCTAD pushed for price stabilization through the negotiation of price floors, below which commodity prices would not be allowed to fall. It proposed a scheme of preferential tariffs that would allow Third World manufactured goods to enter First World markets at lower tariff rates than those applied to exports from the highly industrialized countries. Finally, UNCTAD urged an expansion and acceleration of foreign assistance—which, in its view, was not charity but "compensation, a rebate to the Third World for the years of declining commodity purchasing power."[3] UNCTAD also sought to legiti-mate the use of protectionist trade policy as a mechanism for industrializa-tion and demanded speeded-up transfer of technology to the South. Other key economic agencies of the UN Secretariat, such as the Economic and Social Council and the United Nations Development Program (UNDP), adopted Prebisch's approach. And it became the official program of the UN General Assembly when a Special Session adopted the program of the New International Economic Order in 1974.

The NIEO was one of a set of developments that alarmed northern elites. The oil-price shocks administered by OPEC, and successful national liberation struggles in Indochina and Africa, also deepened their apprehen-sion. These perceived threats from the South, in turn, generated a strategy of political and economic rollback that unfolded in the 1980s, under the leadership of Ronald Reagan and Margaret Thatcher.

ROLLING BACK THE SOUTH

When the Reagan administration assumed power, in 1981, it sought not only to roll back Communism but to discipline the Third World. Over the next eight years, Washington aimed to dismantle the "state-assisted capital-ism" practiced by southern elites and would seek, as well, to weaken drasti-cally the UN development system.

Structural Adjustment and the Bretton Woods Twins

The instruments chosen for rolling back the South were the World Bank and the International Monetary Fund. The project represented an interest-ing transformation particularly for the World Bank, which had been vili-fied by the *Wall Street Journal* as one of the villains responsible for weakening the North's global position and accused by the right of promot-ing Socialism in the Third World through its loans to southern govern-ments. But the ideological right-wingers seeking the closure of the bank were restrained by pragmatic conservatives who wished to use it, instead, as a disciplinarian.

Structural adjustment programs, whose main components were trade liberalization, deregulation, and privatization, constituted the reining-in mechanism, as noted in Chapter 4. SAPs were imposed on Third World governments by the IMF and the bank throughout the 1980s, in return for emergency loans to pay off massive debt to northern commercial banks. By the late 1980s, structural adjustment and shock therapy managed from Washington was common; more than seventy Third World countries submitted to IMF and World Bank programs. While structural adjustment was rationalized as a way for Third World countries to repay their creditors by becoming more efficient exporters, the strategic objective was to eliminate state-assisted capitalism that served as the domestic base for the emerging national capitalist elites in the South. In 1988, a survey by the UN Commission for Africa concluded that the essence of SAPs was the "reduction/removal of direct state intervention in the productive and redistributive sectors of the economy."[4]

As for Latin America, one analyst noted that the United States took advantage of "this period of financial strain to insist that debtor countries remove the government from the economy as the price of getting credit."[5] Similarly, a retrospective look at a decade of adjustment, in a work published by the Inter-American Development Bank (IDB) in 1992, identified the removal of the state from economic activity as the centerpiece of the structural reforms of the 1980s.

By the end of the twelve-year era of Ronald Reagan and George H. W. Bush, in January 1993, the South had been transformed: from Argentina to Ghana, state participation in the economy had been drastically curtailed; government enterprises were passing into private hands in the name of efficiency; protectionist barriers to northern imports were being radically reduced; and, through export-first policies, the internal economy was more tightly integrated into the North-dominated capitalist world markets.

Yet the costs were high. The neoclassical economists at the IMF and World Bank had sold structural adjustment as necessary to spark a virtuous circle of growth, rising employment, and prosperity. Instead, developing economies stopped developing; they fell into a "hole," according to the MIT economist Rudiger Dornbusch,[6] in which radically reduced government spending triggered a vicious cycle of increased unemployment, declining consumption, soaring poverty, and rising inequality.

During what came to be known as the "Lost Decade" of the 1980s, most countries in Latin America and Africa experienced either negative growth or no growth in their gross domestic product. The social results were devastating. In Latin America, the impact of structural adjustment struck with special fury, "largely canceling out the progress of the 1960's and 1970's."[7] The number of people living in poverty rose from 130 million in 1980 to 180 million in 1990.[8] In a decade of negative growth, income inequalities—already among the most troubling in the world—worsened. As Enrique Iglesias, president of the IDB, reported, "the bulk of the costs of adjustment fell disproportionately on the middle- and low-income groups, while the top five percent of the population retained or, in some cases, even increased its standard of living."[9] By the end of the decade, the top 20 percent of the continent's population earned 20 times that earned by the poorest 20 percent.[10]

Sub-Saharan Africa was even more grievously injured than Latin America. Cut off from significant capital flows except aid, battered by plunging commodity prices, wracked by famine and civil war, and squeezed by structural adjustment programs, Africa experienced a per capita decline in income of 2.2 percent a year in the 1980s. By 1990, Africa was back where it had started at the time of independence, in the early 1960s.

Structural adjustment programs were one of the chief culprits in the downward spiral of a continent once considered promising because of its abundant natural resources. As one analyst put it:

> Austerity measures were applied, under IMF direction, to economies which had skeletal public services in the first place. These IMF plans were intended to ensure that money kept flowing to service the debts; the plans were insensitive to the effect of the austerity measures on the population at large. By the mid-1990's, at least 40 percent of Africans were living on less than a dollar a day, and the same proportion suffered from malnutrition and hunger . . . Debt in sub-Saharan Africa had reached $250 billion and most countries were devoting more revenue to interest payments than to spending on education and health combined.[11]

By the early 1990s, not surprisingly, the continent's ability to resist devastating epidemics had severely eroded. Cholera advanced at a catastrophic pace, but even more deadly was the spread of HIV-AIDS. Surveys found, for example, that in Zimbabwe, some 50 percent of the armed forces carried the virus; in Kampala, Uganda, more than 25 percent of women seen in maternity clinics were HIV-positive; and in Zambia, 20 to 25 percent of various groups in the capital, Lusaka, were infected.[12]

So massive was Africa's reversal of fortune that the MIT economist Lester Thurow commented, "If God gave it [Africa] to you and made you its economic dictator, the only smart move would be to give it back to him."[13]

Eroding the UN Development System

A key target of the U.S.-led rollback was the UN development system. Wielding the power of the purse, the United States, whose contribution accounts for some 20 to 25 percent of the UN budget, moved to silence NIEO rhetoric in the key UN institutions dealing with the North-South divide: the Economic and Social Council (ECOSOC), the Development Program, and the General Assembly. Pressure from Washington resulted, as well, in the effective dismantling of the UN Center on Transnational Corporations, whose high-quality work in tracking the activities of the TNCs in the South had earned the ire of these conglomerates, whose global reach and scale escaped the control of most governments. Also abolished was the post of director general for international economic cooperation and development, which had represented "one of the few concrete outcomes, and certainly the most noteworthy, of the efforts of the developing countries during the NIEO negotiations to secure a stronger UN presence in support of international economic cooperation and development."[14]

But the focus of the northern counteroffensive was the defanging, if not dismantling, of UNCTAD. During the UNCTAD IV negotiations in Nairobi in 1976, the North had given in to the South by agreeing to the creation of the commodity stabilization scheme known as the Integrated Program for Commodities. But at UNCTAD V in Belgrade, the North refused the South's program of debt cancelation and other measures intended to revive Third World economies and thus contribute to global recovery at a time of worldwide recession.[15] The northern offensive escalated during UNCTAD VIII, held in Cartagena in 1992. At this watershed meeting, the North successfully opposed all linkages of UNCTAD discussions with the Uruguay Round of negotiations for the General Agreement on Tariffs and Trade (GATT) and even managed to call its existence into question.[16] UNCTAD's main function would henceforth be limited to "analysis, consensus building on some trade-related issues, and technical assistance."[17] By 1995, with the emergence of the WTO to manage world trade, UNCTAD, said its critics, had become superfluous.

WHY THE WTO?

Deprived of the leadership provided by the secretariats of UN agencies, the developing countries—except for a few nations like India—had a marginal role in the negotiations that led to the establishment of the World Trade Organization. As George Soros has noted, the Third World "did not have much say in designing the provisions of the Uruguay Round, yet they had to buy into them wholesale because, under WTO rules, a country must be a party to all the negotiated agreements as a single package."[18]

Hardly Present at the Creation

The eight years of negotiations that produced the WTO were dominated by the United States and the European Economic Community; Canada and Japan also played significant roles. Transnational corporations helped draft key agreements: the agro-trade giant Cargill, for agriculture; the pharmaceutical firms, in the Trade-Related Intellectual Property Rights (TRIPs) Agreement; and the auto industry, in the Trade-Related Investment Measures (TRIMs) Agreement.

The resulting documents underpinning the WTO were comprehensive. The new organization covered not only the global trade in industrial and manufactured goods governed by its predecessor, GATT, but also agriculture, services, and nontrade areas like investment and intellectual property rights. The operative principle was, as the consumer activist Ralph Nader put it, "trade über alles,"[19] and since, according to estimates, 30 to 40 percent of global trade occurred among subsidiaries of transnational corporations, it was, in fact, corporate trade over everything else. The ostensible goal of the WTO was global free trade, but the paramount concern was corporate profitability, as evidenced by three of its central agreements, the

Agreement on Agriculture (AOA), TRIPs, and TRIMs. The AOA actually institutionalized the monopolistic competition between the EU and the United States for third-country agricultural markets—that is, effective competition for global markets was limited to rich and powerful agricultural interests in the two economic blocs. The restrictive provisions of TRIPs gave high-tech firms a practical monopoly on technological innovation. And TRIMs, around which the global automobile industry united, created strong barriers to the emergence of new auto manufacturing in developing countries.

In short, the WTO united two contradictory principles, free trade and monopoly, in the overriding interest of corporate profitability.

There was, indeed, a strong sense among developing countries that the WTO was an antidevelopmental organization. However, once negotiations were completed, in 1994, they found it difficult to resist participating in the ratification of the treaty. Nations that were already members of GATT were told that if they did not come in on the ground floor, they would face onerous accession procedures that could take years. Then there was the argument that by refusing to join the WTO, they would isolate themselves from world trade and end up like North Korea.[20] But probably the most persuasive argument for those with the deepest apprehensions was best articulated by former director general Mike Moore:

> The fact remains that the multilateral trading system—for all its imperfections—gives even the smallest and poorest countries far greater leverage than they would ever have outside the system. Multilateral negotiations allow weaker countries to pool their collective influence and interests—as opposed to bilateral or even regional negotiations in which they have virtually no negotiating clout.[21]

The alternative, he said, "is no rules and no impartial dispute settlement—a world where commercial relations are based on economic and political power, where small countries are at the mercy of the largest, the rule of the jungle."[22]

Such pronouncements seemed to be saying that the countries of the South would be better off with the devil they knew than with the devil they didn't know. As Soros has noted, the Single Undertaking approach "may have been necessary to get the Uruguay Round accomplished, but it has given rise to the complaint that many countries did not know what they were signing."[23]

Made for America

Two realizations gradually dawned on developing countries. One was that the emergence of the WTO served not so much to promote global trade as to further the interests of U.S. corporations seeking new markets worldwide. The other was that the WTO was an antidevelopment organization.

International trade did not need the WTO to expand seventeen-fold between 1948 and 1997, from $124 billion to $10,772 billion.[24] The increase took place under the flexible GATT regime. The founding of the WTO, in 1995, did not respond to a collapse or crisis of world trade, like the one in the 1930s. Nor was the organization necessary for global peace, since no world war or trade-related war had taken place during that period. In the seven major interstate wars that occurred in that period— the Korean War (1950–53), the Vietnam War (1945–75), the Suez crisis (1956), the 1967 Arab-Israeli war, the 1973 Arab-Israeli war, the Falklands War (1982), and the Gulf War (1990–91)—trade conflict did not figure even remotely as a cause.

GATT was, in fact, functioning reasonably well as a framework for liberalizing world trade. Its dispute settlement system was flexible, and its recognition of the "special and differential status" of developing nations provided the opportunity, in a global economy, for Third World countries to use trade policy for modernization and industrialization.

Why was the WTO established following the Uruguay Round (1986–94)? Of the major trading powers, Japan was ambivalent. It was concerned with protecting its agriculture, as well as its particular system of industrial production that, through formal and informal mechanisms, gave its local producers primary right to exploit the domestic market. The European Union (EU), well on the way to becoming a self-sufficient trading bloc, was likewise ambivalent, knowing that its highly subsidized system of agriculture would come under attack. Although they desired greater access to northern markets, the developing countries did not see it happening through a comprehensive agreement enforced by a powerful trade bureaucracy. They relied, instead, on discrete negotiations and agreements modeled after the Integrated Program for Commodities (IPCs), the commodity stabilization agreement established under the aegis of UNCTAD in the late 1970s.

The founding of the WTO primarily served the interests of the United States, which became the dominant lobbyist for the comprehensive Uruguay Round and the founding of the WTO in the late 1980s and early 1990s. New, more competitive global conditions had created a situation in which American corporate interests demanded a fresh approach to the political economy of trade.

In the 1950s, the United States threatened to leave GATT if it was not allowed to maintain protective mechanisms for its milk and other farm products. Agricultural trade was duly exempted from GATT rules. Several decades later, Washington brought agriculture into the GATT–WTO system. And the reason for its change of mind was quite candidly articulated by Secretary of Agriculture John Block at the start of the Uruguay Round negotiations, in 1986: "[The] idea that developing countries should feed themselves is an anachronism from a bygone era. They could better ensure their food security by relying on U.S. agricultural products, which are available, in most cases, at much lower cost."[25] Block, of course, did not have only emerging markets in mind but also those of Japan, South Korea, and the EU.

It was mainly the United States, moreover, that pushed to bring services under WTO coverage. Washington concluded that in the burgeoning area of international services, and particularly in financial services, American corporations' lead should be preserved. It was also the United States that sought to expand WTO jurisdiction to include the TRIMs and TRIPs. TRIMs eliminated barriers, imposed by developing countries to protect their home-grown industries, to the system of internal cross-border trade of product components among TNC subsidiaries; TRIPs consolidated the U.S. advantage in cutting-edge, knowledge-intensive businesses.

And, probably most important, it was the United States that demanded the creation of the WTO's formidable dispute-resolution and enforcement mechanism. American officials, frustrated with weak efforts under GATT to enforce rulings favorable to the United States, were not eager to see a repeat of that experience. As Washington's academic point man on trade, C. Fred Bergsten, head of the Institute of International Economics, told the

Senate, the strong dispute-settlement mechanism serves American interests because "we can now use the full weight of the international machinery to go after those trade barriers, reduce them, get them eliminated"[26]

In sum, Washington's changing perception of the needs of the business community has shaped and reshaped the international trading regime. It was not global necessity that gave birth to the WTO but Washington's assessment that U.S. corporations needed the sort of powerful, wide-ranging instrument of control that GATT did not provide. From the free-market model that underpins it, to the regulations set forth in the agreements that make up the Uruguay Round, to its system of decision making and accountability, the WTO was regarded, even by many Europeans and Japanese, as a blueprint for the global hegemony of corporate America.

An Antidevelopment Agency

The second lesson developing countries learned was that the WTO was antidevelopment, through and through. They belatedly discovered the following:

1. By agreeing to eliminate import quotas and by accepting the TRIMs accord, which declared such mechanisms as local-content policies and trade-balancing requirements illegal, developing countries had signed away their right to use trade policy as a means of industrialization. When the Indonesians sought to develop their automobile industry in 1997 by resorting to local-content policies, they were immediately told by the United States and the EU that they were making use of a measure that had been banned by the TRIMs Agreement. They threatened to haul Indonesia before the WTO dispute-settlement system. Apparently, Jakarta was unaware that such policies had been outlawed by an agreement it had ratified two years earlier.

2. By signing the TRIPs pact, Third World countries had given high-tech transnationals like Microsoft and Intel the power to monopolize innovation in knowledge-intensive industries through restrictive patent rights, and had provided biotechnology firms like Novartis

and Monsanto the go-ahead to privatize the fruits of eons of creative interaction between human communities and the natural world. One key result will be a redistribution of income: "[F]or very poor countries that have yet to develop IP [intellectual property] industries . . . the main effect will be to transfer income in the form of royalties from poor countries to richer ones, particularly the United States."[27] Also, in a world in which new diseases, such as HIV-AIDS, were rampant, TRIPs placed life-and-death power in the hands of the profit-oriented northern pharmaceutical industry.

3. By signing the Agreement on Agriculture, developing countries had agreed to open up their markets while allowing the agricultural superpowers to consolidate their system of subsidized production. The new regulations institutionalized dumping of surpluses on those very markets, a process that was, in turn, destroying smallholder-based agriculture. The figures spoke for themselves: the level of overall subsidization of agriculture in the Organization for Economic Cooperation and Development countries rose from $182 billion in 1995, to $280 billion in 1997, to $318 billion in 2002! According to Oxfam International, the EU and the United States were spending $9 billion to $10 billion more on subsidies in the years after the adoption of the AOA.[28] Subsidies accounted for 40 percent of the value of agricultural production in the EU and 25 percent in the United States.[29]

Instead of the beginning of a New Deal, the AOA, in the words of a former Philippine secretary of trade, "has perpetuated the unevenness of a playing field which the multilateral trading system has been trying to correct. Moreover, this has placed the burden of adjustment on developing countries relative to countries who can afford to maintain high levels of domestic support and export subsidies."[30]

In contrast to the loose GATT framework, which had allowed some opportunity for progressive initiatives, the comprehensive, tightened Uruguay Round was antidevelopment at its core. This point was evident in the way the GATT-WTO agreements watered down the principle of "special and differential treatment" for the Third World. A central pillar of UNCTAD, SDT held that, because of the critical nexus between trade and development, developing countries should not be subjected to the same expectations, rules, and regulations that govern trade among the wealthy nations. Leveling the playing field to enable poorer states to participate equitably in world trade would include the use both of protective tariffs and of preferential access for their exports to industrialized markets.

While GATT was not concerned primarily with development, it did recognize the "special and differential status" of Third World countries. Perhaps the strongest statement of this belief came in 1973, in the Tokyo Round Declaration, which acknowledged "the importance of the application of differential measures in developing countries in ways which will provide special and more favorable treatment for them in areas of negotiation where this is feasible."[31] The evolving GATT code, for instance, permitted industrializing countries to negotiate lower tariffs for their products entering developed country markets than those imposed on developed country imports in order to promote the establishment of certain industries to use tariffs for economic development and fiscal purposes; to use quantitative restrictions to encourage "infant industries"; and to be exempt from making reciprocal concessions in trade negotiations.[32] The 1979 agreement also provided a permanent legal basis for a general system of preferences, to jump-start exports from developing countries.[33]

The Uruguay Round changed the ground rules. Since GSP schemes were not bound, tariffs could now be raised against Third World imports until they equaled maximum rates allowable to imports from all sources. During the negotiations, the threat to remove preferential tariffs was used as "a form of bilateral pressure on developing countries."[34]

Special and differential treatment was turned inside out. Now it merely granted developing countries some leeway in implementing liberalization measures owing to what was regarded as temporary adjustment difficulties.[35] Measures meant to address the structural inequality of the trading system gave way to ineffectual steps—such as a lower rate of tariff reduction or a longer time frame for implementing decisions—which tacitly viewed the problem of developing countries as simply one of playing catch-up on an essentially level playing field.

Because the neoliberal agenda that underpins the WTO philosophy differs fundamentally from the Keynesian assumptions of GATT, clear-eyed observers would have predicted the policy turn-arounds. There are to be no special rights, and no special protections are needed for development.

The only route to economic growth is radical trade (and investment) liberalization.

Southern disillusionment with the GATT-WTO deepened during the Uruguay Round. According to promoters of the WTO, two key accords were designed to meet the needs of the South: the special ministerial agreement, approved in Marrakech in April 1994, decreed that compensatory measures would be taken to counteract the negative effects of trade liberalization on developing countries who were net importers of food; the Agreement on Textiles and Clothing mandated that the system of quotas on Third World exports of textiles and garments to the North would be dismantled over ten years.

But the decision taken at Marrakech—to offset the reduction of domestic food subsidies—has never been implemented. Although world crude-oil prices more than doubled in 1995–96, the World Bank and the IMF scotched any idea of offsetting aid, arguing that "the price increase was not due to the agreement on agriculture, and besides there was never any agreement anyway on who would be responsible for providing the assistance."[36]

The Agreement on Textiles and Clothing committed the wealthy nations to subject all textile and garment imports to WTO discipline in four stages, ending on January 1, 2005. A key feature was supposed to be the lifting of quotas on imports previously restricted under the multifiber agreement (MFA) and similar schemes designed to stop or slow the penetration of developed country markets by cheap clothing and textile imports from the Third World. However, developed countries retained the right to choose which product lines to liberalize, and when. So, at first, they brought mainly unrestricted products into WTO discipline and postponed dealing with restricted products until much later. Thus, in the initial phase, all restricted products remained under quota; only imports not considered threatening—like felt hats or yarn of carded fine animal hair—were included in the developed countries' notifications. Indeed, "even at the second stage of implementation only a very small proportion" of restricted products would see their quotas lifted.[37]

Given this trend, one expert warned that "the belief is now widely held in the developing world that in 2004, while the MFA may disappear, it may well be replaced by a series of other trade instruments, possibly substantial increases in anti-dumping duties."[38]

THE WTO AND THE SOUTH: A CASE STUDY

Few cases of the WTO's negative impact on development are better documented than that of the Philippines, and illustrate so clearly the full-court press to which U.S. agencies subjected developing countries to get them to make their laws and practices "WTO-consistent."

In 1994, the Philippine government had campaigned for ratification of the GATT-WTO agreement, painting it as a momentous advance in international relations that would promote the rule of law in global trade and constrain the power of the strong. By 2003, the Philippines had become one of the founding members of the Group of 20, a coalition of developing countries that contributed to the collapse of the Fifth Ministerial of the WTO in Cancun; it was no longer willing to countenance the dumping of heavily subsidized agricultural goods by the EU and the United States. Quite a reversal!

Yet Manila had plenty of warning about the consequences of joining the WTO. During the debate on ratification, civil society representatives had argued that the nineteen separate agreements constituting the Uruguay Round were skewed against countries like the Philippines.[39] Among other things, critics of the Uruguay Round asserted the following:

In signing on to the GATT-WTO, the Philippines essentially gave up the ability to use trade policy as a mechanism for industrialization, because the agreement banned quantitative restrictions or quotas on imports; capped or reduced existing industrial tariffs and made tariff increases practically impossible except under import surges; and outlawed trade-related investment restrictions. The policy instruments used by earlier industrializers but now banned included trade-balancing mechanisms, which tied the value of a foreign investor's imports of raw materials and components to the value of its exports of the finished commodity. Also prohibited under the Uruguay Round were local-content regulations, which had mandated that a certain percentage of a product's components had to be sourced locally. Critics argued that TRIPs, with its rigid penalties for the unauthorized use of technology, would make "industrialization by imitation" difficult if not impossible. A key factor in the takeoff of industrial latecomers like the United States, Germany, and Japan was their relatively easy access to cutting-edge technology. But what was, from the point of view of late industrializers, technological diffusion was piracy in the eyes of the dominant industrial power. Dissenters also claimed that TRIPs actually reinforced monopoly through such draconian provisions as the generalized minimum patent protection of twenty years, the increase in the duration of protection for semiconductors and computer chips, punitive border regulations against products judged to be violating intellectual property rights, and the placing of the burden of proof on the accused violator of process patents.

The TRIPs agreement, critics added, would enable corporations to patent living organisms as well as privatize knowledge acquired over centuries by communities through the modification of genetic material. The gene-rich Philippines would be a big loser in this game, as would most of the South. Already, observers warned, patents had been filed in the North on processes for transforming *nata de coco*, a versatile coconut by-product, for industrial use, and extracting the medicinal elements of *lagundi*, a ubiquitous Philippine plant.

Most controversial, however, was the Agreement on Agriculture. Opponents in the Philippines charged that the AOA was the antithesis of free trade—that it functioned simply to legitimize the high levels of protection and the subsidizing of the agricultural markets of the European Union and the United States while opening up the markets of developing countries to the two agricultural superpowers. Death by dumping would be the fate of the Philippines under the AOA, critics said, and faulted AOA and WTO advocates who, in their misconceived quest to make Philippine agriculture more efficient by means of free trade, seemed oblivious to the monopolistic structure of the international agricultural market.

After ratification, opponents observed that the Philippines would have to change at least forty of its laws and regulations and promise to enact new ones. What also became clear is that, at some point, the country would have to amend its constitution, since, in signing on to the WTO agreement, Manila would also have to initial the General Agreement on Trade in Services (GATS), which committed it to providing "national treatment," or nondiscriminatory treatment, to foreign service providers. No less than a major overhaul of the constitution was required, because many key provisions gave citizens preferential treatment as service providers in areas as diverse as advertising, journalism, telecommunications, and transport.

Tightening Intellectual Property Rules

The drive to make Philippine legislation WTO-consistent began immediately. The pressure came from the developed countries that stood to benefit from the WTO, particularly the United States. The dynamics of this process were illustrated by two agreements: TRIPs and TRIMs.

At the time Manila ratified the WTO, the Philippines' treatment of intellectual property rights (IPRs), based as it was on that of the United States, was already relatively comprehensive, protecting patents, trademarks, and copyrights.[40] Nevertheless, the Philippines was quick to promise to "align existing laws on patents, trademarks, and copyrights with TRIPs," "enact new laws on the protection of plant varieties, geographical indications, layout designs of integrated circuits, and undisclosed information," and "strengthen enforcement of IPRs."[41]

Under strong prodding from Washington, the government delivered. Indeed, a U.S. Agency for International Development program called AGILE (Accelerating Growth, Investment, and Liberalization with Equity) practically wrote the key TRIPs-related legislation and shepherded it through the Philippine Congress. Among AGILE's accomplishments were the Intellectual Property Code and the Electronic Commerce Act.[42] The code, passed in 1997, made Philippine legislation WTO-consistent, while the Electronic Commerce Act extended IPR protection to the Internet in 2000.[43] In the following year, President Gloria Macapagal Arroyo signed into law protections of the layout designs (topographies) of integrated circuits, extending the provisions of the Intellectual Property Code to the information industry along the lines desired by the United States and the WTO.

The United States was not satisfied with the WTO alignment process, however. The trade representative complained that "legislation implementing fully the WTO TRIPS Agreement commitments has been slow to develop," and pointed out that the Philippines still had to enact laws "to provide IPR protection to plant varieties as required by the WTO TRIPS obligations that became mandatory for the Philippines on January 1, 2000."[44] AGILE again stepped into the breach. Its consultants had drafted the plant variety protection bill in 1999 for the Department of Agriculture.[45] This bill eventually became the Philippine Plant Variety Protection that was signed into law on June 7, 2002.

Washington kept up the pressure on all fronts, including the judicial arena. In 2001, the Philippine Supreme Court speeded up the prosecution of piracy by mandating forty-eight courts to handle infringements of intellectual property rights—a "notable achievement," according to a report from the U.S. trade representative.[46]

Still dissatisfied with the pace of government movement on TRIPs, the United States, responding to reports, from distributors, of "high levels of pirated optical discs," placed the Philippines on the dreaded Priority Watch List under Section 301 of U.S. Trade Law.[47] This was a move that preceded bilateral retaliatory sanctions—which were themselves illegal under the WTO.

Yet the difficulties of enforcement, even under threat of sanctions, stemmed from contradictions inherent in TRIPs itself. Contrary to the WTO's free-trade rhetoric, TRIPs are an effort to control the market and reinforce monopoly under conditions of high market demand. As one account put it, however, intellectual property violators "are basically harmless. . . . And in a developing country like the Philippines, they are welcomed by the majority of cash-strapped consumers; their products sell, and sell better than the originals. They are in fact considered as allies of the poor—an economic leveler—because they make things affordable to all."[48]

Eliminating Trade Policy as a Tool for Development

Before the WTO, developing countries routinely used trade policy, notably quotas and high tariffs, as a key mechanism for industrialization. In the Philippines, though, the process was sketchy and incoherent, and implementation was spotty. Yet even Manila's weak legislation and enforcement framework was seen as threatening by foreign TNCs. TRIMs provided a means to eliminate it, and, as with TRIPs, it was the U.S. trade representative who acted as the WTO's enforcer for TRIMs.

When the Philippines ratified the WTO agreement, two industries were immediately affected: car manufacturing and the soap and detergent industry.

Local-content and trade-balancing requirements had helped set up rudiments of an indigenous auto industry. Under the Motor Vehicle Development Program, participants had to generate, through exports, a certain percentage of foreign exchange in order to meet import requirements, as well as to locate a larger portion of the content of a vehicle in the Philippines. As in Malaysia, though not as successfully, these trade policy instruments for industrialization were designed to discourage transnational corporations from simply making the country an assembly point for imported components and compel them instead to stimulate the development of component and parts suppliers, companies which would eventually become the core of an integrated industry. Naturally, as in Malaysia, the automobile TNCs hated local-content policies, because they interfered in the regional and international trade among their subsidiaries. For example, transfer pricing to get around taxes and other government levies was disrupted.

The Philippines notified the WTO of its trade policy tools in the automobile industry in 1995, availing itself of the five-year transitional period to phase out these measures. In October 1999, however, the government asked for a five-year extension. Washington, again acting as the WTO's enforcer, objected, forcing Manila to shorten the requested delay. "After extensive consultations on the issue," noted a report from the U.S. trade representative's office, "the United States and the Philippines agreed in November 2001 that the Philippines will discontinue all local-content and exchange balancing requirements . . . by July 1, 2003."[49]

The United States also pushed the Philippines to get rid of trade policy tools in the soap and detergent industry. United States TNCs like Procter and Gamble and Colgate Palmolive complained about a 1987 executive order, EO 259, which required manufacturers to use a minimum of 60 percent of raw materials that do not endanger the environment and prohibited the import of laundry soap and detergents containing less than 60 percent of such raw materials. As the USTR noted, the law had been passed to support the creation of the coconut-processing industry by promoting the use of coconut-based surface-active agents of local origin. It noted approvingly that "the Philippine Department of Justice . . . stated that E.O. 259 conflicts with the country's obligations under the WTO TRIMs Agreement. Since then, the E.O. has not been enforced."[50] Many other trade policy tools were eliminated at the insistence of the United States.

By the beginning of 2003, most Philippine legislation had been made WTO-consistent—although the constitution remained to be amended, something U.S. officials wished would happen soon. The process had been painful and the price was high. The widespread application of technology necessary for self-sustaining industrialization had been severely restricted. The TRIPs regime represents what UNCTAD describes as a "premature strengthening of the intellectual property system . . . that favors monopolistically controlled innovation over broad-based diffusion."[51] And its likely consequence would be to limit the possibility of an "imitative path of technological development" based on methods such as reverse engineering, the adaptation of foreign technology to local conditions, and the improvement of existing innovations.[52]

This antiindustrial bias of the TRIPS regime has been supplemented by legislation that all but eliminates the use of trade policy for industrial development.

Dumping and the Crisis of Philippine Agriculture

The AOA was the most important agreement the Philippines entered into under the WTO. The agricultural sector continued to employ nearly half the labor force and contributed over 20 percent of gross domestic product. Agriculture thus plays "a strategic role in the country's overall economic development through its strong growth linkage effects as a source of food and raw material supply for the rest of the economy, and as a source of demand for nonagricultural inputs and consumer goods and services."[53]

During the national debate on WTO ratification, the government argued that free trade would increase the efficiency of agriculture. Under pressure from the United States, Manila downplayed the impact of the dumping of highly subsidized American farm goods on the Philippines and promised the people that the AOA regime would create 500,000 jobs annually.[54]

The government quickly repealed its Magna Carta for Small Farmers and enacted comprehensive legislation to transform existing quotas into tariff rate quotas (TRQs). The TRQ system covered fifteen lines of "sensitive" agricultural imports, including live animals, fresh and chilled beef, pork, poultry, goat meat, potatoes, coffee, corn, and sugar. For these commodities, the Philippines had to provide "minimum access," at low tariffs, to a volume equivalent to 3 percent of domestic consumption in the first year of WTO implementation, rising to 5 percent in the tenth year. Imports over the quota would be taxed at a much higher rate. For corn, for instance, using the agreed-upon period of 1986–88 as the basis for calculating domestic consumption, the minimum access volume (MAV) eligible to come in at a low tariff of 35 percent would be 65,000 metric tons in 1995, rising to 227,000 in 2004.[55] Beyond the MAV, the tariff rate rose to 65 percent.

Under Annex 5 of the AOA, countries could retain a quota on "a primary agricultural product that is the predominant staple in the traditional diet."[56] In the case of the Philippines, it was rice. Manila was nevertheless required to increase the quota from 1 percent of domestic consumption in the first year to 4 percent in the tenth year—from 30,000 metric tons in 1995 to 227,000 metric tons in 2004.[57]

As with the other agreements in the WTO, the United States served as the local enforcer of the Geneva-based body, watching Philippine legislative and implementation processes with an eagle eye. The surveillance could be quite intrusive. For instance, Washington intervened to stop the issuing of licenses to importers for pork and poultry, accusing the government of allocating "a vast majority of import licenses to domestic producers who had no interest in importing."[58] When the Philippines balked, the United States threatened to suspend the preferential tariffs for Philippine exports covered by the general system of preferences. The Philippines gave in, and after issuing a memorandum of understanding detailing its concessions, "the review of the Philippines' eligibility to receive preferential access under the General System of Preferences . . . was terminated."[59]

By the end of the decade, not only had the promised benefits of AOA membership failed to materialize, but Philippine agriculture was in the throes of crisis.[60]

Contrary to the projections of proratification technocrats that agricultural output would grow by 50 billion pesos (about $885,000,000, at 55.6 pesos to the dollar) by 2002, agricultural production grew by only 12 billion pesos.[61] Far from increasing by 500,000 a year, employment in agriculture actually dropped from 11.2 million people in 1994 to 10.8 million in 2001.[62]

Farm exports, such as coconut products, were supposed to rise with WTO membership, but, in fact, the value of exports registered no significant movement, increasing from $1.9 billion in 1993 to $2.3 billion in 1997, then declining to $1.9 billion in 2000. On the other hand, massive imports, the big fear of GATT-WTO critics, became a reality. The value of imports almost doubled, from $1.6 billion in 1993 to $3.1 billion in 1997, and then registered $2.7 billion in 2000. The status of the Philippines as a net-food-importing country was consolidated as the agricultural trade balance moved from a surplus of $292 million in 1993 to a deficit of $764 million in 1997 and $794 million in 2002.[63]

Thus, as a result of the AOA-mandated entry of foreign goods, key sectors of Philippine agriculture ended up in pretty bad shape—especially traditional items like rice and corn, although the production of poultry, pork, and other livestock was also severely affected. At the same time, government promises that displaced farmers could shift from traditional crops to high-value-added temperate crops, like asparagus and snowpears, failed to materialize because of the tremendous costs of entry into those markets.

The Collapse of the Corn Industry

The social cost of trade liberalization was evident on the island of Mindanao, the Philippines' main corn-producing area. Even before the AOA, the limited liberalization of the late 1980s had left corn production in crisis. As Kevin Watkins of Oxfam noted after a field trip to Mindanao, "increasing imports of corn have been associated with a marked decrease in domestic corn production, and in the area planted. In South Cotabato, where most of Mindanao's corn is produced, there was a 15 percent decrease in production last year."[64]

The trend accelerated after the country's adherence to the AOA. Following a trip to the province of Bukidnon in Mindanao in 1996, more than a year after the Philippines began implementing the AOA, one analyst reported: "I found out that the southern part of the province is steadily being converted from corn to sugar."[65] Several years later, the Focus on the Global South analyst Aileen Kwa claimed that corn farmers in "Mindanao . . . have been wiped out. It is not an uncommon sight to see farmers there leaving their corn to rot in the fields as the domestic corn prices have dropped to levels [at which] they have not been able to compete."[66] Anecdotal evidence was supported by macro data. While production remained stagnant, land devoted to corn across the country contracted sharply, from 3,149,300 hectares in 1993 to 2,510,300 hectares in 2000.[67] Not surprisingly, widespread hunger stalked the corn-producing areas by the beginning of the next millennium.

It was not that the domestic demand for corn had slackened. Rather, thanks to the WTO's Agreement on Agriculture, the local demand for corn was being met by foreign imports, including highly subsidized corn imports from the United States.

At a session of the WTO's Agricultural Committee, in Geneva, a Philippine negotiator eloquently summed up the situation confronting farmers in the Philippines and in other developing nations:

> Our agricultural sectors that are strategic to food and livelihood security and rural employment have already been destabilized as our small producers are being slaughtered by the gross unfairness of the international trading environment. Even as I speak, our small producers are being slaughtered in our own markets, [and] even the more resilient and efficient are in distress.[68]

Indeed, Third World farmers had to survive on less than $400 a year while American and European farmers were receiving, respectively, an average of $21,000 and $16,000 a year in subsidies.[69] The system imposed by the WTO's Agreement on Agriculture amounted to Socialism for the rich.

CONCLUSION

Once, in the era of decolonization, the promise of economic development along lines that would enhance national independence excited the nonindustrialized countries. But it ran up against the desire of the United States to incorporate the newly independent economies as subordinate elements in the global capitalist system.

The multilateral trading system emerged to impose some order on commercial relations among the developed countries and to discipline the developing countries and lay the ground work for their more intensive penetration by global capital. To achieve the second objective, structural adjustment programs were universally implemented in the South, although at great social cost. To the same end, the WTO was established to dismantle trade barriers to commodities produced by TNCs while protecting the monopolistic production practices in northern agriculture and high-tech industry.

The wrenching resubordination of the South inevitably generated resistance. The character and fate of that resistance is the subject of the next two chapters.

CHAPTER 6

The South Rises, and the North Prevails

[The] WTO will not be able to continue in its present form. There has to be fundamental and radical change in order for it to meet the needs and aspirations of all 134 of its members.

STEPHEN BYERS, SECRETARY OF STATE OF THE UNITED KINGDOM, JANUARY 9, 2000

Our world is not for sale, my friend,
Just to keep you satisfied.
You say you'll bring us health and wealth,
Well, we know that you just lied.

SONG OF THE DELEGATES FROM NGOS, OR NONGOVERNMENTAL ORGANIZATIONS, TO THE WTO CANCÚN MINISTERIAL, SEPTEMBER 2003 (SUNG TO THE TUNE OF THE BEATLES' "CAN'T BUY ME LOVE")

In the second half of the 1990s, the North's system of economic control was severely destabilized. Its widely recognized failure to promote development and prosperity triggered resistance from Third World governments and from an increasingly militant civil society. Two ministerials of the WTO, one in Seattle in 1999 and then one in Cancún, Mexico, in 2003, collapsed. The IMF also suffered a crisis of credibility, brought on by its dismal performance during the Asian financial crisis of 1997. Even the World Bank couldn't escape denunciation.

The United States and other wealthy nations began to talk about reform. Few reforms were actually implemented, however, and none were successful. In the end, the credibility of the multilateral system grew still more fragile.

REVOLT IN SEATTLE

Perhaps the most inequitable aspect of the WTO is its wholly undemocratic decision-making procedure. During the WTO ratification process in 1994, partisans of the trade association portrayed it as a one-country/one-vote organization in which the United States would have the same say as the least powerful country. In truth, the WTO was not to operate according to a one-country/one-vote system, as the UN General Assembly does, or even through a system of weighted voting, like the World Bank and the IMF. Its constitution may imply democratic procedures, but in the World Trade Organization, consensus is the reigning process, one that it inherited from the old GATT, where the last vote was taken in 1959.

What happens under consensus, in practice, is that the big trading nations impose their views on the less powerful. As C. Fred Bergsten, a prominent partisan of globalization who heads the Institute of International Economics, put it during Senate hearings on the ratification of the agreement in 1994, the WTO "did not work by voting. It worked via a consensus arrangement which, to tell the truth, is managed by four—the Quads: the United States, Japan, European Union, and Canada. . . . Those countries have to agree if any major steps are going to be made. But no votes."[1]

The Ministerial Meeting and the General Council were, theoretically, the highest decision-making bodies of the WTO, but policies were arrived at not in formal plenaries but in nontransparent backroom sessions known as the Green Room, after the color of the director general's office at the WTO headquarters in Geneva. In such sessions, the Quad countries called the shots, although expressions of dissent by large developing countries like India were duly noted. A representative from an industrializing nation described the dynamics thus:

In my opinion, [the WTO] is not democratic. You are not allowed to gain anything as a small developing country fighting for your legitimate interests unless you manage to get the powerful countries on your side. It does not matter how much effort you put into developing credible position papers, you will get nowhere without the rich countries' backing. You generally have two options if you try to take on this system: you are either excluded, or you are diminished as a person and a country.[2]

Growing discontent marked the run-up to the Third Ministerial, scheduled for Seattle in late 1999. Arriving in the city, negotiators faced a draft ministerial text that reflected deep divisions, mainly between the North and the South. Mike Moore, the director general, captured the tension: "The differences across the Atlantic and North/South were too large to bridge."[3]

Yet two other factors played a key role in the Seattle debacle. One was the smoldering conflict between the United States and the European Union, particularly over agricultural subsidies; the other was the mobilization of more than 50,000 representatives of civil society to prevent the ministerial from taking place at the Sheraton Convention Center. Made up of labor unionists, farmers, environmentalists, students, and other activists, mainly from the North, the mobilization revealed how successful opponents of the WTO had been in linking the organization with the interests of corporations. The prominent free-trade economist Jagdish Bhagwati joked about the increasing isolation of free-trade advocates:

When I was at Seattle and facing a tough Chinese Red Guards–style female demonstrator who was blocking my way illegally down a road and threatening me with body harm if I persisted, my good friend Gary Sampson (a distinguished trade economist, formerly of the GATT and WTO) drew me away from a confrontation that would have surely left me bloodied, saying, "You are the foremost free trader in the world today; we cannot afford to lose you!" It was meant to be funny and it was. But it also was a pointed reference that there were not too many of us out there, fighting the fight for free trade.[4]

The struggle in the streets, and the resistance mounted by developing countries inside the Sheraton Convention Center, dominated the proceedings. Stories circulated about Third World ministers roaming the convention center in a vain quest to locate the "Green Room," not knowing that the name referred not to a real room but to an exclusive process of decision making. The term *Green Room*, in fact, came to symbolize all that was wrong with the WTO. In the end, the ministerial fell apart as the delegates refused to ratify a declaration drafted largely by the wealthy countries.

Shortly after the ministerial collapse, on December 1, 1999, the U.S. trade representative was surprisingly frank in acknowledging the unfairness. At a press conference in Seattle, Charlene Barshefsky described the dynamics and consequences of the Green Room: "The process, including even at Singapore as recently as three years ago, was a rather exclusionary one. All the meetings were held between 20 and 30 key countries. . . . And this meant 100 countries, 100, were never in the room. . . . [T]his led to extraordinarily bad feeling that they were left out of the process and that the results even at Singapore [site of the first WTO Ministerial Meeting] had been dictated to them by the 25 to 30 countries who were in the room."[5]

Barshefsky admitted that "the WTO has outgrown the processes appropriate to an earlier time. An increasing and necessary view, generally shared among the members, was that we needed a process which had a greater degree of internal transparency and inclusion to accommodate a larger and more diverse membership."[6] Secretary of State Stephen Byers of the United Kingdom echoed this perspective: the "WTO will not be able to continue in its present form. There has to be fundamental and radical change in order for it to meet the needs and aspirations of all 134 of its members."[7]

RECOVERY IN DOHA

The big trading powers realized that they could not afford a repetition of a debacle like Seattle. At the same time, they were reluctant to relinquish their prerogatives. As the Fourth Ministerial, slated for Doha, Qatar, in late 2001, approached, they made sure they were in control. Not surprisingly, a deliberate murkiness marked the proceedings.

Most of the developing countries were united around the position that the ministerial would have to focus on issues of implementation and on reviewing key WTO agreements. They opposed a new round of trade liberalization.

Nonetheless, when the draft declaration came out a few weeks before Doha, the emphasis was on the so-called "Singapore issues" or "new issues": competition, investment policy, government procurement, and trade facilitation—the priorities of the rich nations. This initiative represented a bold effort to extend the jurisdiction of the WTO to nontrade areas. "Despite clearly stated positions that the developing countries are unwilling to go into a new round until past implementation and decision-making are addressed," noted Aileen Kwa, who followed the process closely, "the draft declaration favorably positioned the launching of a comprehensive new round with an open agenda."[8]

The draft, authored by the chair of the General Council, was presented as the product of consultations with all WTO members. In fact, the key discussions were conducted among an inner circle of about twenty to twenty-five participants at two exclusive "mini-ministerials," one in Mexico at the end of August and another in Singapore on October 13–14. How one got invited to these meetings was obscure. Kwa cites the experience of an ambassador from a transition economy who was promised an invitation to a Green Room meeting by the WTO secretariat but never received one. Then there was the case of an African ambassador who wanted to attend the Singapore mini-ministerial. When he approached the secretariat for an invitation, he was told that the WTO was not hosting the meeting. When he tried the Singapore mission in Geneva, he was informed that the staff was simply coordinating the meeting and was not in a position to send out invitations.[9]

The Doha ministerial, from November 9 to 14, 2001, took place under terrible conditions. In the first place, the September 11 events provided a perfect opportunity for the U.S. trade representative, Robert Zoellick, and his European Union counterpart, Pascal Lamy, to pressure the developing countries to agree to a new round of trade negotiations. They were necessary, the two men claimed, to offset a global downturn worsened by the terrorist actions. Second, the location of the Fourth Ministerial was unfavorable. Qatar is a monarchy, and dissent could be easily controlled. The WTO secretariat's authority over who would be granted visas to enter Qatar allowed it to radically limit the number of legitimate NGOs to about sixty, to prevent the kind of explosive interaction between Third World resentment and street protest that had taken place in Seattle.[10]

Doha was a low point in the GATT-WTO's history of backroom intimidation, threats, bribery, and clubby exclusion. In Qatar as in Seattle, the actual decision-making process remained off the books; only the formal sessions of the ministerial, reserved for speeches, were recorded. The substantive discussions took place in informal groupings whose meeting places kept shifting, and because there was no paper (or electronic) trail, no one could be held accountable.

As a result, Third World demands were subordinated to the top agenda item of the wealthy powers: the launching of a round of negotiations that would extend WTO jurisdiction into the "new issues." The needs of developing countries for "special and differential treatment," for trade rules that took account of levels of development, were effectively ignored.

Bergsten, the free-trade partisan, once compared the WTO and trade liberalization to a bicycle: it stays up only by moving forward. Doha set the WTO upright once more, but it was still wobbly. However, a great deal of resentment accumulated among the nations who had been manipulated into accepting a declaration running counter to their own interests.

COLLAPSE IN CANCÚN

To many developing countries, the Doha Declaration was a prelude to a major extension of the authority of the WTO. If all went as planned, the expansion would happen at the Fifth Ministerial Meeting in Mexico.

Northern governments, especially the British, claimed that the Doha Round would incorporate development concerns into the trade agenda. Much of the mainstream media—and many northern NGOs—pointed to Article 6 of the declaration, which upheld public health concerns over intellectual property rights, as indicating that the WTO had the potential to become a development-friendly institution (we'll look more closely at Article 6 a little later).

But the eighteen months leading up to the Fifth Ministerial Meeting in Mexico, in mid-September 2003, suggested otherwise. The North pushed a new Agreement on Agriculture; initiated preliminary negotiations on the New Issues; launched talks on industrial tariffs; and pressed to accelerate liberalization of services. The hope was that, at Cancún, trade and trade-related matters would coalesce into a WTO agreement that would be as far-reaching as the Uruguay Round and would give the faltering globalization process some momentum while bypassing the needs of the South.

Even from the standpoint of the central economies, however, progress was maddeningly slow. Between Doha and Cancún, little if any movement occurred in any of the negotiating areas. Agriculture, in particular, presented a knotty problem.

Even before Doha, negotiations had begun to rework the AOA. By the beginning of 2002, though, the talks were getting nowhere. Both the United States and the European Union competed to stymie the talks. Announcing that "we want to be selling our beef and our corn and our beans to people around the world who need to eat," President George W. Bush signed legislation, on May 13, 2002, giving U.S. farming interests $190 billion in subsidies over the next ten years. The measure increased certain subsidies by 80 percent; raised price supports for wheat, cotton, soybeans, rice, and cotton; and created new subsidies for items like lentils, peanuts, and milk.[11]

Equally defiant was the European Union. In October 2002, French president Jacques Chirac and German prime minister Gerhard Schroeder agreed that there would be no cut in agricultural subsidies during the ongoing talks on EU enlargement. Indeed, the overall amount of subsidies was to increase until 2006, and then from 2007 to 2013, spending was to be frozen at 2006 levels.[12]

By the beginning of 2003, so little progress had been registered that many negotiators feared that the impasse would spoil concurrent negotiations in areas like industrial tariffs, services, and the New Issues. A second Seattle loomed. The draft document prepared by WTO farm negotiations chairman Stuart Harbinson produced a stalemate among the superpowers on how much and how fast trade-distorting subsidies would be cut. In the fight between the agro-export giants, the concerns of developing countries were conveniently forgotten. As Aileen Kwa points out, the Harbinson text did not address southern fears that EU and U.S. subsidies would now be mostly shifted to the so-called Green Box, a listing of allowable subsidies.[13]

The Harbinson text, moreover, completely ignored proposals put forward by Argentina and the Philippines, neither of which were invited to a pre-Cancún meeting in Tokyo of representatives of selected countries in February 2003 for "rebalancing/countervailing mechanisms" that would allow developing countries to raise tariffs on crops subsidized by the developed nations, by amounts proportionate to the subsidies.[14] Instead, for developing countries, tariffs greater than 120 percent were to be slashed by 40 percent, while those between 20 and 120 percent would be decreased by 33 percent. There would be no linkage to the subsidies maintained by the wealthy agro-exporters.

The draft also contained no meaningful recommendations for "special and differential treatment" of the Third World countries—that is, to provide their agricultural sectors significant protection, owing to their level of development.[15] True, the Harbinson draft proposed that developing countries might classify some staple products as "strategic" and have them subjected to lower tariff cuts than other commodities. However, the proposal was vague, the number of products that could qualify as strategic was unclear, and the impact would be limited, since the strategic products would still be liable to an average tariff cut of 10 percent.[16] As Kwa noted, the proposal was "no more than wool being pulled over the eyes of trade negotiators and Ministers. It is a fictitious fig leaf offered to entice the less-WTO-savvy decision-makers in the developing world."[17]

Agricultural negotiations remained effectively stalemated all the way up to the Cancún meeting. The situation was much the same in other areas. One of the few positive items in the Doha Ministerial Declaration was the clear statement that "the TRIPs Agreement does not and should not prevent Members from taking measures to protect public health."[18] But the United States squandered a lot of goodwill after Doha, by asserting that only in the case of medications for three epidemics—HIV-AIDS, tuberculosis, and malaria—should patent rights be loosened and that only the poorest nations without a pharmaceutical industry could import inexpensive generic drugs. After the developing countries rejected the U.S. position, a stalemate existed until the very eve of Cancún, when negotiations forged a compromise, which was denounced as loaded down with such tight restrictions as to make the import of low-cost drugs a cumbersome process. Not surprisingly, developing countries viewed U.S. trade policy as hostage to the pharmaceutical lobby, precisely because the technomonopoly promoted by TRIPs represented America's most profitable industry.

Meanwhile, the EU was insisting that negotiations begin on the "new issues." But the developing countries were even more adamant that the Singapore issues be dropped. The question threatened to derail the ministerial. Moreover, agriculture continued to hold everything up.[19] While the United States and the EU wrangled over reductions in export subsidies and over the formulas for lowering agricultural tariffs, several developing countries, led by Brazil, India, South Africa, and China, met on August 20, 2003, to form the Group of 20. It demanded "substantial cuts on trade distorting domestic support, substantial increase in market access, and elimination of export subsidies."[20]

Another group, consisting of thirty-three developing countries, formed around the demand for "special products" that would be exempted from tariff reductions as well as "special safeguard mechanisms" against the highly subsidized agricultural exports from the rich societies.

Still another, and even larger, group, which eventually came to be known as the G-90, were united in their opposition to the start of negotiations on the "new issues" without the explicit consensus of all WTO members.

As the Cancún ministerial opened, on September 10, a showdown seemed inevitable, but the flashpoint turned out to be an unexpected one. It was the question of cotton subsidies, provided to U.S. producers, that had contributed to a collapse of prices. U.S. producers were offloading cotton on world markets at between 20 and 55 percent of the cost of production, leading to a severe crisis for west African and central African cotton farmers.[21] Four African countries—Benin, Burkina Faso, Chad, and Mali— demanded compensation of between $250 million and $1 billion annually and the unilateral elimination of the subsidies.[22] The confrontation was the prelude to a more encompassing impasse.

Discussion started on the "new issues." Japan and South Korea declared themselves unwilling to drop investment and competition policy from the negotiations. G-90 members from Asia and Africa—many of them angered by the U.S.-inspired suggestion that African cotton exporters should diversify away from cotton—fiercely rejected the inclusion of any new issue. Some started to walk out of the meeting. At that point, Mexican Foreign Minister Luis Derbez, who was serving as ministerial chairman, gaveled the proceedings to an end, declaring that the necessary consensus was absent.

NGO delegates and observers near the convention press center erupted in cheers and began singing "Our World Is Not for Sale" to the tune of the Beatles' "Can't Buy Me Love." Demonstrations both inside and outside the convention center and in the town of Cancún continued for almost a week. The tragic denouement of the mass mobilizations was the suicide, at the barricades, of the Korean farmer Lee Kyung Hae, on September 12, to protest the dispossession of southern farmers. The event stunned the ministerial, which observed a minute of silence in his memory.

Despite an effort by Robert Zoellick to pin the blame of the collapse at Cancún on developing countries and by Pascal Lamy to assign it to the "medieval" decision-making rules, most of the media, including the Western press, attributed the debacle to the inflexibility of Washington and the EU on agriculture and Europe's unrelenting push to take up the "new issues."[23]

CRISIS OF LEGITIMACY OF THE BRETTON WOODS SYSTEM

Seattle and Cancún were two key moments in the crisis of globalization. Another was the Asian financial crisis of 1997, which triggered the IMF crisis of legitimacy.

The Asian Financial Crisis and the Unraveling of the IMF

The East Asian economies, whose average rate of growth was predicted to remain at 6 to 8 percent far into the future, were widely heralded as the leaders of the global economy in the twenty-first century. Thus, when these economies crashed in the summer of 1997, the ideological appeal of globalization suffered. Perhaps the most shocking aspect, for people in the developing world, was the social impact of the crisis. As noted earlier, over 1 million people in Thailand and some 21 million people in Indonesia found themselves impoverished in just a few weeks.[24] The IMF, seen as the architect of the capital account liberalization that had created the crisis and of the devastating contraction that followed, was widely discredited.

On January 15, 1998, throughout the global South, the picture of Michel Camdessus, the IMF managing director, arms folded, standing over Indonesian president Suharto as he signed an IMF Letter of Intent, agreeing to the harsh conditions of stabilization demanded by the fund, became an icon of Third World subjugation to a much-hated overlord. So unpopular was the IMF that Thaksin Shinawatra and his Thai Rak Thai political party won a smashing victory by running against the IMF and the Thai regime that had done its bidding. The new government inaugurated anti-IMF expansionary policies that revived the Thai economy. In Malaysia,

Prime Minister Mohamad Mahathir defied the IMF by imposing capital controls, a move that raised a howl from speculative investors but ultimately won the grudging admission of the IMF itself as having stabilized an economy in serious crisis.[25] Many establishment critics agreed that the fund "should have tried unorthodox combinations such as fiscal expansion, monetary contraction, and capital controls."[26]

Indeed, the IMF eventually acknowledged—though in euphemistic terms—that its reliance on fiscal belt-tightening to stabilize the currency and restore investor confidence was mistaken: "[T]he thrust of fiscal policy . . . turned out to be substantially different . . . because . . . the original assumptions for economic growth, capital flows, and exchange rates . . . were proved drastically wrong."[27]

The IMF was further discredited by its close association with the interests of the United States. "In great detail, crisis countries were asked to slash their subsidies, end their local monopolies, reform their tax systems, liberalize their financial systems, and more."[28] The staff of the fund, it was noted, "worked in very close cooperation with the U.S. Treasury in designing the most controversial features of the IMF's programs in Asia."[29]

Japan's proposal for an Asian monetary fund (AMF) exposed the IMF as essentially a tool of the United States. Tokyo suggested the AMF—capitalized at $100 billion—when Southeast Asian currencies were in a free fall. As a multipurpose fund, it would assist Asian societies in defending their currencies against speculators, provide emergency balance-of-payments financing, and make available long-term funding for adjustment needs. As outlined by Japanese officials, notably the influential Eisuke Sakakibara, the AMF would be more flexible than the IMF, by requiring a "less uniform, perhaps less stringent, set of required policy reforms as conditions for receiving help."[30] Not surprisingly, the AMF proposal drew strong support from Southeast Asian governments.

Just as predictably, the AMF aroused the strong opposition of both the IMF and Washington. At the IMF-World Bank annual meeting, in Hong Kong in September 1997, Michel Camdessus and his American deputy Stanley Fischer argued that the AMF, by serving as an alternate source of financing, would subvert the IMF's ability to secure tough economic reforms from Asian countries in trouble. Because of congressional constraints on the president's power to commit U.S. bilateral funds to international initiatives, the United States had become "more dependent on its power in the IMF to exercise influence on financial matters in Asia. In this context, an Asian Monetary Fund in which Japan was the major player would be a blow to the U.S. role in the region."[31] Indeed, the analyst Eric Altbach claims that "some Treasury officials accordingly saw the AMF as more than just a bad idea; they interpreted it as a threat to America's influence in Asia. Not surprisingly, Washington made considerable efforts to kill Tokyo's proposal."[32] Unwilling to lead an Asian coalition against U.S. wishes, Japan abandoned the proposal, which might have prevented the collapse of the Asian economies. Without a doubt, the episode left many Asians resentful of both the IMF and the United States.

Revisiting Structural Adjustment

The performance of the IMF during the Asian financial crisis led to a widespread reappraisal of its role in the Third World in the 1980s and early 1990s, the period during which structural adjustment programs covered ninety developing and transition, or post-Socialist, economies. Fifteen years down the road, it was hard to point to more than a handful as successes, among them the highly questionable case of Augusto Pinochet's Chile. As noted earlier, poverty and inequality in most adjusted economies increased. Beyond that, structural adjustment institutionalized stagnation in Africa, Latin America, and other parts of the Third World. A study by the Center for Economic and Policy Research shows that 77 percent of countries for which data are available saw their per capita rate of growth fall significantly from 1980 to 2000. In Latin America, income expanded by 75 percent during the 1960s and 1970s, when the region's economies were relatively closed, but grew by only 6 percent in the next two decades.[33] Robert Pollin's analysis shows that, excluding China from the equation, the overall growth rate in developing countries during the interventionist, developmental state era (1961–80) was 5.5 percent, compared with 2.6 percent in the neoliberal era. In terms of the growth rate of per capita income, the figures were 3.2 percent in the developmental state era and 0.7 in the neoliberal era.[34]

No longer could the IMF hide the fact that adjustment had been a disaster in Africa, Latin America, and South Asia. During the World Bank-IMF meetings in September 1999, the fund conceded failure by renaming the extended structural adjustment facility (ESAF) the "poverty reduction and growth facility" and promised to learn from the World Bank in making the elimination of poverty the centerpiece of its programs. But such attempts at self-reform were too little, too late, and too incredible.

Indeed, among the key consequences of the IMF's calamitous record in East Asia and elsewhere was its exposure of the long-simmering conflict within elite circles over the role of the fund. The American right denounced the agency for promoting moral hazard, or irresponsible lending; some, including former U.S. Treasury secretary George Shultz, called for its abolition. Meanwhile, orthodox liberals like Jeffrey Sachs and Jagdish Bhagwati attacked the fund as a threat to global macroeconomic stability and prosperity. Late in 1998, a rare conservative-liberal alliance in Congress came within a hairbreadth of denying the IMF a $14.5 billion increase in the U.S. quota. Arm-twisting on the part of the Clinton administration salvaged the quota, but clearly the longtime internationalist consensus among American elites that had supported the fund for more than five decades was unraveling.

The World Bank in Question

In an eventuality that had hardly been anticipated a decade earlier, the World Bank shared in the IMF's delegitimation. Australian-turned-American James Wolfensohn assumed the presidency of the bank in 1995 and opened up channels of communication with the nongovernmental organizations. Assisted by a well-oiled public relations machine, he tried to recast the bank's image as an institution that was not only moving away from structural adjustment but also making the elimination of poverty its central mission, along with promoting good governance and environmentally sensitive lending.

But in early February 2000, a report by a commission mandated by Congress to look at the international financial institutions unsettled the bank. Headed by academic Alan Meltzer, the commission came up with a number of devastating findings: 70 percent of the bank's nongrant lending was concentrated in 11 member countries, with 145 other members left to scramble for the remaining 30 percent; 80 percent of the bank's resources were devoted not to the poorest countries but to the better-off ones that enjoyed positive credit ratings and, according to the commission, could therefore raise their funds in international capital markets; the failure rate of bank projects was 65–70 percent in the poorest societies and 55–60 percent in all developing countries. In short, the World Bank was irrelevant to the achievement of its avowed mission: alleviating global poverty.[35]

And what to do with the bank? The commission urged that most of the lending activities be offloaded to regional development banks. Readers of the report soon realized that, as one of the commission's members revealed, it "'essentially wants to abolish the International Monetary Fund and the World Bank,' a goal that had "significant pockets of support . . . in our Congress."[36]

Much to the chagrin of Wolfensohn, few people came to the bank's defense. More interesting was that many critics, from across the spectrum—the left, right, and center—agreed with the report's findings although not necessarily with its recommendations.

The realities concealed beneath the verbiage of the bank's expanded mission statement were made public in the months leading up to the World Bank-IMF meeting in Prague in September 2000.[37] The claim that the bank was concerned about "good governance" was contradicted by its profound involvement with the Suharto regime in Indonesia, to which it had funneled more than $30 billion over thirty years. According to several reports, the bank accepted false government statistics, legitimized the dictatorship by passing it off as a model for other countries, and was complacent about the state of human rights and the monopolistic control of the economy. According to Jeffrey Winters, a specialist in Indonesia, one of the galling aspects of the situation was that the bank leadership tolerated the corruption:

> [Julian Schweitzer,] a senior official at the Bank, went even further in our joint interview, making direct reference to the estimate that a third of the Bank's funds loaned to Indonesia had been stolen and became criminal debt. "If you take the amount of 30 per cent loss," Schweitzer stated, "it means 70 cents [on the dollar] got used for development after all. That's a lot better than some places with only 10 cents on the dollar." He was referring to certain Bank clients in Africa where nearly all of the loan funds are misallocated, diverted, unaccounted for, or simply stolen.[38]

That this close embrace of the Suharto regime continued well into the Wolfensohn era was particularly damning.

Although the image of an environmentally sensitive bank under Wolfensohn was buried under the avalanche of criticism that followed the Meltzer report, it, too, reflected the gap between the bank's public relations efforts and its lending practices. The bank was a staunch backer of the controversial Chad-Cameroon pipeline, which would seriously damage ecologically fragile areas like Cameroon's Atlantic Littoral Forest.[39] Furthermore, bank management was caught violating its own rules on environment and resettlement when it tried to push through the China Western Poverty Reduction Project, which would have transformed an arid ecosystem supporting minority Tibetan and Mongolian sheepherders into agricultural land for people from other parts of China. Global pressure from NGOs forced a cancelation of some of the worst aspects of this program. But other environmentally destabilizing components were approved.[40]

A look at the bank's loan portfolio revealed the reality behind the rhetoric: loans for the environment as a percentage of total loans declined from 3.6 percent in fiscal year 1994 to 1.02 percent in 1998; funds allocated to environmental projects declined by 32.7 percent between 1998 and 1999; and in 1998 more than half of all lending by the World Bank's private sector divisions went to environmentally harmful projects like dams, roads, and power plants.[41] So marginalized was the bank's environmental staff within the bureaucracy that Herman Daly, the distinguished ecological economist, left the bank because he felt that he and other in-house environmentalists had no impact on agency policy.

Confronted with a list of thoroughly documented charges at a debate with critics in Prague in September 2000, Wolfensohn was reduced to meaningless cheerleading: "I and my colleagues feel good about going to work every day."[42] It was an answer that underlined the depth of the Bretton Woods crisis of legitimacy, and was matched only by IMF managing director Horst Koehler's famous line, also at the Prague Castle debate: "I also have a heart, but I have to use my head in making decisions."[43]

REFORM: PROMISE VERSUS REALITY

As the crisis of legitimacy deepened, the need for reform was felt acutely. A reworking of the prevailing international financial architecture, debt relief, and a new approach to development topped the agenda.

No Changes in the Global Financial Architecture

Calls for financial restructuring to reduce the volatility of the trillions of speculative capital roaming the world in pursuit of narrow but significant interest rate differentials came from many quarters. But the United States argued that the existing mechanisms were basically sound. Instead of a major overhaul, what was needed, Washington said, was a technical jiggering, a new "wiring of the system." Although there were some differences on details, this position was shared by the other members of the G-7, a grouping of the most economically powerful northern countries.

This approach advocated tougher bankruptcy laws to eliminate moral hazard, and prudential regulations based on a set of core principles, such as transparency of accounts. The G-7 called for greater inflow of foreign currency, as well, not only to recapitalize shattered banks but also to stabilize the local financial system by making foreign interests integral to it. This practice would allow foreign banks to freely buy up local institutions or set up their fully owned subsidiaries.

The G-7 also trumpeted the creation of a financial stability forum. As originally proposed, this body had no representation from the less developed economies. When this failing generated criticism, the G-7 issued an invitation to Singapore and Hong Kong to join the forum. Because Third World nations were still not satisfied, the G-7 created the G-20,* with more representation from the South. As Andy Knight noted, however, even the G-20 had no representation from the poorest countries.[44] He continued: "The G-20 also lacks any mechanism for reporting or for accountability to the broader international community; its origins in the G-7 reduce its legitimacy; its membership is not fully representative; its mandate is narrow; its procedures are not inclusive enough to allow for participation by non-governmental organizations; and its operations are not all that transparent either."[45]

Tobin taxes, or similar controls designed to slow down capital flows by imposing fees on them at various points in the global financial network, were strongly resisted. Even when the IMF admitted that capital controls worked to stabilize the Malaysian economy during the 1997 financial crisis, resistance to capital controls remained, including the most market-friendly

---

*This grouping is not the same as the G-20 that was established prior to the Cancún WTO summit in September 2003.

kind, like the Chilean *encaja*. That mechanism applied holding-period taxes, or their equivalent, noninterest-bearing deposit requirements, on all capital inflows, to ensure that they would remain in country for a period of time and thus avoid volatile movements that could destabilize an economy.[46] As Barry Eichengreen noted,

> This advice ought not to be controversial, although it continues to be regarded as such. If the experience of the 1990's taught us one thing, it is that throwing open the capital account before [developed country standards and practices of prudential supervision] have been put in place is a recipe for disaster. Moreover, developing the relevant mechanisms and capacities is no easy task. It follows that these interim measures may have to be retained for some time.[47]

Despite the IMF's poor record, the G-7 supported the expansion of its powers to manage financial crises. It gave the fund the authority to compel private creditors to carry some of the costs of a rescue program—that is, to bail them in instead of bailing them out, an approach that was tried during the Korean crisis. This requirement was a modest response to a chorus of complaints from both the right and the left that because the fund had been used in the past to bail out private creditors, it encouraged irresponsible lending.

The G-7 also authorized the creation of a contingency credit line, to be made available to nations that are likely to be subjected to speculative attack. Access to these funds would depend on a country's track record for observing good macroeconomic fundamentals, as traditionally stipulated by the fund. The only problem was that no one wanted to take advantage of this precrisis credit line, rightly worried that speculative investors would take this move as a sign of crisis, pull their capital out of the country, and thus accelerate the crisis that the precrisis credit line was supposed to avert in the first place.

Probably the most far-reaching proposal came, surprisingly, from the American deputy director of the fund, Anne Krueger, who proposed an orderly workout process similar to Chapter 11 bankruptcy proceedings: the sovereign debt restructuring mechanism. A government suffering a financial crisis would apply for protection. If the IMF found that the country was dealing with its creditors in good faith, it would grant a standstill in its payments. Protected in this fashion, the debtor would negotiate new terms of repayment, with the IMF providing emergency funding to finance its imports of goods and services. The IMF then would oversee the creation of a tribunal, independent of the fund, that would adjudicate disputes between the debtor and the creditors, as well as among creditors, and come out with a debt restructuring program that would be binding on everybody.[48] According to Eichengreen,

> The merit of this proposal is that it addressed head-on the key problems to be resolved in order to make debt restructurings more orderly and predictable and thereby create an alternative to large-scale multilateral [emergency] lending. It would shelter the country from disruptive litigation. It would allow a qualified majority of the creditors to bind in an uncooperative minority. And it would lay down clear rules and procedures governing that restructuring process.[49]

Proposed during the height of the Argentine crisis, the restructuring measure was viewed as inadequate by most developing countries. But its greatest problem was that powerful interests in Washington and in the financial community were dead set against it. The day after Krueger made her proposal public, John Taylor, the undersecretary of the Treasury for international affairs, registered his disagreement, saying that the "most practical and broadly acceptable reform would be to have sovereign borrowers and their creditors put a package of new clauses in the debt contracts."[50] In other words, maintain the status quo, in which the creditors tend to unite and have tremendous advantage over the debtor.

Krueger apparently had the support of Secretary of the Treasury Paul O'Neill. Ron Suskind's account of O'Neill's tenure provides a sense of the conflict the proposal provoked:

> Anne Krueger, the progressive number two at the IMF, and O'Neill had become something of an odd couple as well, trumpeting the virtues of extending to troubled nations the same reasonable protections that multinationals enjoy in Chapter 11. Banks and investment houses hated the idea, saying they wouldn't extend credit to the developing countries of Africa,

Asia, and South America if those countries were protected from creditors. O'Neill's response was that over the past decade their investments had been risk-free, because they knew the U.S. Treasury would bail them out in a crisis.[51]

When O'Neill was fired by President Bush in December 2002, however, Krueger lost her strongest supporter. At the April 2003 meeting of the IMF's International Monetary and Finance Committee, the United States squelched the proposal.

The lack of any real movement in reforming the international financial architecture prompted warnings by, of all people, Robert Rubin, that "[f]inancial crises have continued to rock emerging markets and are likely to remain a factor in the decades ahead."[52]

HIPC and PRSPs

Nor was there any progress in moving toward more effective development strategies. The G-7 committed itself to achieve, under the leadership of the World Bank, a significant reduction in the debt servicing of the forty-one highly indebted poor countries (HIPC). This commitment was most loudly proclaimed at the G-7 meeting in Cologne in July 1999. Yet at the Okinawa summit the following year, debt reduction for the poor nations did not figure in the agenda, and during the Genoa summit in July 2001, it received only perfunctory mention in the final communiqué.

The turnabout was not surprising, because the actual debt reduction achieved by HIPC since it began in 1996 was only $1 billion—a reduction of debt service by only 3 percent in four and a half years.[53] Another estimate, by the British nonprofit organization Christian Aid, is that only 6.4 percent of the total debt of the world's poorest countries would be tackled by the HIPC initiative,[54] a far cry from the IMF's projection that HIPC would result in a debt reduction of "$41 billion over time."[55]

A joint submission to the IMF and the World Bank by four British NGOs offered a detailed breakdown of HIPC's meager results:

1. Out of twenty HIPCs that have already reached HIPC decision point, four countries (Mali, Niger, Sierra Leone, and Zambia) will have annual debt service payments due in 2003–05 that

will actually be higher than their annual debt services paid in 1998–2000.

2. Five countries will be paying almost as much in debt service as before HIPC (Ethiopia, Guinea-Bissau, Honduras, Nicaragua, Uganda).

3. In six countries, annual debt serviced will be reduced by a modest $15 million in 2003–05.

4. The medium- to long-term projections on debt servicing are also alarming—Senegal's jumps by 61 percent in 2004; Nicaragua's rises by 60 percent in 2002; Mauritania's rises by 46 percent in 2007; and Honduras faces an increase of 93 percent in 2002.[56]

The report warned that "in the absence of radical reform, HIPC will join a long list of failed poverty reduction initiatives."[57] As if to confirm these fears, the World Bank itself admitted that, because of lower export prices, half the countries covered by HIPC would still have unsustainable debt loads at the end of the program; the scheduled debt reduction would be too small to have an impact on the overall debt level.[58]

At the World Bank–IMF meeting in the fall of 1999, the extended structural adjustment facility (ESAF) was renamed the Comprehensive Development Framework or the Poverty Reduction Strategy Paper. The shift in nomenclature was supposed to augur a basic change in approach. As U.S. Treasury secretary Lawrence Summers put it, the policy would consist of "moving away from an IMF-centered process that has too often focused on narrow macroeconomic objectives at the expense of broader human development."[59] The reconfiguration would engender "a new, more inclusive process that would involve multiple international organizations and give national policy makers and civil society groups a more central role."[60]

But on closer inspection, the new approach turned out to be suspiciously like the old one. Summers stated that the new IMF must have, as one of its priorities, "strong support for market opening and trade liberalization."[61] Trade liberalization, he continued,

is often a key component of IMF arrangements. In the course of negotiations, the IMF has sought continued compliance with existing trade obligations and further commitments to market opening measures as part of a strategy of spurring growth. For example: As part of its IMF program, Indonesia has abolished import monopolies for soybeans and wheat; agreed to phase out all non-tariff barriers affecting imports; dissolved all cartels for plywood, cement, and paper; removed restrictions on foreign investments in the wholesale and resale trades; and allowed foreign banks to buy domestic ones. Zambia's 1999 program with the IMF commits the government to reducing the weighted average tariff on foreign goods to ten percent, and to cutting the maximum tariff from 25 to 20 percent in 2001. In July, the import ban on wheat flour was eliminated.[62]

In other words, beneath the antipoverty rhetoric not much had changed.

In recent years, several comprehensive studies of PRSPs have been released. Probably the most favorable survey was commissioned by the Strategic Partnership for Africa (SPA). Yet a close reading shows little real progress. In summing up the results of PRSPs in eight African countries, the study notes, "Many of the corresponding gains in terms of performance and results remain potential rather than actual. Decisive further steps will be necessary to realize the potential."[63] It asserts:

Even today, after countries' full PRSPs have in most cases been agreed by cabinets and endorsed by the Joint Boards of the Bank and the Fund, the impact on public consciousness—even at the level of opinion leaders—remains shallow. Awareness of the existence of a PRSP (as distinct from the myriad of donor-supported projects and programs) still tends to be limited to a few layers of officialdom in central governments and to a limited range of non-governmental actors. Clear understanding of the distinctive features of the approach, and the degree to which it does or does not constitute a break with the past, is especially scarce.[64]

Given the crucial role assigned to "national ownership"—that is, the process of assuring citizens that the program is not imposed on them from the outside—the report notes that while "ownership is quite strong in the 'technocratic' dimension," in most countries this "has so far been rather narrowly shared." The more general case, the survey continues, is that "the political dimensions of ownership does not match technocratic commitment, and this is a potential source of real difficulty."[65] Thus technocrats might think they have formulated the program, but the people continue to view it as an external imposition.

One of the few positive elements noted by the report is that PRSPs have achieved "a useful mainstreaming of anti-poverty efforts in national policy processes in Africa," although exactly what that means is unclear. But what is clear to the authors at this stage is that "whether or not vicious circles of patrimonial politics, state weakness and ineffectual aid can be replaced with virtuous ones, based on greater national ownership of anti-poverty effort, is still uncertain."[66]

Most other assessments are much more negative. A study by the Economic Policy Empowerment Program of the European Network on Debt and Development noted that while the PRSPs stress the importance of social safety nets and poverty reduction, the prescribed macroeconomic reforms to achieve them are "undiscussed" and are indistinguishable from the previous macroeconomic frameworks that focused on rapid growth via liberalization and privatization.[67] The "disjuncture" between the goal of reducing poverty and the underlying macroeconomic framework might, in fact, be the wedge with which the World Bank, the IMF, and other multilaterals, like the United Nations Development Program, expand their influence over national life: "Beyond macroeconomic policy, the traditional domain of the IMF, the PRSP emphasis on 'good governance' has now brought the whole national plan for poverty reduction, under the endorsement of the World Bank and the IMF."[68]

As for the "process" itself, most studies confirm one analyst's contention that the so-called participatory approach of the PRSPs involve

> little more than consultations with a few prominent and liberal CSO's [civil society organizations] rather than broad-based, substantive public dialogue about the causes of incidence of poverty. Local, vernacular forms of civil society organization such as labor unions, peasant organizations, social movements, women's groups, and indigenous people's organizations have not been invited into the process, and the little public discussion that

has taken place has been limited to well resourced national and international non-governmental organizations.[69]

A detailed look at the PRSPs for three countries—Vietnam, Laos, and Cambodia—reinforces the observations discussed here. The PRSP approach reveals the same one-size-fits-all formula emphasizing rapid growth, the deregulation of monetary policy, the tearing down of the state sector in favor of private enterprises, looser foreign investment laws, trade liberalization, export-oriented growth, and commercialization of land and resource rights. This time, however, the antipoverty rhetoric is deployed to drag in NGOs and people's movements so as to lend the whole business legitimacy.

"The PRSP is upheld by the World Bank and the IMF as a comprehensive approach," note the authors of the Southeast Asian survey. "That it certainly is," they conclude, "but not for poverty reduction. The PRSP is a comprehensive program for structural adjustment, in the name of the poor."[70]

Institutional Feudalism Lives On

As for structural reforms designed to make the World Bank and the IMF more democratic, there's not much progress to report. In both institutions, voting power depends on the size of one's capital subscriptions. At the World Bank, the U.S. share is 17.6 percent, somewhat above the critical 15 percent it needs to exercise a veto over major lending decisions. At the IMF, similarly, Washington controls 19 percent of the vote, comfortably above the 15 percent necessary for vetoing vital policy and budgetary decisions.

Even mild proposals have little chance of passing. For instance, Joseph Stiglitz has proposed that "pending a reexamination of the allocation of voting, the direct voice of the borrowing countries in the executive boards of the IFIs [international financial institutions] be increased, e.g., by establishing two additional seats with half votes or repackaging constituencies."[71] Why such reasonable proposals, in terms of equity, cannot make it to first base is explained by Mark Zacher:

> [I]t is very unlikely that the major donor states [namely, the Western industrialized countries] are going to sacrifice their veto

power (15, 30, 50 percent of total votes, depending on the issue) over the amount of money that they contribute or the policies concerning loans and grants to recipient countries. They may be willing to make some modest changes in the distribution of votes and the majorities that are required for particular types of decisions; but they are not going to sacrifice their ability to block decisions that concern contributions to the IMF and the IMF's dispersements [sic] of these funds.[72]

In light of the controversy swirling around the relevance of the two institutions, one would have thought that the rich minority might be willing to do away with a particularly aggravating custom—the head of the fund is always a European and that of the bank is always an American. Twice in the last few years, in 2000 and 2004, the European bloc had a chance to make the selection of the managing director by merit, not nationality. On both occasions, Europeans were chosen: the German Horst Koehler in 2000 and the Spaniard Rodrigo Rato in 2004.

The Europeans were not alone. When James Wolfensohn's current term is up, Washington has no intention of yielding the position of president of the World Bank to anybody but an American.

By the turn of the millennium, reform of the Bretton Woods system had come to be regarded, by most developing states, as a sick joke. In civil society, moreover, the failure of reform made the demand to abolish the IMF, the World Bank, and the WTO more than a rhetorical outburst from the far left. What would take the place of these multilateral agencies became a respectable topic even among establishment academics. The institutions might limp along over the next few years, but the damage to their credibility appeared to be lasting.

CHAPTER 7

George W. Bush and Rollback Economics

The rhetoric of the "won't do" overwhelmed the concerted efforts of the "can do." "Won't do" led to the impasse.

As the WTO members ponder the future, the US will not wait: we will move towards free trade with can-do countries.

ROBERT ZOELLICK, U.S. TRADE REPRESENTATIVE, ON OUTCOME OF WTO CANCÚN MINISTERIAL, SEPTEMBER 2003

Efforts at international economic reform were already stumbling badly when the Bush administration came to power. Its actions over the next four years deepened the crisis of multilateralism.

On the political front, George W. Bush was unequivocally committed to unilateralism. His economic policies did not initially signal a radical break with the proglobalization policies of the Clinton era, however. Washington worked with Brussels to get the WTO back on its feet after the debacle in Seattle in 1999, and they were moderately successful in Doha, two years later. Secretary of the Treasury Paul O'Neill appeared to warm toward debt relief and massive aid to the developing world, especially after a trip to Africa with the U2 rock star Bono in the spring of 2002. And at the IMF, Anne Krueger, the No. 2, was toying with the sovereign debt restructuring mechanism.

These moves turned out to be misleading indicators. The new administration was ultrasensitive to the needs of its corporate-class constituency. When the Cabinet debated the steel tariffs in 2002, most members were against an increase. But two heavyweights finely attuned to corporate donations and to politics were on the other side—the trade representative, Robert Zoellick, and Vice President Dick Cheney. The result was the controversial 30 percent increase in tariffs on imported steel that pushed the United States to the brink of trade war with the European Union and other steel-producing countries.[1]

According to O'Neill, "steel was mostly about politics, not about economics or the principles of free trade. There were political debts to pay."[2] The same could be said of the Farm Bill of 2002, which increased government subsidies to powerful agricultural interests by $180 billion over ten years. And then, of course, there was blatant favoritism accorded to firms like Halliburton and Bechtel in the awarding of war contracts in Iraq.

RETREAT FROM GLOBALIZATION

Since early 2001, a distinctive Bushite political economy emerged. Its main features include the following:

1. Unlike the Clinton administration and even of the Bush I administration, Bush II aggressively put the interests of U.S. corporations ahead of the concerns of the global capitalist class, even at the risk of serious disharmony.
2. Bush's political outlook is wary of any steps toward globalization that are not managed by the U.S. government so as to ensure that the process does not dilute the economic power of the United States. After all, a totally free market might victimize key corporations and thus compromise U.S. economic interests. Despite the free-market rhetoric, Washington is highly protectionist in the areas of trade, investment, and the management of government contracts. Apparently the motto of the Bushites is "Protectionism for the United States and free trade for the rest of the world."
3. The Bush inner circle is deeply skeptical of multilateralism. Its members are fearful because even though multilateralism may pro-

mote the interests of the global capitalist class in general, it may, in many instances, go against particular U.S. corporate interests. The administration's growing ambivalence toward the WTO stems from the fact that the United States has lost a number of rulings there—rulings that hurt U.S. capital and augmented the regulation of intercapitalist competition.

4. For the Bush people, politics is key, not only in the sense of using state power to repay political favors to corporate interests but, even more important, in the sense that for them, strategic power is the ultimate form of power. The neoconservatives and nationalists that command enormous influence in the administration see economic power as a means to achieve strategic power. Economic arrangements, like trade deals and the WTO, are judged less by their adherence to free trade than by the extent to which they contribute to the strategic power of the United States.

5. While the Bush administration is dedicated to advancing the interests of U.S. capital as a whole, it is especially concerned about what might be called the hard economy, which includes firms that are tied to government leaders by direct business connections, as is the case of the oil industry; industries that can subsist only with massive subsidies from the government, like steel and agribusiness; and those that operate outside the free market and depend, instead, on secure government contracts that function on a risk-free, cost-plus basis. These latter businesses make up the military-industrial complex, the most powerful bloc among corporate lobbyists in Washington today. Since many of the capitalists supporting Bush are not subject to the rigors of the free market, they regard it and free trade as no more than rhetorical weapons that may be deployed against external competitors but need not be taken seriously in conducting their own affairs.

KEY ECONOMIC POLICY THRUSTS

If these notions represent the premises for action in the Bush administration, then the following elements of recent U.S. economic policy make sense:

1. *Achieving control over Middle East oil.* While this goal did not exhaust the aims of the administration in invading Iraq, it was certainly high on the list. U.S. management of petroleum resources is, in part, aimed at potential European competitors. But perhaps, as discussed earlier, the far-sighted intention was to preempt the region's resources in order to control access to them by energy-poor China, which was still identified as a threat in the 2002 National Security Strategy Paper.[3]

2. *Applying aggressive protectionism in trade and investment matters.* The Bush administration has, in fact, not hesitated to destabilize multilateral trade in order to protect U.S. corporate interests. In addition to pushing for massive farm subsidies and raising steel tariffs, it defied the Doha Declaration that health should take priority over intellectual property claims. Responding to its powerful pharmaceutical lobby, the administration sought to limit the easing of patent controls to just three diseases. Since the Doha ministerial, in fact, Washington has put less energy into making the WTO a success. It prefers to pour its efforts into bilateral or multilateral trade deals, such as the Free Trade Area of the Americas treaty or the Central American Free Trade Agreement. Indeed, the term *free-trade agreements* is a misnomer, because these are actually preferential deals designed to severely disadvantage parties outside their purview, like the European Union.

3. *Incorporating strategic considerations into trade agreements.* In a recent speech, U.S. trade representative Robert Zoellick stated explicitly that "countries that seek free-trade agreements with the United States must pass muster on more than trade and economic criteria in order to be eligible. At a minimum, these countries must cooperate with the United States on its foreign policy and national security goals, as part of 13 criteria that will guide the U.S. selection of potential FTA partners." For example, New Zealand, a government committed to free trade, has nevertheless not been offered a free-trade deal because it has a policy that prevents visits by nuclear ships.[4]

4. *Manipulating the dollar's value to shift the costs of economic crisis to rivals among the center economies and improve the competitiveness of the U.S. economy.* As discussed in Chapter 3, exchange rate manipulation is a convenient instrument for displacing the costs of adjustment to one's competitors in a global economy marked by overcapacity.

5. *Making the other center economies, as well as developing countries, bear the burden of adjusting to the environmental crisis.* The Bush inner circle is divided between those who do not believe there is an environmental crisis and those who know that the current rate of global greenhouse emissions is unsustainable. The latter group, however, wants other nations to bear the brunt of adjustment, since that policy would not only exempt environmentally inefficient U.S. industry from the costs of adjustment but would hobble Europe, Asia, Africa, and Latin America with greater costs. Raw economic realpolitik, not fundamentalist fanaticism, lies at the root of Washington's decision not to sign the Kyoto Protocol on Climate Change.

6. *Aggressively manipulating multilateral agencies both to promote the interests of U.S. capital and to encourage a reliance on bilateral aid as a way to force change on poor countries.* Because of the strength of the European Union and other trading powers, the instrumental employment of a multilateral agency like the WTO may not be easy to achieve; such control can more readily be accomplished at the World Bank and the IMF, where U.S. dominance is institutionalized. In 2003, despite support for the proposal from many European governments, as noted in Chapter 6, the U.S. Treasury torpedoed the IMF proposal for a sovereign debt restructuring mechanism to enable developing countries to restructure their debt while giving them a measure of protection from creditors. Already a weak mechanism from the point of view of developing countries, the SDRM was vetoed by the Treasury in the interest of U.S. banks.[5]

Washington has also made the World Bank an instrument of its bilateral aid and development initiatives, including the unprecedented effort known as the Private Sector Development. Nancy Alexander's account of how the agency came to accept this revolutionary program is instructive:

Initially, most of the Bank's Board of Directors opposed the PSD Strategy's proposal to launch a third generation of adjustment focused on investment and to privatize services, especially health, education, and water. Gradually, outright opposition dissipated as Board members described the hard, uncompromising, "you're with us or against us" attitude of U.S. officials. The

PSD Strategy, which was finally approved by the Board on February 26, 2002, calls for a radical transformation of the form and functions of the World Bank group in order to promote the private sector. The Bank is now promoting investor rights while, at the same time, liberalizing and privatizing services, especially in low-income countries where regulatory regimes are generally weak to non-existent.[6]

Perhaps even more important, the United States, by roping the World Bank and the IMF into providing public financing for its so-called reconstruction efforts in both Afghanistan and Iraq, is using international taxpayers' money to stabilize economies devastated by U.S. wars. Both agencies are not only being asked to come up with money, however, but to help manage the privatization effort, particularly in Iraq, which mainly benefits—scandalously so—U.S. firms like Halliburton and Bechtel.

Indeed, bilateral rather than multilateral aid has become the main conduit of U.S. aid policy. Bilateral grant aid, Bush's foreign policy experts argued, is more easily controlled and tailored to one's purposes. "Grants can be tied more effectively to performance in a way that longer-term loans simply cannot. You have to keep delivering the service or you don't get the grant," said John Taylor, undersecretary of the Treasury.

Probably the most ambitious bilateral aid program unveiled by the administration was the Millennium Challenge Account (MCA), which called for a $5 billion increase in aid, above the average of $10 billion now regularly appropriated. For a nation to qualify for aid under the new program and to continue to receive aid, it had to get passing grades on sixteen criteria that included trade policy, "days needed to start a business," inflation, budget deficit, control of corruption, rule of law, civil liberties, and immunization rate.[7] The World Bank, along with conservative private NGOs like Freedom House and the Heritage Foundation, was supposed to assess a country's eligibility for aid. The aid process itself would be conducted like a business venture, as the State Department made clear:

> [T]he MCA will use time-limited, business-like contracts that represent a commitment between the U.S. and the developing country to meet agreed performance benchmarks. Developing countries will set their own priorities and identify their own

greatest hurdles to development. They will do so by engaging their citizens, businesses, and governments in an open debate, which will result in a proposal for MCA funding. This proposal will include objectives, a plan and timetable for achieving them, benchmarks for assessing progress and how results will be sustained at the end of the contract, delineation of the responsibilities of the MCA and the MCA country, the role of civil society, business and other donors, and a plan for ensuring financial accountability for funds used. The MCA will review the proposal, consulting with the MCA country. The Board will approve all contracts.[8]

The aim of this right-wing transformation of aid policy was not just to accelerate market reform but, equally, to push political reform along narrow Western lines.[9]

VENDETTA DIPLOMACY AND ITS LIMITS

The South bears the brunt of the unilateralist offensive in the area of foreign economic policy.

The most brazen manifestation of unilateralism came in the wake of the Cancún debacle, with an all-out assault by Washington to destroy the newly formed Group of 20. A U.S. official disdainfully branded the formation the "Group of the Paralyzed."[10] He characterized the creation of the G-20 as a return to the antagonistic politics of the "New International Economic Order" of the 1970s.[11]

The G-20's reasonable proposals to correct the flaws of the world trading system were dismissed as "welfare measures" that had no place in a trade organization. A concerted campaign was launched to split the group. "Weak links" like Colombia, Mexico, Chile, Costa Rica, Thailand, and El Salvador were subjected to a full court press. Appalled by their government's tactics, NGOs revealed that Washington's tactics included "backroom coercion, calls from the White House, and threats to terminate other trade benefits and stop ongoing negotiations."[12] So intense was the pressure that the Brazilian delegation was compelled to issue a statement asking the delegations "to negotiate and not direct our energies at attacking countries or groups of countries."[13]

Alongside the government trade team, the corporate lobby went to work to split the G-20. Consumer Alert, a business group masking as a consumer organization, said that "while ostensibly representing the views of developing countries," the G-20 program "better represents the positions of several powerful exporting countries, who want greater market access, without opening up their own countries' markets to importers."[14]

But despite the intimidation, the United States managed to detach only one country from the group: El Salvador. Failing to split the G-20 during the negotiations, U.S. trade representative Robert Zoellick then tried to isolate the alliance by blaming it for the collapse of the Cancún ministerial: "The rhetoric of the 'won't do' overwhelmed the concerted efforts of the 'can do.' 'Won't do' led to the impasse."[15] His unilateralism knew no bounds: "As the WTO members ponder the future, the U.S. will not wait: we will move towards free trade with can-do countries."[16] But the Bush administration's blame game failed. Even the *Wall Street Journal* laid the responsibility for the collapse on the intransigence of the United States and the European Union over the question of agricultural subsidies.[17]

Nonetheless, Washington intensified its efforts to destroy the G-20. In a post-Cancún visit to Colombia, Senator Norm Coleman warned President Alvaro Uribe that "remaining in that Group will not lead to good relations between Colombia and the United States." The Minnesota Republican also alleged that he had gotten the commitment of the Colombian president to eventually leave the group.[18]

Similarly, the negotiations around the proposed Central American Free Trade Area were used by the United States to try to break the Group of 20. On a visit to the region post-Cancún, Zoellick bluntly warned that the negotiations were endangered by Costa Rica and Guatemala's membership in the G-20. "I told them that the emergence of the G-20 might pose a big problem to this agreement since our Congress resents the fact that members of CAFTA are also in the G-20," he stated. "If we want to construct a common future with them, resistance and protest do not constitute an effective strategy. In my talks with some of these countries, I sense that they are drawing the right conclusions." Moreover, Zoellick urged the Central American governments to look after their own interests, since Brazil "is a big country that can defend its interests by itself."[19]

Charles Grassley, Republican from Iowa and chairman of the Senate Finance Committee, added his warning that the United States would "take note" of those countries that "torpedoed" the negotiations in Cancún and would look closely at the attitude adopted by Costa Rica and Guatemala.[20] Costa Rica, in particular, became the object of tremendous pressure in the last weeks of 2003. That relentless prodding was accompanied by Zoellick's demand that the country privatize its energy and telecommunications sectors, which were currently under state control. The fear in the region was that to punish Costa Rica and Guatemala, Washington would push for a CAFTA that included only Nicaragua, El Salvador, and Honduras—a development that would reduce even further what little leverage these Central American countries have.

A month after the Cancún summit, the United States had forced Colombia, Peru, El Salvador, Guatemala, and Costa Rica out of the G-20.

The U.S. corporate community also made efforts to isolate and neutralize Brazil, Argentina, Venezuela, and other Latin American members of G-20, in the days leading up to the FTAA negotiations in Miami in November 2003. On September 23, in a letter addressed to Commerce secretary Donald Evans and Zoellick, a broad coalition of U.S. business groups declared:

> [W]e strongly urge you and your negotiating team to stay the course and continue to fight for a comprehensive and commercially meaningful FTAA that incorporates high standards, similar to those the United States has achieved in its free trade agreements with Canada, Mexico, Chile, and Singapore. We strongly oppose, therefore, attempts by some U.S. trading partners in the region to forge a more limited trade agreement by leaving several difficult, but highly important issues off the negotiating table entirely or addressing them in a less than commercially meaningful way.[21]

This was clearly a reference to the efforts of Brazil and other countries to protect their regimes from Washington's draconian investment proposals, which posed the specter of denationalization of industry and made any kind of industrial policy impossible.

Among the signatories were the heavies of the business lobby: the Emergency Committee for American Trade, Council for International Business, U.S. Chamber of Commerce, National Foreign Trade Council, National

Association of Manufacturers, Coalition of Service Industries, and the Pharmaceutical Research and Manufacturers of America.

The attack on the G-20 focused on Brazil, which was increasingly seen as a rival, both regionally and globally. Brazil was painted as obstructionist. In a widely publicized article, the head of the Inter-American Dialogue, known as a mouthpiece of official Washington, depicted Brazil as "defending an anti-trade, anti-U.S. ideology" and warned that "if it stays on its current course, Brazil will be sidelined. It will miss its opportunity for leadership, lose important economic benefits, and find itself in a costly confrontation with the U.S."[22] The aim was to isolate or break Brazil before the crucial mid-November 2003 meeting of trade ministers in Miami.

Washington tried to spin the Miami meeting as a victory for free trade, but the reality was quite the opposite. The declaration issuing from the ministerial, which was held amid raucous street protests on November 20, clearly retreated from the original FTAA vision. "The U.S. wanted a binding, comprehensive agreement with disciplines all the way through," said one official delegate from a Latin American country who participated in the negotiations. "The draft declaration coming out of the Trade Negotiations Committee clearly is a retreat from that."[23]

Instead, the declaration proposed a "flexible" process in which governments can exclude some economic areas from FTAA negotiations regarding liberalization, even as other governments negotiate liberalization in these same areas. As the document unambiguously stated, "Ministers recognize that countries may assume different levels of commitments. . . . In addition, negotiations should allow for countries that so choose, within the FTAA, to agree to additional obligations and benefits."[24]

The flexibility would allow Brazil and the other members of the Mercosur trade area to withdraw from negotiations on investment, intellectual property, government procurement, services, competition policy, and other arenas they do not wish to subject to mandatory multilateral liberalization. At the same time, it would allow the United States to continue massive subsidies to American agriculture by not joining negotiations to liberalize agriculture. The result is what pundits have called "FTAA lite" or "FTAA à la carte."

If any country won, it was Brazil: "Brazil was saying, look, 2003 is different from 1994, when Clinton launched the FTAA negotiations. Free trade policies have brought about bad results throughout Latin America. People have ousted neoliberal governments. There was no way the U.S. was going to get the comprehensive free trade agreement it wanted today."[25]

To the surprise of many, Washington agreed to the Brazilian compromise a few weeks before Miami. It had no choice, apparently. According to one participant, the alternative was "another Cancún." That would have been a high-profile setback the Bush administration could ill afford facing an election. Yet, in what was now a standard tactic, Washington tried to mask its defeat at the FTAA by threatening to launch negotiations for bilateral free-trade pacts with the Dominican Republic, Panama, Bolivia, Colombia, Ecuador, and Peru.

But to Sarah Anderson, an analyst with the Institute for Policy Studies, this turn to bilateral deals was a confession of weakness: "They're admitting they can't get what they want via the FTAA, and that's because people and governments are resisting throughout the Americas."[26] According to the *Financial Times*, the U.S. threat to focus on bilateral deals was also an empty one, for slightly different reasons: the most attractive markets would not bite, and even smaller markets would find the terms quite unattractive:

> If the U.S. really wants to expand bilateral trade, logic calls for deals with bigger economies. But strained U.S. relations with Brazil, China, and India make such ties with the leading emerging markets improbable. . . .
>
> This has left Mr. Zoellick trawling for tiddlers. His targets at present are mainly a motley collection of poor and backward countries in Africa, the Middle East, and Central America, with a negligible share of world output and trade. Even Australia, much the richest prospective U.S. partner, accounts for only 1 per cent of world imports—and its market is already fairly open.
>
> The U.S. has further narrowed its options by subordinating trade to politics. Mr. Zoellick and congressional leaders say bilateral partners will be judged by their loyalty to U.S. interests. If they step out of line, they can expect no mercy. Egypt is a case in point. After hailing the country as a prime candidate for a deal, Mr. Zoellick struck it from the list because Egypt failed to

support a U.S. challenge to the EU's genetically modified food regime.[27]

Cancún and Miami demonstrated the limits of U.S. hegemony and revealed how unilateralist economic diplomacy might backfire.

TACTICAL SHIFT

By the spring of 2004, however, Washington realized that its dual strategy was running into trouble. The Free Trade Area of the Americas that it wanted failed to transpire in Miami in November. Washington also began to realize that bilateral agreements could complement but never substitute for a comprehensive multilateral free-trade framework. At the same time, despite the initial defections, the G-20 held firm.

Unlike Washington's military policies in Iraq, U.S. trade strategy under Zoellick was flexible. To get the WTO restarted, Zoellick reached out to his friend Pascal Lamy, the trade commissioner of the European Union. Instead of trying to destroy or undermine the G-20, they moved to make its leaders, Brazil and India, a central part of the negotiations in agriculture, which was the key obstacle to any further moves at liberalization. Thus was formed in early April the informal grouping called the Five Interested Parties (FIPS), composed of the United States, the EU, Australia, Brazil, and India to deal with the biggest problem: agriculture. It was in close consultation with this grouping that Agriculture Committee chairman Tim Groser produced the Agriculture Text for the crucial meeting of the WTO General Council at the end of July 2004.

A shift in strategy was also evident toward other formations. Instead of spurning their invitations to the meeting of the big southern caucus, the G-90, held in Mauritus in mid-July 2004, the EU and the United States sent high-level delegates, including Zoellick. There, confrontational language gave way to rhetorical efforts to get the developing countries not only to come to a compromise on agriculture but also to get talks moving on bringing down nonagricultural tariffs, starting talks on trade facilitation, and getting the negotiations on services under way. But perhaps the strongest message that the developing countries heard was that this was the last chance to get the multilateral system moving, that they would be held responsible if the General Council talks held in late July in Geneva failed.

The U.S.-EU drive to restart the WTO succeeded brilliantly in Geneva. The United States and the EU were the main beneficiaries of an agreement to cut nonagricultural tariffs. Indeed, Zoellick went around trumpeting the claim that the accord on nonagricultural tariffs was a massive victory for U.S. corporations since it was but the beginning of a process that would reduce industrial and manufacturing tariffs to zero. Both the EU and the United States scored a victory by getting the developing countries to agree to begin talks on trade facilitation, one of the "new issues" that the developing countries rejected in Cancún. But it was the United States that scored the biggest gains, by getting an expanded "Blue Box" (a set of subsidies exempted from elimination or significant reductions) in which to house a considerable portion of the subsidies to its farmers legislated under the U.S. Farm Bill of 2002.

The key to the victorious U.S. strategy was bringing in Brazil and India to be part of the core group of the negotiations, then acceding to these countries' core demands in order to detach them from the rest of the developing countries. India's key concern was to avoid a formula that would require it to bring down its agricultural tariffs substantially. The EU and the United States conceded this. Removing agricultural subsidies was the main Brazilian concern, and here it seemed to get its way. The final text affirmed the phaseout of export subsidies as well as certain categories of export credits, making Brazil the big gainer, with some estimates placing its gains as some $10 billion.

The other developing countries got hardly anything, which resulted in much consternation and accusations from other developing countries that Brazil and India had betrayed them.

The United States learned from the debacle in Cancún and the failure of its hardline post-Cancún approach. The shift from a confrontational strategy to one of cooptation and subtle divide-and-rule was able to rip apart a superficial Third World unity that came out of Cancún. The centerpiece of the strategy was to bring India and Brazil into the center of the negotiations and to play to their specific interests. The two Third World leaders fell into the trap. Moreover, having become central players as members of the exclusive Five Interested Parties, their ability to repudiate large parts of a text that they had been consulted on prior to its release to the General Council was limited. That would have invited the onus of their being responsible for the "collapse" of the Doha Round and the multilateral trading system.

The strategy was masterful, but it was simply a tactical shift for Washington, not a retreat from its largely unilateralist approach in its foreign economic policy. The developing countries were not so much accommodated as outmaneuvered by a wily tactic. The result was to make many of them even more frustrated.[28]

A return to liberal multilateralism seemed very unlikely, following Bush's victory in the 2004 presidential election. Financier George Soros's appeal for a reform of the IMF, the World Bank, and the WTO to promote a more equitable form of globalization may seem sound.[29] But it won't appeal to the dominant business interests, which, after all, torpedoed the WTO talks with their aggressive protectionist posture on agriculture, intellectual property rights, and steel tariffs, and their bullying posture toward other economies in the areas of investment rights, capital mobility, and the export of genetically modified products. Behind the ideological smokescreen of free trade, the U.S. corporate establishment is, in fact, likely to become even more protectionist and mercantilist in the new era of deflation, diminishing profits, and stagnation.

CHAPTER 8

Crisis of Legitimacy

If I can get you to want to do what I want, then I do not have to force
you to do what you do not want to do.

JOSEPH NYE

In a worst case scenario, historians will someday have to explain why
the golden age of Western democracy, like the age of the Antonines,
lasted only about two hundred years.

RICHARD RORTY

Imperial systems cohere through force, but also because they are perceived as legitimate by those over whom they rule. Indeed, legitimacy is often the more critical element of power. The Roman Empire lasted seven hundred years, according to sociologist Michael Mann, thanks to the Roman invention of territorial citizenship. "Citizenship was granted to loyal allies and added to the intensive, Greek-style citizenship of Rome itself to produce what was probably the widest extent of collective commitment yet mobilized."[1]

An American empire faces a particularly vexing problem when it comes to establishing it own legitimacy. After all, the country was born through an anti-imperialist insurgency directed against the British Empire. Americans have long seen themselves as representatives of a new society, a democratic republic, leading the fight against authoritarian political systems of which empire constitutes a subspecies. Thus traditional colonialism was out of the question for the United States. Instead, the nation led the way in elaborating types of rule that would maintain the essence of empire while abjuring its form.

For American citizens it is important that the imperial process be made to seem consistent with democratic values. It is in this sense that the United States is an "imperial democracy." The imperial enterprise enjoys a measure of domestic approval because it purports to extend the political blessings of the homeland to the unfortunate and oppressed around the world. Winning consent from those outside the boundaries of the United States is, of course, more problematic. The same ideology that goes down so well at home runs up against the day-to-day realities of foreign domination. The big question for the U.S. imperial elite, then, is: "How do we sustain a belief in the common interests and values of the oppressor and the oppressed?" The failure of this quixotic undertaking presents the biggest threat to the future of the imperial order.

THE PHILIPPINE PARADIGM

The U.S. experience in the Philippines from 1900 to 1946 is instructive. There, American elites first labored to produce a postcolonial form of government that would legitimize control by and dependency on Washington.

The United States annexed the Philippines after the bitter and bloody suppression of Asia's first modern war of national liberation, a war that cost the lives of over 200,000 Filipinos and over 4,000 U.S. troops. The solution was classically American: Prepare the Filipinos for "responsible independence" by exporting the institutions of American democracy. That formula legitimated forty-six years of colonial rule and set the basis for the postcolonial relationship between the two countries.

The wholesale transplant of formal political institutions began shortly after the conquest. U.S. colonial authorities and missionaries served as instructors, and an indigenous Philippine upper class constituted a dutiful student body. By the time of independence, in 1946, the Philippine political system was a mirror image of the American. It included a presidency, the separation of powers, and a two-party system.

Actually, however, Philippine democracy married the feudal paternalism of the Philippine elite to a Chicago-style machine politics. Electoral politics was enthusiastically embraced by wealthy landowners, those whom the United States had detached from the national liberation struggle and formed into a ruling class. But it was hardly a belief in representative government that turned this elite into eager students. Rather, democratic elections provided a means for a fractious upper class to compete, relatively peacefully, for political office and to alternate in power. The upper class realized that the genius of the American political system lay in the way it harnessed elections to socially conservative ends. Because running for high office, in both countries, cost a fortune, only the wealthy or those backed by wealth could think about running for office. In the American system, elections made voters active participants in legitimizing the social and economic status quo. In the Philippines, as in the United States, democracy did not extend to the economic sphere. Electoral politics unfolded atop an immobile class structure, in which the distribution of income was one of the worst in Asia.

Nonetheless, having created the local elite, having provided access to the U.S. market for its agricultural products, and having socialized both the elite and the population-at-large to formal democratic practices, the United States felt confident that the formal independence granted in 1946 would not result in an unfriendly regime. And it did not. The Philippine experience had perhaps its greatest impact on the American political psyche: what happened in the Philippines reconciled the drive for U.S. strategic and economic expansion with America's democratic mission.

CONTAINMENT AND THE DEMOCRATIC MISSION

During the Cold War, the Philippines provided a model for America's approach to other countries in the region. The historic contradiction between America's disdain for colonies and its desire for control now reproduced itself on a global scale. The United States, Neil Sheehan points out, "did not seek colonies as such":

> Having overt colonies was not acceptable to the American political conscience. Americans were convinced that their imperial system did not victimize foreign peoples. . . . It was thought to be neither exploitative, like the nineteenth-century-style colonialism

of the European empires, nor destructive of personal freedom and other worthy human values, like the totalitarianism of the Soviet Union and China and their Communist allies. Instead of formal colonies, the United States sought local governments amenable to American wishes and, where possible, subject to indirect control from behind the scenes. Washington wanted native regimes that would act as surrogates for American power. The goal was to achieve the sway over allies and dependencies which every imperial nation needs to work its will in world affairs without the structure of old-fashioned colonialism.[2]

And, as in the case of the Philippines, formal democracy controlled by local elites tied to the United States provided both the mechanism of influence and the justification for intervention in the affairs of a Third World country. As Frances Fitzgerald pointed out:

> The idea that the mission of the United States was to build democracy around the world had become a convention of American politics in the 1950's. Among certain circles it was more or less assumed that democracy, that is, electoral democracy combined with private ownership and civil liberties, was what the United States had to offer the Third World. Democracy provided not only the basis for American opposition to Communism but the practical method to make sure that opposition worked.[3]

Efforts to set up Philippine-style formal democracies failed in most places in East Asia, however, just where the historic struggle for hearts and minds between capitalism and Communism was sharpest. With democracy stillborn in places like South Korea and Vietnam, U.S. officials underwent a democratic disillusionment. They sought, instead, to base relations with developing countries mainly on their skill in serving American strategic and economic interests. A turning point of sorts occurred when, in the early 1970s, authoritarian regimes dismantled democratic practices in two countries once promoted by Washington as showcases of democracy in the Third World: Chile and the Philippines. In both cases, the turn to dictatorship had the blessing of the Nixon administration.

SUPPORTING REPRESSIVE REGIMES

Samuel P. Huntington's celebrated *Political Order in Changing Societies* codified this retreat from democratic messianism. In the chaotic Third World, Huntington argued, it was quixotic to expect democratic government to emerge from a tradition that lacked democracy. Rather, the building of a strong central authority must necessarily precede the question of democratic representation.[4] The book not only contained the operative philosophy in the Washington diplomatic establishment but it quickly became a bible of Third World autocrats like Ferdinand Marcos, who claimed to have broken the "democratic deadlock" in the Philippines. Parroting Huntington, Marcos said, "All that people ask is some kind of authority that can enforce the simple law of civil society. . . . Only an authoritarian system will be able to carry forth the mass consent and to exercise the authority necessary to implement new values, measures, and sacrifices."[5]

The Huntington thesis foreshadowed the full-blown justification, in what came to be known as the Kirkpatrick doctrine, for supporting repressive regimes. Writing in the neoconservative organ *Commentary*, Jeane Kirkpatrick argued that dictators like Marcos and Anastasio Somoza Debayle, president of Nicaragua in the 1960s and 1970s, needed support. "The fabric of authority unravels quickly when the power and status of the man at the top are undermined or eliminated. The longer the autocrat had held power, and the more pervasive his personal influence, the more dependent a nation's institutions will be on him. Without him, the organized life of society will collapse, like an arch from which the keystone has been removed."[6] Kirkpatrick went on to become the U.S. ambassador to the United Nations, and the Reagan administration adopted her view of authoritarian politicians in its relations with its Third World allies.

DESTABILIZING THE NEW DEMOCRACIES

Meanwhile, events in the global South were moving in the opposite direction. The trend away from dictatorship and toward democracy in the Third

World—the so-called third wave of democratization—took place in spite of, and not because of, the United States. For example, the Reagan regime stuck with Marcos during the People's Power Revolution in 1986 in the Philippines until State Department pragmatists like Michael Armacost were able to persuade the president that backing Marcos tied U.S. interests to a sinking ship.[7] As a former envoy to Manila put it, the State Department realists "saved the Reagan administration from its worst instincts and stopped it from snatching defeat from the jaws of victory."[8]

The pragmatic abandonment of Marcos was typical of the United States as democracies displaced dictatorships in the 1980s. Washington had to change its tune or lose influence with the new governments. But the democratic movements were deeply suspicious of a superpower that until recently had forgotten about human rights and democracy and based its posture toward developing countries purely on strategic interests, corporate expansion, and anti-Communism. For Filipinos, to cite an example mentioned in Chapter 1, democratic rhetoric emanating from Washington was Orwellian double-talk, as epitomized by then-Vice President George H. W. Bush's toasting of Marcos during a 1981 visit to Manila: "We love you, sir. . . . we love your adherence to democratic rights and processes."

The fears of the new democracies were well founded. Although the United States backed away from dictatorships during the late 1980s, it did so because they proved incapable of imposing stabilization and free-market policies demanded by the IMF and the World Bank. They lacked the legitimacy to foist those measures on their subject populations. In Brazil and Argentina, for instance, tight monetary and fiscal policies drew opposition in the early 1980s not only from labor and other members of civil society but also from business groups that had once benefited from labor-repressive policies imposed by military dictatorships. Now, however, business circles distanced themselves from repressive governments when neoliberal policies failed to produce the promised economic growth. As Stephen Haggard and Robert Kaufman observed:

> With economic problems mounting, business elites began to reevaluate the costs and benefits of the technocratic decision-making style that characterized authoritarian rule. Business groups had complained periodically about their lack of access to the remote technocrats who conducted macroeconomic policy,

but such concerns had been offset by particularistic benefits and the fact that governments were willing to repress popular sector challenges. The private sector's gradual disaffection did not reflect a democratic epiphany, but a pragmatic response to changing circumstances. With authoritarian governments increasingly unable to deliver their side of the bargain, "voice" began to appear increasingly important to business groups, even if it meant reopening the arena to the previously excluded popular sectors.[9]

Even so, the democratic governments that displaced authoritarian regimes faced their own dilemma. Redistributive policies were blocked by elites who had joined the reform coalition. At the same time, expansionary fiscal policies were discouraged by the World Bank and the IMF. It soon became clear that what the multilateral agencies wanted them to do was to use their democratic legitimacy to impose structural adjustment programs. In Argentina, for instance, the international financial institutions pressured the new government of Raul Alfonsín to abandon neo-Keynesian policies, implement tax reforms, liberalize trade, and privatize public enterprises. When the regime quailed, the World Bank "concluded that the government had not made sufficient progress toward its reform goals and suspended disbursements on a structural adjustment loan."[10]

Democracy of this specific variety became the prime mechanism for the imposition of stabilization or structural adjustment programs in Jamaica, the Philippines, Peru, and Pakistan. In Jamaica, the progressive Michael Manley government suffered a devastating loss of legitimacy when it caved in to pressure to impose an IMF stabilization program blessed by Washington. The program, which eroded living standards, led to Manley's crushing defeat in the 1980 elections. In Peru, the government of Alberto Fujimori was elected on a populist, anti-IMF platform, but proceeded to impose a neoliberal "shock" program that included steep price increases in the rates charged by state enterprises as well as radical trade liberalization.[11] These measures provoked a deep recession, leading to popular discontent that in turn provoked Fujimori to suspend the constitution, close Congress, and rule as a strongman with little respect for legal restraints, until he was ousted in 2000, after a decade in office.

In the Philippines, Washington abandoned Marcos when it realized that the dictatorship's lack of legitimacy made it an ineffective instrument for

repaying the $26 billion foreign debt and for implementing IMF stabili-
zation policies. But not even the economic crisis that accompanied the end
of the regime stopped the World Bank and the IMF from demanding that
the fledgling democratic government of President Corazon Aquino, who
became president in 1986, make debt repayment its top economic priority.
The government submitted, issuing a decree that affirmed the "automatic
appropriation" of the full amount needed to service the foreign debt from
the national budget. The 40 to 50 percent of the budget going to service the
debt precluded most development and drastically reduced the funds needed
to improve the country's physical, technical, and educational infrastructure.
In some years, 10 percent of the country's GDP was spent meeting its foreign obligations. It is hardly surprising, then, that the Philippines registered
average growth of below 1.5 percent a year between 1983 and 1993.

In 1991, five years after the end of the dictatorship, the percentage of the
population living below the poverty line had dipped only slightly, from
49.3 to 46.5 percent. Income distribution worsened as the share of wealth
going to the lowest 20 percent of families fell from 5.2 to 4.7 percent, while
that captured by the top 10 percent rose from 36.4 to 38.6 percent. Lower-
class alienation from the country's revived democracy was pervasive; it cul-
minated in an aborted uprising on May 1, 2001.[12]

As in Peru, Argentina, and the Philippines, the return of democracy to
Brazil in the 1980s was accompanied by scarcely veiled warnings from the
IMF and the United States that the first order of business for the new
regime was to accomplish what the exiting military regime had failed to
do—that is, to impose stabilization programs raising interest rates, cutting
back government expenditures, devaluing the currency, and liberalizing
trade. Thus, democratic rule in the largest country in Latin America suffered a severe crisis of legitimacy lasting from the mid-1980s to 2002, as
government after government did the bidding of the IMF and Washington
and earned the enmity of impoverished peoples.[13]

The IMF's latest victim was the government of Lula—Luis Inácio da
Silva—of the Brazilian Workers' Party, one of the most committed antineoliberal parties on the continent. Even before he won the presidential
elections in the fall of 2002, Lula did the unprecedented in Latin America:
under duress, he promised the IMF that he would honor the high-interest,
expenditure-restrictive conditions of a stabilization loan negotiated with

the outgoing president, Fernando Henrique Cardoso. The fund made it clear it would not release the remaining $24 billion of the stabilization loan unless he behaved.

Lula was true to his word. Consequently, in 2003, Lula's first year in office, Brazilian GDP contracted by 0.2 percent; unemployment surged to a record 13 percent. This bitter medicine for the Brazilian people was, however, a tonic for foreign investors. In the first eight months of the year, even though the economy remained depressed, Brazilian stocks soared by over 58 percent, prompting *Business Week* to advise speculative investors: "Don't leave this party yet."[14] As for Lula, he faced mounting criticism from within his Workers' Party and governing coalition, as well as from ordinary voters; by the spring of 2004, only 28 percent of the population voiced support for his government.[15]

Everywhere fealty to international financial interests eroded democracy's political capital. In a poll conducted by the UN Development Program in 2004, 54.7 percent of Latin Americans said they would support authoritarian governments over democracy if the shift would solve their economic woes.[16]

In Latin America, reversal of the third wave of democratization loomed as a threat. In South Asia it was a reality. When General Pervez Musharraf seized power in Pakistan in October 1999 and sent Prime Minister Nawaz Sharif packing, he ended eleven years of unstable democracy. The implications of the Pakistani events worried many. As the analyst Larry Diamond wrote: "Pakistan [may] not be the last high-profile country to suffer a breakdown of democracy. Indeed, if there is a 'third reverse wave,' its origin may well be dated to 12 October 1999."[17]

Postmortems of Pakistan's parliamentary democracy tend to focus on corruption, collapse of the rule of law, ethnic and religious polarization, and economic failure. Yet the United States and the multilateral agencies were key factors in the breakdown, in two ways.

First, traditionally strong support for the Pakistani military from the Pentagon and the CIA helped convert it into a state within a state, for all intents and purposes outside the control of civilian authorities. These special ties were forged before the 1980s, but they were strengthened as the Pakistani Army served as a liaison between the Pentagon and CIA and the Islamic mujahideen, or guerrillas, during the war against the Soviet forces occupying Afghanistan in the early 1980s. So while the Clinton administration registered disapproval at first, the Pentagon made it clear that it was not at all worried about the coup that deposed Sharif.

Second, as in Latin America and the Philippines, the IMF and the World Bank pushed the democratic regimes of both Benazir Bhutto and Nawaz Sharif to impose stabilization and structural adjustment programs that contributed significantly to the rise in poverty and inequality as well as a fall in the growth rate.[18] As one respected Pakistani economist noted: "The almost obsessive concern with short-term macroeconomic stabilization has with it the danger . . . that some of our basic social programs might be affected, and this would have inter-generational consequences on development in Pakistan."[19] Since democracy became associated with a rise in poverty and economic stagnation, it is not surprising that the coup was viewed with relief by most Pakistanis, from both the middle classes and the working masses.

THE CRISIS OF AMERICAN DEMOCRACY

Sensitive to the legitimacy question, the Clinton administration made promoting democracy and "enlarging the community of free nations" the rhetorical centerpiece of its policy toward the global South, along with a reemphasis on multilateralism.[20] Not taking the ideological dimension seriously would invite trouble, said Clinton's deputy secretary of State Strobe Talbott, because the "American people have never accepted traditional geopolitics or pure balance of power calculations as sufficient reason to expand national treasure or to dispatch American soldiers to foreign lands."[21] But twenty years of Washington's cultivation of dictatorships left millions skeptical. Moreover, the Democrats undermined their stated objectives when they advocated free-market globalization as their principal foreign policy, since globalization entailed intensifying the ongoing processes of liberalization and adjustment that were already undermining democratic regimes in the South.

But there was a new feature to this Third World skepticism. Orthodox "democracy studies" continued to evaluate the governments of the South according to whether they lived up to the standards of democratic practice in the West. But people in the South were wondering if those political practices were really worth emulating. Something was rotten back home in the U.S. of A.

Democracy showed symptoms of decay even in its self-proclaimed homeland. The influence of powerful interest groups, which the Washington style of electoral competition institutionalized, reached massive proportions. In the 1980s and 1990s, increasing numbers of Americans came to recognize that their liberal democracy had been so thoroughly corrupted by corporate money that it might better be described as a plutocracy. Indeed, as the liberal columnist William Pfaff noted, "Nothing on the scale of the American system of political expenditure and influence exists anywhere."[22]

Charges that the government seemed accountable to no one surfaced at both ends of the political spectrum. As the conservative writer Fareed Zakaria observed, "The American people believe that they have no real control over government. What they do not realize is that the politicians have no control, either. Most representatives and senators believe that they operate in a political system in which any serious attempts at change produce instant, well-organized opposition from the small minority who are hurt by the change. And it is these minorities who really run Washington."[23] Campaign finance reform propelled the candidacy of Arizona senator John McCain, who made a strong run for the Republican nomination in the spring of 2000. In the same year, the overbearing influence of corporate money was the issue on which the progressive consumer activist Ralph Nader ran the most vigorous third-party candidacy in years.

The corrupting role of corporate money in political life was one symptom of a gathering crisis whose dimensions included racial tensions masked as a problem of law and order, the most lopsided distribution of income in the industrial world, an increasingly bitter cultural war between right-wing fundamentalists and liberals, and the growing power of the unaccountable national security establishment. The last phenomenon is worth singling out. It suggested that traditional democratic procedures could no longer deal with the realities of power. While in classic Montesquieuan fashion, Congress and the executive were busy checkmating each other on the issue of Clinton's sexual mores, neither branch was able to cope with the accumulation of authority by the Pentagon. As a consequence, Pfaff pointed out, the "military is already the most powerful institution in American government, in practice largely unaccountable to the executive branch. Now the armed forces are setting the limits of American foreign policy. . . . The United States is not yet 18th-century Prussia, when the military owned the state, [but] the threat is more serious than most Americans realize."[24]

While this may seem to be an exaggeration, it is worth noting that Donald Rumsfeld felt compelled to declare, upon assuming the post of secretary of defense, that his mission was to "reinstitute civilian control of the military."[25] Certainly, when it came to foreign policy, the regional commanders in chief (CINCs) "grew into a powerful force in U.S. foreign policy because of the disproportionate weight of their resources and organization in relation to the assets and influence of other parts of America's foreign policy structure—in particular, the State Department, which was shriveling in size, stature, and spirit even as the military's role expanded."[26]

What really shocked Americans, as well as citizens of developing countries, however, was the presidential election of 2000. In violation of the fundamental democratic dictum of majority rule, the majority's choice—Al Gore, the man who won the popular vote by a not insignificant 540,000 votes, a margin of victory greater than Richard Nixon's in 1968 and five times that of John F. Kennedy in 1960[27]—failed to became chief executive. The outcome revealed the Electoral College to be what New York University law professor Ronald Dworkin described as an "anachronistic and dangerous eighteenth-century" system designed precisely to prevent the direct election of the president and vice president and to insulate the system from the allegedly unhealthy consequences of a process that had become normal in most other democracies.[28]

The circumstances surrounding the vote in the disputed counties in Florida symbolized the effective disenfranchisement of poor people. When the Republican appointees who constituted the majority on the Supreme Court stopped the Florida recount, it was as clear to the rest of the world as to many Americans that the country's democratic heritage had suffered a damaging blow.[29] What many southern nations had long suspected seemed to be confirmed. Daniel Lazare's commentary on the loss of credibility and moral stature of the U.S. democratic system was hardly exaggerated:

> "The U.S. may be the most technologically advanced country but our electoral system is any day better," observed M. S. Gill, India's chief election commissioner, on the heels of the Florida fiasco. But then, scores of other electoral systems are better as

well. As a joke making the rounds of the Third World had it, perhaps it would be up to Haiti (or Russia, Serbia, Mozambique, etc.) to send observers to the United States to see to it that the governor of Florida did not again steal the election on his brother's behalf. In parts of the world where the natives are used to hanging their heads in shame whenever Jimmy Carter or Madeleine Albright lectures them on their democratic shortcomings, the schadenfreude was running at high tide.[30]

THE CRISIS OF THE LIBERAL ORDER

The U.S. system, many of its admirers remind us, is not merely rule by the majority but a distinctively liberal form of democracy. "Constitutional liberalism," according to Zakaria, "is about the limitation of power; democracy is about its accumulation and use."[31] Maintaining a healthy tension between the two principles is said to be the key to the vitality of the democratic system. If the election of 2000 discredited the "democracy" in U.S. liberal democracy, the post-September 11 events threw into question the other half of that equation.

The Patriot Act, passed in October 2001, gave the federal government sweeping powers to conduct the war against terror—so sweeping, in fact, that they placed constitutionally guaranteed rights in dire jeopardy. The act, among other things, permitted secret break-ins by federal agents, allowed them to access the most personal information about citizens, including financial records, and granted broad authority to monitor individuals' phone calls and Internet use.[32]

Outrage at the Patriot Act mainly came from liberals and progressives. However, opposition from conservative quarters was not absent. In a biting criticism, Andrew Napolitano, a former Superior Court judge who now serves as the senior judicial analyst of the right-wing Fox News Channel, wrote in the *Wall Street Journal:*

> The U.S. Constitution prohibits invasions of privacy by the government by denying it the power to engage in unreasonable searches and seizures absent a warrant issued upon probable cause. Prior to September 11, 2001, Americans could actually

enjoy that right. But in October 2001, the Patriot Act changed all this. In addition to other violations of the Constitution which it purports to sanction, the Act authorizes intelligence agencies to give what they obtain without probable cause to prosecutors; and it authorizes prosecutors to use the information thus received in ordinary criminal prosecutions. Even worse, the custodians of the records are now prohibited from telling you that your records were sought or surrendered.[33]

Opinion in liberal quarters echoed the same concerns. Harvard professor Elaine Scarry characterized the Patriot Act as "a gigantic license to search and seize that violates the Fourth Amendment."[34] Comparing the act to the pre-Revolutionary Writs of Assistance issued by the British Crown to enable royal officers to search houses at will for smuggled goods, Scarry claims that the "Patriot Act is a many-page-long permission slip to search and seize everywhere and anywhere for four years and beyond, guided not by court-validated standards but by Justice Department hunches and racially inflected intuitions."[35]

While posing a threat to the constitutional rights of all Americans, moreover, the Patriot Act undermines the rights of noncitizens in particular—an issue of great concern to countries in the South. For instance, Section 412 allows the incarceration of noncitizens for seven days without charge and "for six-month periods indefinitely without access to counsel" if the attorney general "determines release would endanger either the country or individual persons." This provision is bad enough, but the reality is, in fact, worse, since various loopholes in the law release the executive from the seven-day constraint, allowing the Attorney General, according to Michael McCarthy, to "detain indefinitely not only those convicted of crimes or immigration offenses . . . but also any person the Attorney General has reasonable grounds to believe is a terrorist or is engaged in any other activity that endangers the national security."[36]

What Congress refused to provide in the Patriot Act, the government has seized by executive fiat. The While House has asserted its right to detain indefinitely anyone, citizen or noncitizen, whom it deems an "enemy combatant." In the Bush administration, the Patriot Act, an all-embracing extension of executive privilege, and a disdain for international law have combined to create systematic violations of traditionally recognized human rights. While the annual State Department Human Rights report castigates southern governments for human rights abuses, in the three years since September 11, the U.S. government has done the following:

- launched a massive manhunt to track down eight thousand young Muslim men on no other basis than their religious affiliation;
- expanded the use of wiretaps, secret searches, and collection of personal information;
- sought to establish secret military tribunals to try non-U.S. citizens;
- allowed the use of secret evidence, in immigration proceedings, that noncitizens could not confront or rebut;
- gave the Justice Department the authority to overrule immigration judges;
- destroyed the secrecy of the client-lawyer relationship by allowing the government to listen into conversations;
- institutionalized racial and ethnic profiling;
- established concentration camps where "enemy combatants" who were not legally classified as prisoners of war were indefinitely incarcerated, with no access to counsel and no assurance that they were covered by the Geneva Conventions regarding the treatment of captives; and
- engaged in torture and other forms of abuse to extract information, in Abu Ghraib and other detention centers, in violation of the Geneva Conventions, the Torture Convention, the U.S. Torture Statute, and the U.S. War Crimes Act.

ABU GHRAIB AND THE END OF THE MORAL MISSION

The perspective that ultimately sanctioned the hellhole of Abu Ghraib was contained in an opinion drafted for George W. Bush by his lawyer Alberto Gonzales, who told the president that the war on terror "is unique, that it renders obsolete Geneva's strict limitations on questioning of enemy prisoners and renders quaint some of its provisions."[37] With the administration hesitant to assert definitively whether or not "enemy combatants" were covered by the Geneva Conventions, no clear rules could be formulated on how to treat them, especially for the purpose of extracting information. Then the national security establishment fatefully crossed the line from interrogation to torture and systemic abuse.

While the Bush administration tried to describe these acts and paint the abuses at Abu Ghraib as the work of a few enlisted men and women, the events at Abu Ghraib and elsewhere were seen by many Americans and the rest of the world as systematic acts of torture that undermined the credibility of the nation's moral mission to liberate and democratize Iraq.

CONCLUSION

The Bush administration has been nothing if not bold. It cast itself as the leader of an imperial democracy. That is to say, it conceals neither its imperial ambitions nor its missionary zeal to implant democracy in what it considers "benighted regions" of the world, especially the Middle East. But the Abu Ghraib horrors shredded whatever legitimacy still attached to the American imperial enterprise. The chief of Central Command, John Abizaid, said that Abu Ghraib was a "defeat for the U.S. Army."[38] But it was more than that. It was a profound ideological defeat as well.

The good opinion of mankind no longer held America in high regard, thanks to its misadventure in Iraq. A prominent U.S. ally in Latin America, former Mexican foreign minister Jorge Castañeda, noted that "America's friends . . . are feeling the fire of this anti-American wrath. They are finding themselves forced to shift their own rhetoric and attitude in order to dampen their defense of policies viewed as pro-American or U.S.-inspired, and to stiffen their resistance to Washington's demands and desires."[39]

For many in the developing world, the trends in the United States were all too clear. After September 11, America and other Western countries seemed headed away from liberal democracy. Indeed, they were taking on a disturbing likeness to some of the regimes so long derided by Western theorists. In the view of the philosopher Richard Rorty:

> At the end of this process of erosion, democracy [in the United States and Europe] would have been replaced by something quite different. This would probably be neither military dictator-

ship nor Orwellian totalitarianism, but rather a relatively benevolent despotism, imposed by what would gradually become a hereditary nomenklatura.

That sort of power structure survived the end of the Soviet Union and is now resolidifying under Putin and his fellow KGB alumni. The same structure seems to be taking shape in China and in Southeast Asia. In countries run in this way, public opinion does not greatly matter. Elections may still be held, but opposition parties are not allowed to pose any serious threat to the powers that be. Careers are less open to talent, and more dependent on connections with powerful persons. Since the courts and police review boards are relatively powerless, it is often necessary for shopkeepers to pay protection money to the police, or to criminals tolerated by the police, in order to stay in business. It is dangerous for citizens to complain about corruption or about abuse of power by public officials. High culture is restricted to areas that are irrelevant to politics. . . . No more uncensored media. No more student demonstrations. Not much in the way of civil society. In short, a return to something like the Ancien Regime, with the national security establishment of each country playing the role of the court at Versailles.[40]

This is a bleak, nearly dystopian vision, not yet applicable to the United States. But as empire eats away at the foundations of democracy, no one can be confident about the future. Indeed, the reelection of Bush and the emergence of a more right-wing House of Representatives and Senate promised an acceleration of legal and administrative efforts to curtail traditional liberties in the name of security. There is one certainty: U.S. democracy, celebrated by liberal writers like Joseph Nye, as the main source of Washington's "soft power," has long ceased to be a model for the rest of the world.

CONCLUSION

The Way Forward

DECLINE AND OPPORTUNITY

Although the idea may have been unimaginable just a few years ago, the empire is now on the defensive on almost every front. Once regarded by an arrogant Washington elite as a walkover, Iraq has become the Achilles heel of the American imperium.

So what does the future hold? Despite Bush's victory in the 2004 presidential election—or perhaps because of it—the empire will continue to unravel, but not all of a sudden. Yet an unraveling there will be, and it will entail a multidimensional weakening of the economic, political, and ideological foundations of the imperial undertaking.

THE ECONOMICS OF IMPERIAL DECLINE

The crisis of overproduction and overcapacity will continue to haunt the global economy. Financial crises will increase in number and intensity. These will eat away at the leading role of the U.S. economy.

The United States is likely to remain the dominant power over the next two decades. In terms of relative economic strength, however, the nation is on the decline. Analysts estimate that, barring a massive downturn or a political catastrophe, China will have an economy larger than that of the United States perhaps within two or three decades, and one 50 percent larger by 2050.[1]

Moreover, as a result of the country's industrial overcapacity and large inflows of speculative capital, growth will remain heavily dependent on the financial sector. Right now, the United States and Europe may be fighting for each other's markets, but the former is, as Jeffrey Sachs points out, in "deep and growing debt to Asia."[2] In their efforts to prop up the value of the dollar so as to keep their currencies and products competitive in the U.S. market, Asian governments are hoarding U.S. currency and Treasury bills. Japan's foreign exchange reserves now come to $750 billion, much of it in Treasury bills. And together, China, Hong Kong, India, Korea, Singapore, and Taiwan have another $1.1 trillion in reserves.[3]

America will continue to decline economically because the global framework for transnational capitalist cooperation to which the WTO is central is eroding. Bilateral and regional trade arrangements are likely to proliferate. But the most dynamic hookups may not be those that integrate weak economies with one superpower, like the United States or the European Union. Regional economic collaborations among Third World countries—or, in the parlance of development economics, "South-South cooperation"—are the wave of the future. Such alliances as Mercosur in Latin America, the Association of Southeast Asian Nations (ASEAN), and the Group of 20 will increasingly embody the key lessons that developing countries have learned over the last 25 years: that trade policy must be subordinated to development; that technology must be liberated from stringent intellectual property rules; that capital controls are necessary; that development demands not less but more state intervention; and, above all, that the weak must hang together or they will hang separately—this was the lesson of Cancún and Miami, and it will not be forgotten despite the setback at the WTO meeting in Geneva in July 2004.

Economic competition between the EU and the United States is bound to intensify. More and more, governments will protect and subsidize their own industries and keep out regional or national competitors like Microsoft, the U.S. steel industry, and Airbus. The transatlantic balance of corporate power is shifting, according to Charles Kupchan:

> Airbus (a French, German, British, Italian, and Spanish conglomerate) has already passed Boeing as the world's number one supplier of civilian aircraft. The largest maker of cell phones in the world is Finland's Nokia, well ahead of America's Motorola. After years of U.S. corporations acquiring foreign companies,

the tables are turning. In 2000, British and French corporations ranked ahead of their American counterparts in terms of the aggregate value of their international acquisitions. Germany has also been coming on strong. Bertelsmann is the largest book publisher in the world, having bought Random House and other prominent U.S. houses. Daimler Benz acquired Chrysler in 1998 and Deutsche Telekom purchased VoiceStream in May 2001.[4]

Competition between Japan and the United States has been muted in recent years. But it is likely to heat up again with Japan's economic recovery and renewed efforts in Washington to do away with what trade negotiators call the "structural impediments" (such as Japan's mom-and-pop stores) to U.S. penetration of the Japanese market.

Together with Japan, Europe, and, increasingly, China, Washington will find it necessary to maintain its current beggar-my-neighbor policies not only in trade but in exchange rates. Most probably, exchange rate warfare will become a permanent fixture of the international economy. In the years to come, policies originating in enlightened self-interest—such as the strong dollar maintained by the Clinton-Rubin regime—are likely to be a rarity.

Among the developing countries, China is, of course, in a category by itself. Indeed, China is one of the winners of the Bush era. On key economic and political conflicts, it has managed to be on the side of everybody and thus on the side of nobody but China. As the United States has become ensnared in wars without end, China has deftly maneuvered to stay free of entangling commitments, the better to pursue rapid growth, technological prowess, and political stability.

The diplomatic skills of the Chinese leadership, based on the principle that nations have no permanent friends but only permanent interests, have been highly successful, as witness Beijing's achievements on the economic front. Although the Chinese have joined the WTO, they're likely to bend the rules and get away with it. The Chinese as well as the WTO know that in its current state of disarray, the organization needs China more than China needs the WTO. Beijing is a charter member of the Group of 20, yet it has encouraged Brasília to act as the leader of the alliance, making sure, among other things, that Brazil, not China, draws flak from Washington. Furthermore, the Chinese have toned down their propaganda attacks on the United States over Taiwan, preferring, instead, to point to the "mutual benefit" expanded economic ties between the two nations are likely to deliver. And yet, at strategic points, they have not hesitated to cash in their chips, as they did in February 2004, when the Taiwanese government's plan to hold a referendum on independence was slapped down by none other than George W. Bush himself, during a state visit to Washington by Chinese prime minister Hu Jintao.

THE IDEOLOGICAL DILEMMA

Ideologically, claims by the United States that it is building democracy in the global South will sound increasingly hollow as its own political system shows signs of becoming authoritarian, especially as it pursues the war against terror. Elections are apt to be determined even more by contributions from powerful, wealthy groups and individuals. Overseas, American elites may recommend dropping all the democratic rhetoric so as not to be judged by it. Many will be attracted to George Kennan's classic espousal of a hard-nosed foreign policy:

> [W]e would be better off to dispense now with a number of concepts which have underlined our thinking. . . . We should dispense with the aspiration to "be liked" or to be regarded as the repository of a high-minded altruism. We should stop putting ourselves in the position of being our brother's keeper and refrain from offering moral and ideological advice. We should cease to talk about vague and . . . unreal objectives such as human rights, the raising of living standards, and democratization. The day is not far off when we are going to have to deal in straight power concepts. The less we are hampered by idealistic slogans, the better.[5]

With George Bush opting for the hard-boiled realist Condoleeza Rice as his second secretary of state, there is a possibility that idealistic slogans might indeed be jettisoned.

The problem, of course, is that an American empire without its democratic rationale would be fragile indeed and perhaps impossible to sustain. An imperial elite that dispenses with the myth of extending democracy must face the loss of popular support at home. Unlike the Roman Empire, the United States never developed the mechanism of extending citizenship to win the loyalty of those it subjugated. Unlike the traditional colonial powers, it cannot follow the advice of Kennan—and Henry Kissinger—to deal in "straight power concepts." Washington is stuck with its democratic messianism at a time when the rest of the world sees it as sheer hypocrisy.

CONTINUING OVERSTRETCH

Militarily, there is no doubt that Washington will retain absolute superiority in all the gross indices of military might, such as nuclear warheads, conventional weaponry, and aircraft carriers. But the ability to transform military power into effective intervention will decline. The Iraq syndrome is here to stay. Both nuclear and conventional power, including airpower, will be as useful as a sledgehammer in swatting flies. Ground troops will continue to be the key, and troop deployments against motivated insurgents in far-flung reaches of the empire will simply not fly with an increasingly skeptical public.

Thus, geopolitically, the crisis of overextension will intensify. Iraq has already been branded with the Q word—*quagmire*—and the rest of the Middle East may follow suit. Even as insurgents grind down the U.S. military machine in Iraq and Afghanistan, the battle to expel American troops from Saudi Arabia will begin in earnest. Washington's isolation in a radicalized Islamic world will deepen because of its inability to detach itself from Israel's Likud Party. And as the war turns against Washington, the pro-U.S. regimes in Jordan, Egypt, and Tunisia will lose what little public support they have left.

Political rebellion against Washington and neoliberal economics will gain strength throughout Latin America. So far the unrest has led to victory through the ballot box, as in Brazil, Ecuador, Uruguay, and Argentina. Hugo Chavez's tremendous victory in a referendum on his rule in August 2004 was an electoral slap not only to the Venezuelan right but to the latter's backers in Washington as well. But successful uprisings against U.S.-allied regimes, such as the one that ousted the government of Gonzalo Sánchez de Lozada in Bolivia, might become less rare. What is certain is that to survive politically, even conservative elites must adopt anti-American postures.

As China injects a new diplomatic dynamic into East Asian affairs, the United States will find it more difficult to maintain military bases in South Korea and Japan. The foreign policy establishment will see the emerging power on the Asian landmass as a strategic threat, however, and the Pentagon's unwillingness to close the bases will only increase the dangers of conventional or nuclear confrontation with China.

In Southeast Asia, notably Indonesia, Malaysia, the Philippines, and Thailand, Islamic movements will increasingly challenge the regimes in power, some of which, like those in Thailand and the Philippines, are allied to Washington in the war against terror. Such movements are likely to make common cause with the secular left, whose goal is to promote economic justice and national sovereignty, that will revive in societies that, no longer tiger economies, face worsening poverty, inequality, and economic stagnation. Whether peaceful or violent, these insurgencies may put even greater pressure on Washington to deploy ground troops in support of beleaguered allies.

However, in the imperial heartland, the disastrous experience in Iraq will create major roadblocks for the hegemonic project. Even Bush and his clique will be hesitant to translate their recent electoral victory into more imperial adventures. Support will falter for prolonged ground-troop interventions, even for police missions like drug interdiction in, say, Colombia or Bolivia. Indeed, the immediate problem will be to deal with protest marches, from New York to California, demanding the withdrawal of troops from existing areas of deployment like Saudi Arabia, the Balkans, and the Philippines.

If, as may well be the case, isolationism captures the mood of the country, the imperial elite would be hard-pressed to undertake new foreign adventures. Although neoconservatives will prattle, predictably, about "anarchy" or "vacuums of power," the retreat of imperial hubris would be good for the world. Indeed, imperial retreat would allow the nations of the South to breathe, maneuver, and develop along the lines of their own choosing. A weakened Bretton Woods–WTO system, for instance, coupled with the strengthening of such institutions as the UN Conference on Trade and Development, the International Labor Organization, regional economic blocs, and multilateral environmental agreements, would create a more pluralistic world, with multiple checks and balances, that will enhance the economic, political, and cultural flowering of societies that have long been under the thumb of the United States.

There is no blueprint for sustained peace. But we can say, nevertheless, that a weakened empire is a precondition for the effective functioning of the United Nations as a true community of nations relating to one another as equals. Under imperialism, the rules favoring one group of countries at the expense of the majority breed instability and resentment. A weakened imperial center would create the conditions for the phasing out of global double standards. Such hypocrisy—for instance, the tacit understanding that it is legitimate for the United States and the other big powers to maintain nuclear arsenals but it is illegitimate for others to do so—is a fundamental cause of international conflict. In the medium and long term, equality and peaceful intercourse among nations go together.

But the crisis of the empire bodes well not only for the rest of the world. It may also benefit the people of the United States. It opens up the possibility of Americans relating to other peoples as equals and not as masters. Failure of the empire is, moreover, a precondition for the reemergence of a democratic republic. That was the American promise before it was hijacked by imperial democracy.

NOTES

Introduction: A Southern Perspective on the Crisis of Empire

1. Walden Bello, "Endless War," *Focus on Trade*, no. 67, Sept. 2001.
2. Walden Bello, "Pax Romana versus Pax Americana: Contrasting Strategies of Imperial Management," *Foreign Policy in Focus*, Interhemispheric Resource Center, May 12, 2003.

Chapter 1: The Road to Baghdad

1. Ivo Daalder and James Lindsay, "Bush's Flawed Revolution," *The American Prospect*, Nov. 2003, p. 43.
2. G. John Ikenberry, "Imperial Ambitions," in Andrew Bacevich, ed., *The Imperial Tense* (Chicago: Ivan R. Dee, 2003), p. 188.
3. G. John Ikenberry, "Multilateralism and U.S. Grand Strategy," in Stewart Patrick and Shepard Forman, eds., *Multilateralism and U.S. Foreign Policy* (Boulder: Lynne Rienner, 2002), p. 130.
4. Quoted in Thomas Powers, *The Man Who Kept the Secrets* (New York: Pocket Books, 1979), p. 250.
5. Stewart Patrick, "Multilateralism and Its Discontents: The Causes and Consequences of U.S. Ambivalence," in Patrick and Forman, p. 13.
6. Cited in Department of Defense, *United States Security Strategy for the East Asia Pacific Region* (Washington: Office of International Security Affairs, Feb. 1995), p. 13.
7. Larry Niksch, *Regional Security Consultative Organizations in East Asia and Their Implications for the United States*, CRS Report for Congress (Washington: Congressional Research Service, Jan. 14, 1994), pp. 13–14.
8. Robert Tucker, "The Future of a Contradiction," *The National Interest*, no. 43 (Spring 1996), p. 26.
9. John Newhouse, *Imperial America: The Bush Assault on the World Order* (New York: Knopf, 2003), p. 112.

10. Ruth Wedgwood, "Unilateral Action in a Multilateral World," in Patrick and Forman, p. 183.
11. *Ibid.*, p. 185.
12. Tucker, p. 26.
13. See Walden Bello, "U.S. Imperialism in the Asia-Pacific," *Peace Review*, vol. 10, no. 3 (Sept. 1998), pp. 367–73.
14. George Kennan, "The Sources of Soviet Conduct," *Foreign Affairs*, July 1947; reprinted in Thomas Etzold and James Gaddis, eds., *Containment: Documents on American Policy and Strategy* (New York: Columbia University Press, 1978), p. 87.
15. U.S. National Security Council, "United States Objectives and Programs for National Security," NSC 68, Apr. 14, 1950, in Etzold and Gaddis, p. 441.
16. Kissinger wrote: "The late 1960's had marked the end of the period of American dominance based on overwhelming nuclear and economic supremacy. The Soviet nuclear stockpile was inevitably approaching parity. The economic strength of Europe and Japan was bound to lead them to seek larger political influence. The new, developing nations pressed their claims to greater power and participation. The United States would have to learn to base its foreign policy on premises analogous to those on which other nations conducted theirs. Still the strongest nation in the world but no longer preeminent, we would have to take seriously the world balance of power, for it tilted against us and might prove irreversible." Kissinger, *Years of Upheaval* (Boston: Little, Brown, 1977), p. 238.
17. Jerry Sanders, "Breaking Out of the Containment Syndrome," *World Policy Journal*, vol. 1, no. 1 (Fall 1983), p. 113.
18. *Ibid.*
19. As one conservative analyst observed, "It was not the Carter administration that concluded the first SALT agreements within the terms of which the Soviet Union was able by 1977 to develop a clearly superior counterforce capability. Nor was it the Carter administration that inaugurated détente in 1972 and claimed that in doing so it had laid the foundations of a stable and lasting structure of peace.... These were the actions of the predecessors of the present [Nixon] administration. In their effects, they compromised American interests and power to an extent we can only now fully appreciate." Robert Tucker, *The Purposes of American Power* (New York: Praeger, 1981), pp. 7–8.
20. Richard Pipes, "How to Cope with the Soviet Threat: A Long-Term Strategy for the West," *Commentary*, Aug. 1984, p. 14.
21. Strobe Talbott, *Deadly Gambits: The Reagan Administration and the Stalemate in Nuclear Arms* (New York: Knopf, 1984), p. 16, note 61.
22. John Mearsheimer, *The Tragedy of Great Power Politics* (New York: Norton, 2001), p. 227.
23. Caspar Weinberger, *Annual Report to the Congress for FY 1983* (Washington: Government Printing Office, 1982), p. 1–15.

24. John Lehman, "Rebirth of a U.S. Naval Strategy," *Strategic Review*, Summer 1981, p. 13.

25. Edward Luck, "The United States, International Organizations, and the Quest for Legitimacy," in Patrick and Forman, p. 62.

26. Quoted in Jan Nederveen Pieterse, *Globalization or Empire* (New York: Routledge, 2004), p. 21.

27. *Ibid.*, p. 23.

28. Senate Armed Services Committee, *Department of Defense Authorization for Appropriations for FY 1985*, Hearings, Part 2 (Washington: Government Printing Office, 1984), p. 919.

29. Jeffrey Record, "Limited War, Limited Means," *Baltimore Sun*, Aug. 3, 1984, p. 13.

30. As summed up in Philip Bobbitt, *The Shield of Achilles* (London: Penguin, 2003), p. 297.

31. Andrew Bacevich, *American Empire: The Reality and Consequences of U.S. Diplomacy* (Cambridge: Harvard University Press, 2002), p. 59.

32. Bobbitt, p. 248.

33. *Ibid.*, p. 341.

34. Quoted in Bacevich, *American Empire*, p. 96.

35. *Ibid.*, p. 88.

36. *Ibid.*, p. 31.

37. Princeton Lyman, "The Growing Influence of Domestic Factors," in Patrick and Forman, p. 77.

38. *Ibid.*, p. 78.

39. Cover story, *Time*, Feb. 15, 1999.

40. Strobe Talbott, "Democracy and the National Interest," *Foreign Affairs*, Nov.–Dec. 1996, p. 57.

41. Anthony Lake, quoted in Bacevich, *American Empire*, p. 99.

42. Quoted in David Halberstam, *War in a Time of Peace* (New York: Scribner, 2001), p. 265.

43. Bacevich, *American Empire*, p. 157.

44. David Shearer, *Private Armies and Military Intervention*, Adelphi Paper 316 (London: Oxford University Press, 1998), quoted in Bacevich, *American Empire*, p. 165.

45. Bobbitt, pp. 297–98.

46. Lawrence Korb, "Rumsfeld's Folly," *The American Prospect*, Nov. 2003, p. 49.

47. Halberstam, pp. 40–42.

48. Bobbitt, p. 298.

49. Madeleine Albright, *Madam Secretary: A Memoir* (New York: Macmillan, 2003), p. 182.

50. Bacevich, *American Empire*, p. 163.

51. Ikenberry, "Multilateralism and U.S. Grand Strategy," pp. 134–35.

52. Halberstam, p. 445.

53. Robert Pape, "The True Worth of Air Power," *Foreign Affairs*, Mar.–Apr. 2004, pp. 116–17.
54. Halberstam, p. 457.
55. Quoted in Albright, p. 421.
56. Pape, p. 125.
57. Michael Mandelbaum, "A Perfect Failure," *Foreign Affairs*, Sept.–Oct. 1999, p. 6.
58. Bacevich, *American Empire,* p. 104.
59. *Ibid.*, p. 105.
60. Quoted in Bobbitt, p. 249.
61. Philip Bobbitt, "Better than Empire" <http://www.gavinsblog.com/mt/archives/00895.html>.
62. *Ibid.*
63. Mandelbaum, p. 5.
64. Hans Binnendijk and Richard Kugler, "Revising the Two-Major Theater War Standard," *Strategic Forum,* no. 179 (Apr. 2001), p. 1.
65. Korb, p. 49.
66. Binnendijk and Kugler, pp. 1–2.
67. Quoted in Daalder and Lindsay, p. 43.
68. Ron Suskind, *The Price of Loyalty: George W. Bush, the White House, and the Education of Paul O'Neill* (New York: Simon and Schuster, 2004), p. 75.
69. Newhouse.
70. Nederveen Pieterse, p. 22.
71. Quoted in Alex Callinicos, *The New Mandarins of American Power* (Cambridge: Polity Press, 2003), pp. 45–46.
72. Newhouse, pp. 32–34.
73. *Ibid.*, p. 31.
74. Callinicos, p. 47.
75. *Ibid.*, p. 45.
76. Newhouse, p. 22.
77. Patricia Greve, "Neoconservative Ideas and Foreign Policy in the Administration of George Bush," American Institute for Contemporary German Studies, Jan. 23, 2004.
78. Nederveen Pieterse, p. 22.
79. Elizabeth Drew, "The Neocons in Power," *New York Review of Books,* June 12, 2003, p. 20.
80. *Ibid.*
81. Drew, p. 20; Greve.
82. Drew, p. 20.
83. Callinicos, p. 48.
84. Suskind, p. 293.
85. Daalder and Lindsay, p. 43.
86. Callinicos, p. 45.
87. Newhouse, p. 15.

88. *Ibid.*

89. Michael Mann, *Incoherent Empire* (London: Verso, 2003), p. 207.

90. Bush was investigated by the Securities and Exchange Commission for possible insider trading in a 1990 deal in which he sold his stocks for $848,560. See James Ridgeway, "George Bush, Failed Corporate Crook," *Village Voice,* July 10–16, 2002 <http://www.villagevoice.com/issues/0228/ridgeway.php>.

91. Nicholas Guyatt, *Another American Century* (London: Zed, 2000), p. 117.

92. Pratap Chaterjee, "Halliburton Makes a Killing on Iraq War," *Corpwatch,* Mar. 20, 2003 <http://www.corpwatch.org/issues/PID.jsp?articeid=6008>.

93. Bacevich, *American Empire,* pp. 159–65. See also "Notes from the Editor," *Monthly Review,* May 2004.

94. Drew, p. 22.

95. Newhouse, p. 29.

96. Harvey Morris, "How Power Was Shifted in Israel's Favor," *Financial Times,* Mar. 2004.

97. Office of the President, *National Security Strategy of the United States* (Washington: Sept. 17, 2002).

98. Quoted in Margaret P. Karns and Karen Mingst, "The United States as 'Deadbeat'? U.S. Policy and the UN Financial Crisis," in Patrick and Forman, p. 276.

99. Office of the President, *National Security Strategy of the United States,* Sept. 17, 2002.

100. *Ibid.*

101. Quoted in Bobbitt, "Better than Empire."

102. Tom Barry, "Hegemony to Imperium," *Foreign Policy in Focus,* Sept. 26, 2002 <http://www.globalpolicy.org/wtc/analysis/2002/0926hege.htm>.

103. Newhouse, pp. 14–15.

Chapter 2: Imperial Hubris/Imperial Overextension

1. Anthony Hall, *The American Empire and the Fourth World* (Montreal and Kingston: McGill-Queen's University Press, 2003), p. xxi.

2. "America Adrift in Iraq," *New York Times,* May 15, 2004 <http://www.nytimes.com/2004/05/15/opinion/15SAT1.html>.

3. *Ibid.*

4. James Fallows, "The Hollow Army," *The Atlantic Monthly,* Mar. 2004, p. 29.

5. Richard Clarke, *Against All Enemies: Inside America's War on Terror* (London: Simon and Schuster, 2004), p. 271.

6. William Arkin, "Not a Magic Bullet," Opinion section, *Los Angeles Times,* Feb. 22, 2004, p. M6.

7. Anthony Blinken, "From Preemption to Engagement," *Survival,* vol. 45, no. 4 (Winter 2003–04), p. 45.

8. Quoted in John Newhouse, *Imperial America: The Bush Assault on the World Order* (New York: Knopf, 2003), p. 29.

9. Philip Gordon, "Bush's Middle East Vision," *Survival*, vol. 45, no. 1 (Spring 2003), p. 159.

10. *Ibid.*

11. Quoted in Elizabeth Drew, "The Neocons in Power," *New York Review of Books*, June 12, 2003, p. 22.

12. *Ibid.*

13. Lawrence Korb, "Rumsfeld's Folly," *The American Prospect*, Nov. 2003, p. 50.

14. Harvey Morris, "How Power Was Shifted in Israel's Favor," *Financial Times*, Mar. 2004.

15. *Ibid.*

16. Stephen Kinzer, "Regime Change: The Legacy," *The American Prospect*, Nov. 2003, p. 42.

17. Clarke, pp. 265–66.

18. Jeffrey Sachs, "America's Disastrous Energy Plan," *Financial Times*, Dec. 23, 2003 <http://www.earthinstitute.columbia.edu/about/director/pubs/ft122303.pdf>.

19. *Ibid.*

20. Quoted in David Usborne, "WMD Just a Convenient Excuse for War, Admits Wolfowitz," reproduced in *Independent Digital*, in *Truthout*, May 31, 2003 <http://www.truthout.org/docs[ru5]03.html>.

21. Quoted in George Wright, "Wolfowitz: Iraq War about Oil?" *Guardian*, June 5, 2003, reproduced in *Truthout* <http://www.truthout.org/docs_03.html>.

22. Chalmers Johnson, *The Sorrows of Empire: Militarism, Secrecy, and the End of the Republic* (New York: Metropolitan Books, 2004), pp. 183–85.

23. *Ibid.*, pp. 175–85.

24. Patrick Seale, "Is China the Reason for America's Obsession with Iraq?" *Daily Star* (Lebanon), Nov. 25, 2002 <http://sea2fd.sea2.hotmail,msn.com/cgi-bin/getmsg?msg=MSG1038928549.16>.

25. Quoted in Usborne.

26. Ellen Meiksins Wood, *The Empire of Capital* (New Delhi: LeftWord Books, 2003), pp. 144–45.

27. Charles Clover, "The Fighters of Falluja," *FT Magazine*, no. 52 (Apr. 24, 2004), p. 21.

28. *Ibid.*

29. Quoted in Rory McCarthy, "Uneasy Truce in the City of Ghosts," *Guardian*, Apr. 24, 2004.

30. Quoted in Kim Sengupta, "1,700 Extra Troops Could Be Sent to Iraq to Replace Spaniards," *Independent*, Apr. 23, 2004.

31. Jayson Keyser, "U.S. Marines to End Siege of Fallujah," Associated Press, Apr. 29, 2004 <http://story.news.yahoo.com/news?tmpl=story&u=/ap/20040429/ap_on_re_mi_ea/iraq>.

32. Peter Spiegel, "Increase in Troops for Iraq Stretches U.S. Army," *Financial Times*, Apr. 24–25, 2004, p. 6.

33. Charles Clover, "Paul Bremer, a Broker, Not a Fighter," *Financial Times*, Apr. 10–11, 2004, p. 7.

34. Naomi Klein, "The Battle the U.S. Wants to Provoke," *Guardian,* Apr. 6, 2004 <http://www.guardian.co.uk/columnists/column/html>.

35. Fareed Zakaria, "Our Last Real Chance," *Newsweek,* Apr. 19–26, 2004, p. 28.

36. Walden Bello, "The Stalemate in Iraq and the Global Peace Movement," *Focus on Trade,* no. 86 (Apr. 2003) <http://www.focusweb.org/publications/Fot2003/fot86.html>.

37. "U.S. Defeat in Iraq 'Inevitable,'" *News24.com,* Mar. 26, 2003 <http://www.news24.com/News24/World/Iraq/0,6119,2-10-1460_1338708,00.html>.

38. Guy Dinmore, "Questions Grow over When Soldiers Will Come Home," *Financial Times,* Apr. 24–25, 2004, p. 8.

39. U.S. Army, *Hearing: Article 15-6 Investigation of the 800th Military Police Brigade* (undated), also known as "The Taguba Report" <http://www.globalsecurity.org/intell/library/reports/2004/800-mp-bde.htm>.

40. *Ibid.*

41. See, among others, Marjorie Cohn, "The Torturer in Chief, *Truthout,* June 18, 2004 <http://www.truthout.org/docs_04/061804A.shtml>.

42. Korb, p. 51.

43. Quoted in Walden Bello, "The Stalemate in Iraq and the Global Peace Movement," *Focus on Trade,* no. 86, 2003 <http://www.focusweb.org/main/html/article.172.html>.

44. Fallows, p. 30.

45. Spiegel, p. 8.

46. Clarke, p. 271.

47. George Packer, "War after the War," *The New Yorker,* Nov. 24, 2003, p. 73.

48. Statement of the President of the General Assembly Han Seung-Soo (Republic of Korea), SG/SM/7985AFG/149, Oct. 8, 2001 <http://www.un.org/News/Press/docs/2001/gasm274.doc.htm>. According to Phyllis Bennis, an expert on the UN, the Security Council authorized the United States to act in self-defense, though the resolution pointedly failed to invoke the self-defense clause of the UN charter and did not specifically recommend military action. Personal communication, Oct. 31, 2004.

49. Stephen Biddle, "Afghanistan and the Future of Warfare," *Foreign Affairs,* Mar.–Apr. 2003, pp. 43–44.

50. Cited in Michael Mann, *Incoherent Empire* (London: Verso, 2003), p. 130.

51. *Ibid.*

52. William Pfaff, "The War on Terror Turns into a War on Afghanistan," *International Herald Tribune,* Nov. 3–4, 2001.

53. Quoted in Seymour Hersh, "The Other War," *The New Yorker,* May 12, 2004 <http://www.newyorker.com/fact/content/?040412fa_fact>.

54. *Ibid.*

55. Amy Frumin, Morgan Courtney, and Rebecca Linder, *The Road Ahead: Issues for Consideration at the Berlin Donor Conference for Afghanistan, March 31–April 1, 2004* (Washington: CSIS, 2004), p. 22.

56. *Ibid.*

57. Quoted in Hersh.

58. Secretary General, United Nations, *The Situation in Afghanistan and Its Implications for International Peace and Security,* A58/742/S2004/230, p. 4.

59. Thea Fierens, member of the Dutch Parliament, personal communication, Apr. 5, 2004.

60. Frumin, Courtney, and Linder, p. 22.

61. *Ibid.*

62. Hersh.

63. Hersh; Clarke, p. 271.

64. Secretary General, p. 16.

65. *Ibid.*

66. Joe Klein, "How Israel Is Wrapped Up in Iraq," *Time,* Feb. 5, 2003 <http://www .time.com/time/columnist/klein/article/0,9565,419688,00.html>.

67. Interview with Usamah Hamdan, representative of Hamas, Beirut, August 14, 2004.

68. Roula Khalaf and Guy Dinmore, "Reforming the Arab World: 'The U.S. Is Serious— It Wants to Change the Middle East but It Doesn't Know How," *Financial Times,* Mar. 22, 2004.

69. Clarke, p. 96.

70. *Ibid.,* p. 246.

71. "Gaming Out Iraq," *Stratfor Weekly,* Apr. 9, 2004.

72. Briefing, Sunai Phasuk, Forum Asia, Chulalongkorn University, Social Research Institute, May 4, 2004.

73. Robert Kagan, "Power and Weakness," *Policy Review,* no. 113 (June–July 2002) <http://www.policyreview.org/JUN02/kagan.html>.

74. *Ibid.*

75. John Mearsheimer, *The Tragedy of Great Power Politics* (New York: Norton, 2001), pp. 338–44.

76. Ivo Daalder, "The End of Atlanticism," *Survival,* vol. 45, no. 2 (Summer 2003), p. 148.

77. Jolyon Howorth, "France, Britain, and the Euro-Atlantic Crisis," *Survival,* vol. 45, no. 4 (Winter 2003–2004), pp. 184–85.

78. Quoted in Howorth, pp. 184–85.

79. Charles Krauthammer, "The Unipolar Era," in Andrew Bacevich, ed., *The Imperial Tense* (Chicago: Ivan R. Dee, 2003), pp. 47–65.

80. Robert Kagan, "America's Crisis of Legitimacy," *Foreign Affairs,* Mar.–Apr. 2004, p. 87.

81. John Pilger, "Venezuela: The Next Chile?" *New Statesman,* Mar. 11, 2002; reprinted in Gregory Wilpert, ed., *Coup against Chávez* (Caracas: Fundación Venezolana para la Justicia Global, 2003), p. 13.

82. Quoted in Alexander Main, Maximilien Arvelaiz, and Temir Porras Ponceleon, "Virtual Reality, Real Coup," in Wilpert, p. 65.

83. Walden Bello, "Original FTAA Draft Scrapped; People Pour into Miami to Protest FTAA," Daily Report from the FTAA Meeting, Food First, Nov. 20, 2003.

84. "Bolivia Leader Toppled by Bloody Revolt," Reuters, Oct. 17, 2003.

85. Personal communication at dinner at Miraflores Presidential Palace, June 2002.

86. Jorge Castañeda, "Bush and the Neglected Hemisphere," Project Syndicate, *Business World*, June 14, 2004.

87. Newhouse, p. 30.

88. See, among others, "Alone on the Sidelines?" *Newsweek*, Jan. 26, 2004, p. 20.

89. Center for Defense Information, *Fiscal Year 2004 Budget*, Washington, 2004 <http://www.cdi.org/budget/2004/world-military-spending.cfm>.

90. "Kerry Calls for More Troops to Bolster U.S. Military," Bloomberg, May 28, 2004 <http://quote.bloomberg.com/apps/news?pid=71000001&refer=us&sid=a9fnN_L Bp1Ls>.

Chapter 3: Contemporary Capitalism's Classic Crisis

1. Robert Brenner, *The Economics of Global Turbulence*, special issue of *New Left Review*, no. 229 (May–June 1998).

2. Angus Maddison, cited in James Crotty, "Why There Is Chronic Excess Capacity," *Challenge*, Nov.–Dec. 2002, p. 25.

3. *Ibid.*

4. *Ibid.*, p. 145.

5. Brenner, p. 185.

6. Robert Brenner, *The Boom and the Bubble* (New York: Verso, 2002), pp. 48–127.

7. *Ibid.*, p. 127.

8. Robert Blecker, "Why the Dollar Needs to Fall Further," *Challenge*, Sept.–Oct. 2003, pp. 28–29.

9. *Ibid.*, p. 29.

10. Sandra Sugawara, "Excess Capacity Sowing Japan's Recovery," *Washington Post*, Dec. 25, 1998, p. B-9.

11. Barney Jopson, "Recovery May Be Fragile," special report on Japan, *Financial Times*, Oct. 14, 2003.

12. See Maryann Keller, "Consolidation Means More Excess Capacity," *Looksmart*, Apr. 2000 <http://articles.findarticles.com/p/articles/mi_m3012/is_4_180/ai_61892608>.

13. Lawrence Mishel and Jared Bernstein, *The State of Working America: 1992–93* (Washington: Economic Policy Institute, 1993), pp. 3–4.

14. Robert Pollin, *Contours of Descent* (New York: Verso, 2003), p. 61.

15. *Ibid.*, p. 61.

16. Research by Dean Maki and Michael Palumbo, cited in Pollin, p. 67.

17. *Ibid.*

18. Stephen Fidler, "Trouble with Neighbors," *Financial Times*, Feb. 16, 1993, p. 15.

19. World Bank, *Global Economic Prospects and the Developing Countries* (Washington: World Bank, 1993), p. 66.

20. UN Development Program, *Human Development Report 2003* (New York: Oxford University Press, 2003), pp. 33–65.

21. Jacques-Chai Chomthongdi, "The IMF's Asian Legacy," in *Prague 2000: Why We*

Need to Decommission the IMF and the World Bank (Bangkok: Focus on the Global South, 2000), pp. 18, 22.

22. Crotty, "Why There Is Chronic Excess Capacity," p. 37.

23. *Ibid.* p. 24.

24. A. Gary Shilling, *Deflation* (Short Hills, N.J.: Lakeview, 1998), p. 177.

25. Crotty, p. 24.

26. U.S. Mission to the European Union, "OECD Nations Pledge Reductions in Global Steel Capacity," Feb. 8, 2002 <http://www.useu.be/Categories/Trade/Feb0802Steel ReductionsOECD.html>.

27. Quoted in *ibid.*

28. *Economist*, Feb. 20, 1999, p. 15.

29. Crotty, pp. 37–38.

30. Crotty, pp. 42–43.

31. United Nations, *World Investment Report 2000* (New York: United Nations, 2000), p. xx.

32. Maryann Keller.

33. Crotty, pp. 38–39.

34. Crotty, p. 41.

35. Brenner, *The Boom and the Bubble*, p. 195.

36. Clyde Prestowitz, *Rogue Nation* (New York: Basic Books, 2003), p. 58.

37. *Ibid.*

38. Brenner, "Towards the Precipice," *London Review of Books*, Feb. 6, 2003, p. 20.

39. *Ibid.*, p. 21.

40. *Ibid.*

41. Brenner, *The Boom and the Bubble*, p. 192.

42. "When Wealth Is Blown Away," *Business Week*, Mar. 26, 2001, p. 33.

43. Brenner, "Towards the Precipice," p. 21.

44. Quoted in Lee Sustar, "The Limits of Recovery," *Socialist Worker*, Oct. 31, 2004 <http://www.socialistworker.org/2003-2/474/474_08_Recovery.shtml>.

45. *Ibid.*

46. John Mauldin, "Employment Quandary," *Investor Insight* (electronic newsletter), Feb. 6, 2004.

47. Citizens for Tax Justice, cited in Pollin, p. 97.

48. Richard Tomlinson, "Strong Euro, Weak Europe," *Fortune*, Feb. 23, 2004, p. 12.

49. *Business Week*, Mar. 8, 2004, p. 30.

50. "Where Wealth Lies," *Business Week*, Apr. 19, 2004, p. 34.

51. *Ibid.*

52. United Nations, *World Investment Report 2003* (New York: United Nations, 2003), p. 42.

53. *Ibid.*

54. Joel Popkin and Kathryn Kobe, "Securing America's Future," *Challenge*, Nov.–Dec. 2003, p. 88.

55. "Outsourcing of U.S. Jobs to Asia Likely to Slow Down in Election Year," AFP, *Business World*, Mar. 15, 2004, p. 25.
56. Popkin and Kobe, p. 101.
57. *Ibid.*
58. Quoted in "The Job Drain: Is It China's Fault?" *Business Week*, Oct. 13, 2003, p. 34.
59. United Nations, *World Investment Report 2003*, p. 45.
60. "Riding China's Coattails," *Business Week*, Mar. 1, 2004, p. 50.
61. "China the Locomotive," *Straits Times*, Feb. 23, 2004, p. 12.
62. United Nations, *World Investment Report 2003*, p. 44.
63. "Burying the Competition," *Far Eastern Economic Review*, Oct. 17, 2002, p. 30.
64. UN Development Program, *Human Development Report 2003* p. 3.
65. Howard Krawitz, "China's Trade Opening: Implications for Regional Stability," *Strategic Forum*, no. 193 (August 2002), p. 2.
66. Brian Bremer, Dexter Roberts, and Frederik Balfour, "Headed for Crisis?" *Business Week*, May 3, 2004, p. 21.
67. "Is This Boom in Danger?" *Business Week*, Nov. 3, 2003, p. 22.
68. See, among others, Gary Shilling, *Deflation*, pp. 247–54.
69. Philip Anthony O'Hara, "Recent Changes to the IMF, WTO, and SPD: Emerging Global Mode of Regulation in Social Structures of Accumulation for Long-Wave Upswing?" *Review of International Political Economy*, vol. 10, no. 3 (August 2003), p. 496.

Chapter 4: The Ascendancy of Finance

1. "Where Wealth Lives," *Business Week*, Apr. 19, 2004, p. 36.
2. *Ibid.*
3. World Bank, *Managing Capital Flows in East Asia* (Washington: World Bank, 1993), p. 66.
4. Doug Henwood, *Wall Street* (New York: Verso, 1997), pp. 107–8.
5. Ariel Buira, "Key Financial Issues in Capital Flows to Emerging Markets," in *International Finance in a Year of Crisis* (Tokyo: United Nations University, 1998), p. 68.
6. Karin Lissakers, *Bankers, Borrowers, and the Establishment* (New York: Basic Books, 1991), p. 254.
7. *Ibid.*, p. 36.
8. George Soros, *The Crisis of Globalization* (New York: Public Affairs, 1999), p. 108.
9. Lissakers, p. 8.
10. Robert Rubin and Jacob Weisberg, *In an Uncertain World* (New York: Random House, 2003), p. 17.
11. Paul Hirst and Grahame Thompson, *Globalization in Question* (Cambridge: Polity Press, 1996), p. 40.
12. Ian Cooper, "The World of Futures, Forwards, and Swaps," in *Mastering Finance* (London: Financial Times, 1998), p. 40.
13. Hirst and Thompson, p. 41.

14. UNCTAD report quoted in UNCTAD *Trade and Development Report 1998* (Geneva: UNCTAD, 1998), p. 1.

15. Randall Kroszner, "The Market as International Regulator," in *Mastering Finance*, p. 399.

16. Jagdish Bhagwati, "The Capital Myth: The Difference between Trade in Widgets and Dollars," *Foreign Affairs*, May 1998, pp. 7–12.

17. Lissakers, p. 59.

18. Quoted in Henwood, p. 292.

19. Lissakers, p. 45.

20. *Ibid.*, p. 104.

21. Patricio Meller, *Adjustment and Equity in Chile* (Paris: OECD, 1992), pp. 61, 77.

22. Duncan Green, *Silent Revolution: The Rise of Market Economics in Latin America* (London: Cassel, 1995), p. 70.

23. Maxwell Cameron and Vinod Agarwal, "Mexican Meltdown: Markets and Post-NAFTA Financial Turmoil," *Third World Quarterly*, vol. 17, no. 5 (1996), p. 977.

24. Timothy Kessler, "Political Capital: Mexican Policy under Salinas," *World Politics*, vol. 51 (Oct. 1998), p. 57.

25. Justin Fox, "The Great Emerging Markets Rip-off," *Fortune*, May 11, 1998.

26. *Ibid.*

27. *Ibid.*

28. *Ibid.*

29. Min Tang and James Villafuerte, *Capital Flows to Asian and Pacific Developing Countries: Recent Trends and Future Prospects* (Manila: Asian Development Bank, 1995), p. 10.

30. Jose Maria Fanelli, "Financial Liberalization and Capital Account Regime: Notes on the Experience of Developing Countries," in *International Monetary and Financial Issues for the 1990's* (Geneva: UNCTAD, 1998), p. 8.

31. For an account of trends in the real economy, see Walden Bello, Shea Cunningham, and Bill Rau, *Dark Victory* (San Francisco: Food First, 1994), pp. 37–42.

32. Carlos Heredia, quoted in William Greider, *One World, Ready or Not* (New York: Simon and Schuster, 1997), p. 274.

33. Greider, p. 260.

34. Jeffrey Sachs, "Personal View," *Financial Times*, July 30, 1997.

35. Buira, "Key Financial Issues in Capital Flows to Emerging Markets," p. 7.

36. Rubin and Weisberg, p. 8.

37. Buira, *ibid.*

38. Maxwell Cameron and Vinod Aggarwal, "Mexican Meltdown: Markets and Post-NAFTA Turmoil," *Third World Quarterly*, vol. 17, no. 5, pp. 977–78.

39. George Soros, *On Globalization* (New York: Public Affairs, 2002), p. 118.

40. Quoted in Kimberly Ann Elliott and Gary Clyde Hufbauer, "Ambivalent Multilateralism and the Emerging Backlash: The IMF and the WTO," in Stewart Patrick and Shepard Forman, eds., *Multilateralism and U.S. Foreign Policy* (Boulder: Lynne Rienner, 2002), p. 384.

41. *Ibid.*

42. Rubin and Weisberg, p. 34.

43. *Ibid.*

44. Figures provided by Japan Ministry of Finance.

45. Institute of International Finance, *Capital Flows and Emerging Market Economies* (Washington: Institute of International Finance, 1998), p. 3.

46. See HG Asia, *Communique: Thailand—Worth a Nibble Perhaps but Not a Bite* (Hong Kong: HG Asia, 1996).

47. Thanong Kantong, "The Currency War Is the Information War," Talk at the Seminar Workshop on "Improving the Flow of Information in a Time of Crisis: The Challenge to the Southeast Asian Media," Subic, Philippines, Oct. 29–31, 1998.

48. Barry Eichengreen and Donald Mathieson, *Hedge Funds and Financial Market Dynamics*, Occasional Paper 166 (Washington: International Monetary Fund, 1998), p. 17.

49. Jeffrey Winters, "The Financial Crisis in Southeast Asia," Paper delivered at the Conference on the Asian Crisis, Murdoch University, Fremantle, Western Australia, August 1998.

50. *Ibid.*

51. Aon-Am Park, "Korea's Management of Capital Flows in the 1990's," in Stephany Griffith-Jones, Manuel Montes, and Anwar Nasution, eds., *Short-Term Capital Flows and Economic Crises* (Oxford: Oxford University Press, 2001), pp. 80–81.

52. Ravi Arvind Palat, "Miracles of the Day Before?: The Great Asian Meltdown and the Changing World-Economy," *Development and Society*, vol. 28, no. 1 (June 1999), pp. 25–26.

53. Paul Blustein, *The Chastening* (New York: Public Affairs, 2001), pp. 125–26.

54. *Ibid.*, p. 126.

55. Palat, p. 25; Ilene Grabel, "Rejecting Exceptionalism," in Jonathan Michie and John Grieve Smith, *Global Instability: The Political Economy of World Economic Governance* (London: Routledge, 1999), p. 52.

56. Grabel, p. 52.

57. Quoted in Blustein, p. 127.

58. Blustein, pp. 196–205.

59. Grabel, p. 53.

60. Blustein, p. 202.

61. Rubin and Weisberg, p. 241.

62. Joseph Stiglitz, quoted in *The Nation*, May 13, 2000.

63. International Monetary Fund, "IMF-Supported Programs in Indonesia, Korea, and Thailand," IMF Occasional Paper, no. 178 June 30, 1999, p. 62.

64. Chalmers Johnson, *Blowback: The Costs and Consequences of American Empire* (New York: Henry Holt, 2000), p. 206.

65. Testimony of Charlene Barshefsky before the House Ways and Means Subcommittee, Feb. 24, 1998.

66. *Ibid.*
67. *Ibid.*
68. Quoted in "Worsening Financial Flu Lowers Immunity to U.S. Business," *New York Times*, Feb. 1, 1998.
69. Robert Pollin, *Contours of Descent* (New York: Verso, 2003), p. 149.
70. Blustein, *The Chastening*, p. 222.
71. Lawrence Summers, quoted in Walden Bello, "Power, Timidity, and Irresponsibility in Global Finance," *Focus on Trade*, Aug. 1999.
72. Paul Blustein, "Argentina Didn't Fail on Its Own," *Washington Post*, Aug. 3, 2003.
73. George Soros, *On Globalization*, p. 143.
74. Alan Cibils, Mark Weisbrot, and Debayani Kar, *Argentina since Default: The IMF and the Depression* (Washington: Center for Economic and Policy Research, 2002), p. 3.
75. Michael Cohen, "A Season of Hope in Argentina," *Challenge*, Sept.–Oct. 2003, p. 39.
76. "Global Bondholders Meet to Plan Recovery of Losses," *Financial Times*, Feb. 23, 2004, p. 3.
77. Stratfor, Global Market Brief, Feb. 4, 2004.
78. Rubin and Weisberg, p. 257.
79. *Ibid.*
80. *Ibid.*, p. 296.
81. "Argentine Stocks Hit All-Time High," *BBC News*, Oct. 21, 2003.

Chapter 5: The Economics of Antidevelopment

1. George Soros, *On Globalization* (New York: Public Affairs, 2002), p. 35.
2. Ministerial Declaration of Coherence of Multilateral Agencies, Singapore, Dec. 1996.
3. Bernard Nossiter, *The Global Struggle for More* (New York: Harper and Row, 1987), p. 45.
4. Cited in Seamus Cleary, "Towards a New Adjustment in Africa," in "Beyond Adjustment," special issue of *African Environment*, vol. 7, nos. 1–4 (1990), p. 357.
5. John Sheahan, "Development Dichotomies and Economic Development Strategy," in Simon Teitel, ed., *Toward a New Development Strategy for Latin America* (Washington: Inter-American Development Bank, 1992), p. 53.
6. Rudiger Dornbusch, quoted in Jacques Polak, "The Changing Nature of IMF Conditionality," in *Essays in International Finance*, Princeton University, no. 184 (Sept. 1991), p. 47.
7. Enrique Iglesias, *Reflections on Economic Development: Toward a New Latin American Consensus* (Washington: Inter-American Development Bank, 1992), p. 103.
8. Stephen Fidler, "Trouble with Neighbors," *Financial Times*, Feb. 16, 1993, p. 15.
9. Iglesias, p. 103.
10. Fidler, p. 15.
11. Nicholas Guyatt, *Another New American Century* (London: Zed, 2000), pp. 21–22.

12. See Robin Wright and Doyle McManus, *Flashpoints: Promise and Peril in the New World* (New York: Knopf, 1991), p. 207; and UN Development Program, *Human Development Report 1991* (New York: Oxford University Press, 1991), p. 36.

13. Lester Thurow, *Head to Head: The Coming Struggle among Japan, Europe, and the United States* (New York: Morrow, 1992), p. 216.

14. Nassau Adams, "The UN's Neglected Brief—the Advancement of All Peoples," in Erskine Childers, ed., *Challenges of the UN* (New York: St. Martin's Press, 1994), p. 43.

15. South Commission, *The Challenge to the South* (New York: Oxford University Press, 1991), p. 217.

16. Myriam van der Stichele, "World Trade—Free Trade for Whom, Fair Trade for Whom?" in Erskine Childers, p. 69.

17. "South Decries Move to Close UNCTAD, UNIDO," *Third World Resurgence*, no. 56 [no year indicated], p. 41.

18. Soros, *On Globalization*, p. 54.

19. Quote from testimony before U.S. Senate Committee on Commerce, Science, and Technology, Washington, Oct. 13, 1994.

20. This was the government's position during the ratification debate in the Philippines.

21. Mike Moore, *A World without Walls* (Cambridge: Cambridge University Press, 2003), p. 109.

22. *Ibid.*

23. Soros, *On Globalization*, p. 54.

24. Figures from World Trade Organization, *Annual Report 1998: International Trade Statistics* (Geneva: WTO, 1998), p. 12.

25. Quoted in "Cakes and Caviar: The Dunkel Draft and Third World Agriculture," *Ecologist*, vol. 23, no. 6 (Nov.–Dec. 1993), p. 220.

26. C. Fred Bergsten, director, Institute for International Economics, testimony before Senate Committee on Commerce, Science, and Technology, Washington, Oct. 13, 1994.

27. Kimberly Ann Elliott and Gary Clyde Hufbauer, "Ambivalent Multilateralism and the Emerging Backlash: The IMF and WTO," in Stewart Patrick and Shepard Forman, eds., *Multilateralism and U.S. Foreign Policy* (Boulder: Lynne Rienner, 2002), p. 404.

28. Oxfam International, *Rigged Rules and Double Standards* (Oxford: Oxfam International, 2002), p. 12.

29. *Ibid.*

30. Cesar Bautista, speech at the Second Ministerial of the World Trade Organization, Geneva, May 18–20, 1998.

31. Quoted in John Whalley, "Special and Differential Treatment in the Millennium Round," *CSGR Working Paper*, no. 30/99 (May 1999), p. 3.

32. *Ibid.*, p. 4.

33. *Ibid.*, p. 7.

34. *Ibid.*, p. 10.

35. *Ibid.*, p. 14.
36. "More Power to the World Trade Organization," *Panos Briefing*, Nov. 1999, p. 14.
37. South Center, *The Multilateral Trade Agenda and the South* (Geneva: South Center, 1998), p. 32.
38. John Whalley, "Building Poor Countries' Trading Capacity," *CSGR Working Paper Series* (Warwick: CSGR, Mar. 1999).
39. This debate was carried widely in the Philippine media. Among the key documents from this debate are MODE (Management and Organizational Development for Empowerment, Inc.), "Putting Food Security and Environment Sustainability on the Line: The Impact of the Dunkel Act and Blair House Accord on the Philippines," Manila, MODE, 1993; *IPR Sourcebook Philippines* (Manila: University of the Philippines, Los Banos College of Agriculture and MODE, 1994); and Department of Agriculture, *Questions and Answers About GATT: The GATT and Its Implications for Philippine Agriculture* (Manila: Dept. of Agriculture, 1994).
40. Republic of the Philippines, "Individual Action Plan for APEC" (draft), Oct. 31, 1996.
41. *Ibid.*
42. "Democracy as an Illusion? How AGILE/DAI Promotes U.S. Interests at the Expense of Farmers' Rights," *SEARICE Notes,* June 2002.
43. A range of bills and laws, including the Omnibus Power Law, Anti-Dumping Act, and the Anti-Money Laundering Law, were drafted and pushed through the Philippines Congress by the AGILE group, which was supported over five years (June 1998–June 2003) by a $31.2 million appropriation from the U.S. Congress. "Democracy as an Illusion?" p. 1.
44. *Ibid.*
45. *Ibid.*, p. 4.
46. U.S. Trade Representative, *2001 National Trade Estimates* (Washington: USTR, 2001), p. 346.
47. *Ibid.*, pp. 345, 346.
48. "Earning from Others' Intellectual Creations," *Philippine Daily Inquirer,* Feb. 17, 2003, p. C7.
49. *2001 National Trade Estimates*, p. 350.
50. *Ibid.*
51. UNCTAD, *Trade and Development Report 1991* (New York: United Nations, 1991), p. 191.
52. *Ibid.*
53. *Ibid.*
54. Francisco Pascual and Arze Glipo, "WTO and Philippine Agriculture," *Development Forum,* no. 1 (Series 2002), p. 5.
55. Department of Agriculture, Rules and Regulations for the Implementation of the Agricultural Minimum Access Volume (MAV), Manila, 1996.
56. World Trade Organization, *The Results of the Uruguay Round of Multilateral Trade Negotiations: The Legal Texts* (WTO: Geneva, 1995), p. 66.

57. Department of Agriculture. During the Uruguay Round negotiations, the quota for rice, for the first year, was set at a different figure: 59,000 metric tons.

58. U.S. Trade Representative, *2000 National Trade Estimates* (Washington: USTR, 2000), p. 330.

59. *Ibid.,* p. 328.

60. Why was there such a contrast between the rosy predictions and the dismal outcomes? Apparently the statistics were simply manufactured for the government to win the WTO ratification debate.

61. Riza Bernabe, quoted in "Accounting of Farmers' WTO Safety Net Sought," *Business World,* Sept. 18, 2003, p. 6.

62. *Selected Agricultural Statistics, 1998 and 2002* (Quezon City: Dept. of Agriculture, 1998, 2002).

63. *Ibid.*

64. Kevin Watkins, *Field Trip Report: The Philippines* (Manila: Oxfam UK, 1995).

65. Charmaine Ramos, "Discussion Points: Trends and Prospects in the Cereals and Grains Sector of the Philippines." Lecture delivered at the KSP Study Session on the Medium-Term Development Plan, St. Vincent Seminary, Quezon City, May 6, 1996.

66. Aileen Kwa, "A Guide to the WTO's Doha Work Programme: The 'Development' Agenda Undermines Development," Focus on the Global South, Bangkok, Jan. 2003.

67. *Selected Agricultural Statistics, 1998 and 2002.*

68. Submission of Republic of the Philippines, WTO Committee on Agriculture, Geneva, July 1, 2003.

69. Oxfam International, p. 12.

Chapter 6: The South Rises, and the North Revails

1. Testimony before the Senate Committee on Commerce, Science, and Technology, Washington, Oct. 13, 1994.

2. Unnamed developing-country trade negotiator, cited by Fatoumata Jawara and Aileen Kwa, in *Behind the Scenes at the WTO: The Real World of International Trade Negotiations* (London: Zed and Focus on the Global South, 2003), p. 21.

3. *Ibid.,* p. 98.

4. Jagdish Bhagwati, *Free Trade Today* (New Delhi: Oxford University Press, 2002), p. 10.

5. Press briefing, Seattle, Wash., Dec. 2, 1999.

6. *Ibid.*

7. Quoted in "Deadline Set for WTO Reforms," *Guardian News Service,* Jan. 10, 2000.

8. Aileen Kwa, "Crisis in WTO Talks," *Focus on Trade,* no. 68 (Oct. 2001).

9. *Ibid.*

10. This was my estimate. I was representing my organization Focus on the Global South.

11. Emad Mekay, "Opponents Unite to Decry U.S. Farm Subsidies," Interpress Service, May 13, 2002.

12. Aileen Kwa, "A Guide to the WTO's Doha Work Programme: The 'Development' Agenda Undermines Development," Focus on the Global South, Bangkok, Jan. 2003.

13. Aileen Kwa, "WTO Agriculture Talks Set to Exacerbate World Hunger: Second-Guessing Mr. Harbinson's Next Strike," Focus on the Global South, Bangkok, Mar. 2003.

14. A paper from the Philippine delegation said that the proposal would allow developing nations to impose the tariff equivalent of export subsidies and domestic support on agricultural imports from the developed countries. This was seen as a "discipline mechanism" that would "balance and interlink reform commitments in market access, export subsidies, and production- and trade-distorting domestic support." Republic of the Philippines, "Integration of Reforms in Export Competition, Domestic Support, and Market Access in World Agricultural Trade," statement at the Informal Special Session of the WTO Committee on Agriculture, Geneva, Sept. 2, 2002.

15. Kwa, "WTO Agriculture Talks Set to Exacerbate World Hunger."

16. *Ibid.*

17. *Ibid.*

18. World Trade Organization, "Ministerial Declaration on the TRIPs Agreement and Public Health," Nov. 14, 2001.

19. The chairman's statement reads as follows: "Let me say that with respect to the reference to an 'explicit consensus' being needed, in these paragraphs, for a decision to be taken at the Fifth Session of the Ministerial Conference, my understanding is that, at that session, a decision would indeed need to be taken by explicit consensus, before negotiations on trade and investment and trade and competition policy, transparency in government procurement, and trade facilitation could proceed. . . . In my view, this would give each member the right to take a position on the modalities that would prevent negotiations from proceeding after the Fifth Session of the Ministerial Conference until that member is prepared to join in an explicit consensus." Chairman's statement, Nov. 14, 2001. Text provided by WTO secretariat at Conference Media Center.

20. Group of 20, "Ministerial Communiqué," Sept. 9, 2003.

21. "Trade Talks Round Going Nowhere sans Progress in Farm Reform," *Business World*, Sept. 8, 2003, p. 15.

22. Robert Zoellick, "America Will Not Wait for the Won't-Do Countries," *Financial Times*, Sept. 21, 2003.

23. See, for instance, "The Hypocrisy of Rich Countries Blocks Trade Liberalization," editorial, *Financial Times*, Sept. 16, 2003; "Cancún's Silver Lining," editorial, *Wall Street Journal*, Sept. 17, 2003; and "The WTO under Fire," *Economist*, Sept. 18, 2003.

24. Jacques-Chai Chomthongdi, "The IMF's Asian Legacy," in *Prague 2000: Why We Need to Decommission the IMF and the World Bank* (Bangkok: Focus on the Global South, 2000), pp. 18, 22.

25. International Monetary Fund, "IMF-Supported Programs in Indonesia, Korea, and Thailand," *IMF Occasional Paper*, no. 178, Washington, June 30, 1999, p. 38; quoted in George Soros, *On Globalization* (New York: Public Affairs, 2002), p. 119.

26. Kimberly Ann Elliott and Gary Clyde Hufbauer, "Ambivalent Multilateralism and the Emerging Backlash: The IMF and the WTO," in Stewart Patrick and Shepard Forman, eds., *Multilateralism and U.S. Foreign Policy* (Boulder: Lynne Rienner, 2002), p. 385.

27. *Ibid.*

28. *Ibid.*

29. *Ibid.*

30. Eric Altbach, "The Asian Monetary Fund Proposal: A Case Study of Japanese Regional Leadership," *Japan Economic Institute Report*, no. 47A (1997), p. 8.

31. *Ibid.*

32. *Ibid.*

33. "Global Capitalism: Can It Be Made to Work Better?" *Business Week*, Nov. 6, 2000, pp. 42–43.

34. Robert Pollin, *Contours of Descent* (London: Verso, 2003), p. 131. Pollin excluded China on the grounds that during the 1981–99 era, it did not follow neoliberal policies but, much like the other Asian NICs (newly industrializing countries), put into motion heavily interventionist programs even as it integrated into the capitalist world economy. Also, Walden Bello and Stephanie Rosenfeld, *Dragons in Distress, Asia's Miracle Economies in Crisis* (London: Penguin, 1992).

35. International Financial Institutions Advisory Commission (Meltzer Commission), *Report* (Washington: U.S. Congress, 2000).

36. C. Fred Bergsten, "The Backlash against Globalization," speech given at the Meeting of the Trilateral Commission, Tokyo, April 2000.

37. The following facts and statistics were drawn from various sources and brought together in Walden Bello, "Hard Answers, Please, Mr. Wolfensohn and Mr. Koehler," speech delivered at the Prague Castle Debate, Sept. 23, 2000.

38. Jeffrey Winters, "Combating Corruption in the Multilateral Development Banks," statement before the Senate Committee on Foreign Relations, Washington, May 13, 2004.

39. "World Bank Sticks by Chad-Cameroon Pipeline," Reuters, Dec. 9, 2002 <http://www.planetark.com/avantgo/dailynewsstroy.cfm?newsid=17729>.

40. Bank Information Center, "Problem Project Alert #4: China Western Poverty Reduction Project" <http://mirrors/zpok.hu/www.bucusa.or/asia/ppa_tibet1.htm>.

41. Friends of the Earth USA fact sheet, 2000.

42. Statement at the Prague Castle Debate, Sept. 23, 2000.

43. *Ibid.*

44. W. Andy Knight, "Multilevel Economic Governance through Subsidiarity: Remodeling the Global Financial Architecture," paper prepared for the Conference on the International Financial Architecture, Center for Global Studies, University of Victoria, British Columbia, Aug. 29–30, 2001.

45. *Ibid.*

46. Barry Eichengreen, *Financial Crises and What to Do about Them* (Oxford: Oxford University Press, 2002), p. 137.

47. *Ibid.*, pp. 137–38.

48. See Anne Krueger, "International Financial Architecture for 2002: A New Approach to Sovereign Debt Restructuring," address at the American Enterprise Institute, International Monetary Fund, Washington <http://www.imf.or/external/np/speeches/2001/112601.htm>; also Eichengreen, pp. 148–56.

49. Eichengreen, *Ibid.*, p. 150.

50. Quoted in Nicola Bullard, "The Puppet Master Shows His Hand," *Focus on Trade*, no. 76 (Apr. 2002), pp. 3–4 (electronic bulletin, pdf.file).

51. Ron Suskind, *The Price of Loyalty: George W. Bush, the White House, and the Education of Paul O'Neill* (New York: Simon and Schuster, 2004), pp. 243–44.

52. Robert Rubin and Jacob Weisberg, *In an Uncertain World* (New York: Random House, 2003), p. 265.

53. These estimates come from Eric Toussaint of CADTM, 2001.

54. Cited in "HIPC: The Official Debt Relief Program," Jubilee 2000/USA Fact Sheet, June 2002.

55. Cited in CAFOD, Oxfam, Christian Aid, and European Network on Debt and Development (Eurodad), "A Joint Submission to the World Bank and IMF Review of HIPC and Debt Sustainability," Aug. 2002, p. 7.

56. CAFOD et al., p. 7.

57. *Ibid.*

58. Cited in Soren Ambrose and Mara Vanderslice, "G7 Debt Relief Plan: More Grief than Relief," Spotlight, Jubilee U.S. Network, June 2002.

59. Op-ed piece in *Washington Post*, reprinted in *Today* (Philippines), Nov. 15, 1999.

60. *Ibid.*

61. Lawrence Summers, testimony before the Senate Committee on Foreign Relations, Washington, Nov. 5, 1999.

62. *Ibid.*

63. David Booth, "Introduction and Overview," *Development Policy Review*, vol. 21, no. 2 (2003), p. 141.

64. *Ibid.*

65. *Ibid.*, p. 157.

66. *Ibid.*, p. 131.

67. Rafael Pereira Gomes, Sadaf Lakhani, and Jacqueline Woodman, "PRSP—Politics, Power, and Poverty: A Civil Society Perspective," Economic Policy Empowerment Program, Eurodad, 2002, pp. 5–6.

68. *Ibid.*

69. *Ibid.*

70. Jenina Joy Chavez Malaluan and Shalmali Guttal, "Structural Adjustment in the Name of the Poor: The PRSP Experience in the Lao PDR, Cambodia, and Vietnam," Focus on the Global South, Bangkok, Jan. 2002, p. 18.

71. Proposal presented at the Conference on International Financial Architecture, Center for Global Studies, University of Victoria, British Columbia, Aug. 29–30, 2001.

72. Mark Zacher, "Redesigning the International Financial Architecture: Voting Power

and Power Sharing in the IMF," paper delivered at the Conference on International Financial Architecture," Center for Global Studies, University of Victoria, British Columbia, Aug. 29–30, 2001.

Chapter 7: George W. Bush and Rollback Economics

1. Ron Suskind, *The Price of Loyalty: George W. Bush, the White House, and the Education of Paul O'Neill* (New York: Simon and Schuster, 2004, pp. 218–21.

2. *Ibid.*, p. 217.

3. David Harvey, speech at Conference on Trends in Globalization, University of California at Santa Barbara, May 1–4, 2003.

4. "Zoellick Says FTA Candidates Must Support U.S. Foreign Policy," *Inside U.S. Trade*, May 16, 2003. This article summarizes a May 8, 2003, speech by Zoellick.

5. For the sharpening conflicts between the Treasury Department and IMF officials, see Nicola Bullard, "The Puppet Master Shows His Hand," *Focus on Trade*, Apr. 2002 <http://focusweb.prg/popups/articleswindow.php?id=41>.

6. Nancy Alexander, "The U.S. on the World Stage: Reshaping Development, Finance, and Trade Initiatives," Citizens' Network on Essential Services, Washington, Oct. 2002.

7. Susanne Soederberg, "American Empire and 'Excluded States': The Millennium Challenge Account and the Shift to Preemptive Development," *Third World Quarterly*, vol. 25, no. 2 (2004), p. 295.

8. Quoted in *ibid*.

9. *Ibid.*

10. Briefing, USTR, Sept. 12, 2003.

11. *Ibid.*

12. "U.S. Groups Call Attacks on G-23 Shameful," Cancún, Mexico, Sept. 13, 2003.

13. Giovernment of Brazil, press release, Cancún, Mexico, Sept. 12, 2003.

14. Consumer Alert, "Group of 21 Proposal Harms Their Own Consumers, Says Consumer Group," Cancún, Mexico, Sept. 12, 2003.

15. Robert Zoellick, press briefing, Sept. 14, 2003.

16. Robert Zoellick, "America Will Not Wait for the Won't-Do Countries," *Financial Times*, Sept. 21, 2003.

17. "Cancún's Silver Lining," *Wall Street Journal*, Sept. 17, 2003.

18. "We Demand a Halt to U.S. and EU Bullying and Intimidation of the G-20," statement of some groups belonging to the Our World Is Not for Sale Coalition <http://fosusweb.org/sign-on-g20>.

19. *Ibid.*

20. David Leal, quoted in "Costa Rica siente presion por ser parte de G-20 en Cancún," article from *La Nación* (Costa Rica), disseminated by comercio@redes.org.uy.

21. Quoted in "We Demand a Halt."

22. Peter Hakim, "Towards a More Positive Brazilian Trade Policy," *Financial Times*, Oct. 22, 2003.

23. Briefing for NGOs conducted by a delegate from Venezuela, Nov. 19, 2003.

24. Ministerial declaration on the FTAA, Miami, Nov. 18, 2003.

25. Briefing by the delegate from Venezuela, Nov. 19, 2003.

26. Statement at NGO workshop on the Central American Free Trade Area, Miami, Nov. 18, 2003.

27. "U.S. Bilateral Deals Are Unlikely to Net Much of a Catch," *Financial Times,* Sept. 29, 2003.

28. For a more detailed discussion of the Geneva negotiations, see Walden Bello and Aileen Kwa, "Washington's Triumph in Geneva: How the Leaders of the Group of 20 Succumbed to the United States' Divide-and-Rule Tactics," *Bangkok Post,* Aug. 14, 2004.

29. See George Soros, *America's Role in the World* (New York: Public Affairs, 2004).

Chapter 8: Crisis of Legitimacy

1. Michael Mann, *The Sources of Social Power,* vol. 1 (Cambridge: Cambridge University Press, 1986), p. 254.

2. Neil Sheehan, *A Bright Shining Lie* (New York: Random House, 1988), p. 131.

3. Frances Fitzgerald, *Fire in the Lake* (New York: Random House, 1973), p. 116.

4. Samuel P. Huntington, *Political Order in Changing Societies* (New Haven: Yale University Press, 1968).

5. Ferdinand Marcos, *The Third World Alternative* (Manila: Ministry of Public Information, 1980), p. 1.

6. Jeanne Kirkpatrick, "Dictatorships and Double Standards," *Commentary,* July 1979, p. 37.

7. See Walden Bello, *U.S.-Sponsored Low-Intensity Conflict in the Philippines* (San Francisco: Institute for Food and Development Policy, 1987), pp. 66–67.

8. William Sullivan, remarks at Conference on the Philippines, sponsored by the Washington Institute for Values in Public Policy, Washington, Apr. 30–May 1, 1986.

9. Stephen Haggard and Robert Kaufman, *The Political Economy of Democratic Transitions* (Princeton: Princeton University Press, 1995), pp. 59–60.

10. *Ibid.,* p. 192.

11. Evelyn Huber and John Stephens, "The Bourgeoisie and Democracy: Historical and Contemporary Perspectives from Europe and Latin America," paper delivered at the meeting of the Latin American Studies Association, Guadalajara, Mexico, Apr. 17–19, 1997, p. 8.

12. This account of the Philippines is drawn from Walden Bello et al., *The Anti-Development State: The Political Economy of Permanent Crisis in the Philippines* (Quezon City: University of the Philippines, Department of Sociology, and Focus on the Global South, 2004), pp. 9–31.

13. See, among others, Maria Rocha Geisa, "Neo-Dependency in Brazil," *New Left Review,* no. 16, 2nd series (July–Aug. 2002), pp. 5–33; see also Haggard and Kaufman, pp. 193–96, 209–11.

14. "Don't Leave This Party Yet," *Business Week,* Sept. 8, 2003, p. 63.

15. "Is Lula's Honeymoon Winding Down?" *Business Week*, Apr. 26, 2004, p. 31. See also Roger Burbach, "Brazilian Fiscal Conservatives in Lula's Government under Attack Along with International Monetary Fund," Center for the Study of the Americas (CENSA), Berkeley, Mar. 22, 20004.

16. Geri Smith, "Democracy on the Ropes," *Business Week*, May 19, 2004.

17. Larry Diamond, "Is Pakistan the (Reverse) Wave of the Future?" in Larry Diamond and Marc Plattner, *The Global Divergence of Democracies* (Baltimore: Johns Hopkins University Press, 2001), p. 358.

18. A. R. Kemal, "Structural Adjustment, Macroeconomic Policies, and Poverty Trends in Pakistan," paper delivered at the Asia and Pacific Forum on Poverty, Reforming Policies and Institutions for Poverty Reduction, Asian Development Bank, Manila, Feb. 5–9, 2001.

19. Keane Shore, "The Impact of Structural Adjustment Programs on Pakistan's Social Development," IDRC Reports, June 7, 1999.

20. Strobe Talbot, "Democracy and the National Interest," *Foreign Affairs*, Nov.–Dec. 1996, pp. 47–63.

21. *Ibid.*, p. 50.

22. William Pfaff, "Money Politics Is Winning the American Election," *International Herald Tribune*, Mar. 11–12, 2000.

23. Fareed Zakaria, *The Future of Freedom: Illiberal Democracy at Home and Abroad* (New York: Norton, 2003), p. 177.

24. William Pfaff, "The Pentagon, Not Congress or the President, Calls the Shots," *International Herald Tribune*, Aug. 6, 2001.

25. Dana Priest, *The Mission: Waging War and Keep Peace with America's Military* (New York: W. W. Norton and Co., 2003), p. 24.

26. *Ibid.*, pp. 16–17.

27. Daniel Lazare, *Velvet Coup* (London: Verso, 2001), p. 4.

28. Ronald Dworkin, quoted in Lazare, p. 113.

29. *Ibid.*, p. 4.

30. *Ibid.*, pp. 6–7.

31. Zakaria, pp. 101–2.

32. "The Patriot Act," *Philadelphia Inquirer*, May 27, 2004.

33. Andrew Napolitano, "Repeal the Patriot Act," *Asian Wall Street Journal*, Mar. 8, 2004.

34. Elaine Scarry, "Resolving to Resist," *Boston Review*, vol. 29, no. 1 (Feb.–Mar. 2004), p. 12.

35. *Ibid.*

36. Quoted in Scarry, p. 8.

37. Majorie Cohn, "The Torturer in Chief," *Truthout*, June 18, 2004 <http://www.truthout.org/docs_04/061804A.shtml>.

38. Gen. John Abizaid, comment to CNN, June 18, 2004.

39. Jorge Castañeda, "Bush and the Neglected Hemisphere," Project Syndicate, *Business World*, June 14, 2004.

40. Richard Rorty, "Post-Democracy," *London Review of Books*, vol. 26, no. 7 (Apr. 1, 2004), p. 10.

Conclusion: The Way Forward

1. Jeffrey Sachs, "The Decline of America," Project Syndicate, Mar. 2004.

2. *Ibid.*

3. *Ibid.*

4. Charles Kupchan, *The End of the American Era* (New York: Vintage Books, 2002), p. 137.

5. George Kennan, "Document PPS 23," State Department Policy Planning Staff, Feb. 21, 1948 <http://www.firesthistime.org/georgekennanpps23.htm>.

ACKNOWLEDGMENTS

The idea for this book came from Steve Fraser and Tom Engelhardt, the editors of Metropolitan's *American Empire* series. I am grateful to both, as well as to Sara Bershtel of Metropolitan for her support of the project. Steve was the perfect editor: patient, sensitive to what I was trying to say, yet willing to wield the knife to do away with the nonessential or the obscure.

This book brings together ideas and analysis developed in dialogue with many friends, colleagues, and fellow activists over the years. Among the many I am indebted to are Robin Broad, John Cavanagh, Richard Falk, Alejandro Bendana, Lyuba Zarsky, Robert Brenner, Chalmers Johnson, Tom Mertes, James O'Connor, Peter Hayes, Marybeth Brangen, Susan George, Jim Heddle, Naomi Klein, Anuradha Mittal, Teddy Goldsmith, Martin Khor, Elmar Altvater, Jayati Ghosh, Joel Rocamora, Muto Ichiyo, Randy David, Conrad de Quiros, C. P. Chandrasekhar, Ed Snyder, Suthy Prasartsert, Yoko Kitazawa, Alex Callinicos, Peter Rosset, Reiko Inoue, Barbara Gaerlan, Suranuch Thongsila, Ronald Llamas, Ria Pugeda, Nicky Perlas, Angie Tran, Vandana Shiva, David Korten, Etta Rosales, Jerry Mander, Mia Adjali, Phyllis Bennis, Francisco Nemenzo, Christopher Aguiton, Debi Barker, Ed Rodriguez, Dick Ng, Elsie Castrence, and Roberto Castrence.

Especially to be noted are the support and encouragement given by my present and past colleagues at Focus on the Global South, among them Nicola Bullard, Shalmali Guttal, Chanida Bamford, Praphai Jundee, Joy Chavez, Soontaree Nakaviroj, Anoop Sukurmaran, Jacques-Chai Chomthongdi, Raghav Narsalay, Mayuree Reuchakiattikul, Minar Pimple, Marco

Mezzera, Herbert Docena, Marylou Malig, Meena Menon, and Kamal Malhotra.

I am particularly grateful for the stimulating insights on trade negotiations and other matters of my dear friend Aileen Kwa, who also offered warm support at difficult moments.

Julie de los Reyes provided invaluable research assistance and was always there to take over my classes so I could write. Rita Quintas and Kate Levin served as dependable links between Metropolitan and me during the final stages of the editing.

Angkarb Kanjapat Korsieporn, Laura Samson, Cynthia Bautista, Esther de la Cruz, Amara Pongsapich, Suwattana Thadanithi, Giles Ungpakorn, Surichai Wan Geao, and other colleagues at the University of the Philippines and Chulalongkorn University in Thailand were instrumental in providing a supportive academic context for the critical research and writing represented by the book.

Finally, as always, a very special thank-you to my wife, Marilen Abesamis, and to Ami, Annette, Willie Abesamis, and Carlos Abesamis.

While all these fine individuals contributed greatly to charting the direction of this book, they are in no way responsible for its shortcomings, for which I take full blame.

INDEX

INDEX *253*

Pinochet, Augusto, 109, 166
Pipes, Richard, 23
Plaza Accord of 1985, 80, 81, 114
Political Order in Changing Societies
　(Huntington), 197
Pollin, Robert, 84, 166
poverty, global, 84
　highly indebted poor countries (HIPC),
　　173–74
　Poverty Reduction Strategy Papers
　　(PRSPs) and, 166–67, 174–77
　structural adjustment policies and, 134,
　　135, 202
　World Bank and, 167
Poverty Reduction Strategy Paper (PRSPs),
　166–67, 174–77
Powell, General Colin, 32–34, 64
　Gulf War and, 26, 33
　as secretary of state, 39, 40, 49, 50, 63
Powell doctrine, 32–34, 36, 62, 66
Prebisch, Raul, 132, 133
preemption doctrine, 14, 23, 46, 47
presidential election of 2000, 204, 205
"Pressure Point" exercise, 25
Prestowitz, Clyde, 89
Private Sector Development strategy of
　World Bank, 183–84
privatization of state enterprises, 9, 122,
　123, 134, 199
Procter and Gamble, 149
productivity, 92, 98
Project for a New American Century, 24, 26
protectionism, 133, 134, 180, 182, 192, 212
Putin, Vladimir, 209

Qaeda, Al, 18, 40, 64–65, 69–70
Qatar, 159
Qwest, 90

Random House, 213
Rato, Rodrigo, 178
Reagan, Ronald, and Reagan
　administration, 44, 133
　authoritarian governments and, 197, 198
　Cold War foreign policy, 8, 23–25, 47
　economic policy, 80, 83, 92–93, 133, 134
real estate, foreign capital investments in,
　115–16
regional development banks, 168
regional trade agreements, 212
Republican Party, 16, 17
　sources of support for, 24–25, 44–45
Rice, Condoleeza, 214
rich and poor, gap between, 5, 93, 131–32,
　134, 135, 166
Riefenstahl, Leni, 49

Rite Aid, 91
Ritter, Scott, 60
rollback policy, 21–22, 23–25
　Bush II administration and, 39–47
　economic, 133–37, 179–92
　struggle between containment and, 5, 21,
　　22
Roman Empire, 193
Roosevelt, Franklin D., 22
Rorty, Richard, 193, 208–9
Rove, Karl, 44, 45
Rubin, Robert, 29, 81, 101, 107, 112, 113,
　121, 127–28, 173, 213
Rumsfeld, Donald, 39, 42, 66, 204
　Iraq invasion and, 58, 62, 63
Russia, post-Soviet, 29, 73, 89
Rwanda, genocide in, 32

Sachs, Jeffrey, 54, 112, 167, 212
Sadr, Muqtad al-, 58
Sakakibara, Eisuke, 165–66
Salomon Brothers, 105
Sam, Kim Young, 119
Samoza, Anastasio, 197
Sampson, Gary, 157
Sanchez, Lieutenant General Ricardo, 64
Sanders, Jerry, 22
Sandinistas, 9, 24
Saudi Arabia, 8, 53
　authoritarian regime of, 30
　removal of U.S. troops from, 54, 215, 216
　terrorist attacks in, 69
Scarry, Elaine, 206
Schroeder, Gerhard, 161
Schweitzer, Julian, 168
Scowcroft, Brent, 44
Seale, Patrick, 55
securitization and international capital
　markets, 105
Senegal, 174
September 11, 40, 159
　civil rights after, 205–7
　Iraq war as revenge for, 53
　reactions to, 2, 64
Sharif, Nawaz, 201, 202
Sharon, Ariel, 45, 52, 68–69, 75
Sheehan, Neil, 195–96
Shelton, General, 39
Shilling, Gary, 97
Shinawatra, Thaksin, 164
Shinseki, General Eric, 62
Short, General Mike, 35
Shultz, George, 167
Sierra Leone, 173–74
Silva, Luis Inácio da (Lula), 74, 200–201
Singapore, 78–79, 212

ABOUT THE AUTHOR

WALDEN BELLO, a professor of sociology and public administration at the University of the Philippines, is the author of numerous books on globalization. Also an award-winning peace and human rights activist, he lives in Quezon City.